COAL DUST IN THEIR BLOOD:

The Work and Lives of Underground Coal Miners

AMS STUDIES IN ANTHROPOLOGY: No. 6

ISSN 0738-064X

Series Editor: Robert J. Theodoratus
Department of Anthropology, Colorado State University

COAL DUST IN THEIR BLOOD:

The Work and Lives of Underground Coal Miners

by

Bruce T. Williams

AMS PRESS

New York

Library of Congress Cataloging-in-Publication Data

Williams, Bruce T.
    Coal dust in their blood : the work and lives of underground coal miners /
by Bruce T. Williams
    Revision of: Underground bituminous coal miners of Cambria County,
Pennsylvania—an anthropological study. Thesis (Ph.D.)—University of
Pittsburgh, 1975.
    Bibliography: p.
    Includes index.
    ISBN 0-404-62606-8
    1. Coal miners—Pennsylvania—Cambria County.   I. Title.

HD8039.M62U694 1991
338.7'622334'0974877—dc19   89-31159
                                               CIP

AMS Press, Inc.
56 East 13th Street
New York, N.Y. 10003

Manufactured in the United States of America
TP

TABLE OF CONTENTS

For the coal miners of Cambria County, Pennsylvania,
whose hard work has contributed so much to the region
and to our country.

For the families of the coal miners who were an
integral part of their struggle.

FOREWORD

A major portion of the material contained in this text was originally submitted to the Graduate Faculty of Arts and Sciences at the University of Pittsburgh in partial fulfillment for the degree of Doctor of Philosophy in Anthropology. This was done in November, 1975. The original title was: *Underground Bituminous Coal Miners of Cambria County, Pennsylvania: An Anthropological Study.*

While this is not a completely new version of the original, attempts have been made to do three things. First, it has been revised so as to make it more simple and readable and hopefully more accessible to many more people than it was originally intended. A Ph.D. thesis is a scholarly work conforming to certain rules of the academy which make it awkward in its form and for most people unattractive and foreboding. Second, there has been an attempt to emphasize the descriptive or ethnographic dimension of the original thesis. What do underground bituminous coal miners do when they work? What are their communities like? What are they and their families like? In short, an attempt has been made to describe the culture of the underground coal miners of northern Appalachia. Third, an effort has been made to make this revised work more current while at the time preserving the intent of the original. Consequently, comments which have been added are distinguished from the original text by an asterisk joined to an existing footnote to update conditions from the time of the original research. It is felt that the revisions while not extensive have been done in such a way that it will be obvious to the reader where, and for what reasons, they have been included and that taken as a whole they strengthen and increase the relevancy of this work. At no time has statistical data from the original thesis been changed: rather, it has simply been supplemented. Furthermore, an effort has been made to locate new bibliographic materials relevant to the original story and these have been included wherever appropriate within the text and have been added as a supplement to the original bibliography.

PREFACE

JOHN ORLOVSKY'S WORK DAY

John Orlovsky awoke at 6:35 on a Thursday morning and readied himself for work at the coal mine as he had done thousands of times before. Except for four years in the army during the Korean Conflict and a few brief periods in the middle 1950's when many coal mines in northern Cambria County were closed, he had worked steadily as an underground bituminous miner and so he claimed about twenty-six years of experience. He gave no thought to the work ahead but simply shaved, washed, and put on an old pair of green work pants, a bright yellow short-sleeved shirt and a worn pair of black shoes.

After dressing, he went down the steep narrow stairs into the kitchen. He and his wife, Catherine, now lived alone in this house built by a mining company some fifty-five years ago. Although they owned the house, they occupied only the right half and rented out the other side to a young couple with one child. Their half of the house was identical to the other side and contained six rooms, all renovated and modernized. The two of them had plenty of room, but John Orlovsky sometimes wondered how he had raised his three sons and a daughter in such limited space.

In the kitchen, Catherine was placing his lunch into a battered
miner's bucket: the strips of red reflecting tape on its side were torn
and curled and the scratches and dents were evidence of its long service
and rough treatment.   She put in two large sandwiches wrapped in wax
paper, three cookies, and a box of Skoal snuff, sweet staff of a miner's
life.   John did not have much to say and just mumbled something about going
shopping when he got home from work, or perhaps working in his vegetable
garden.   He took his bucket and went out to the 1973 Chevy Blazer which was
parked half off the road in front of his half of the house.   As he turned
the motor over, his son, Paul, drove by and tooted his horn.   Like his
father, Paul lived in Bakerton and worked in a coal mine, though not the
same one as John.

On his way to work, John stopped at the M&M Coffee Shop in Barnesboro.
While it was 7:10 a.m. and getting late, he still stopped for a quick cup
of black coffee and a doughnut.   Then he ordered a cup to go for the
remaining eight miles to the North mine of Greenwich Collieries.   He
enjoyed having his coffee out in the morning, although he really did not
know why.   It occurred to him that a few years back he would never have
allowed himself to spend nearly a dollar on something like coffee and a
doughnut when he had not even worked yet.   He pulled into the large dusty
parking lot of the mine at 7:35, and walked to the locker room.   It was a
clean modern facility, bustling with the activity of earlier arrivals.
Most of the men had removed their street clothes and were moving ahead to
join those who had already gone into the second dressing area located away
from the lockers which were designed to hold only the clean street clothes

of the men. John hurried along and did not speak to anyone since he did
not know anyone around him very well. He hung his clothes in his locker
and then quickly shut it. There were no locks. He hurried through the
shower area and into the second dressing area where some eighty men were in
various stages of dressing into their work clothes, preparing for the day
ahead.

Even after years of work, the odor of the coal dust which clung to the
miners' clothes was pungent and offensive to John's nostrils. He wrinkled
his nose to adjust but after a couple of breaths he noticed it no longer.
Quickly he pulled down and unhitched the long metal chain which reached
some twenty feet to the ceiling to a large wire mesh basket with metal
hooks on the sides in which he had stored his gear and mining clothes.
Slowly he lowered the basket down until he could reach it. His clothes,
dampened with perspiration from yesterday's work, had dried overnight from
the gentle flow of hot air which was circulated over them by fans and
heaters at the top of the locker room. Now the odor of coal dust was
renewed and he could smell the dry sweat from his last three days' work.
He put on the bottoms and then the tops of his thermal underwear. Next, he
put on the grey athletic socks, which had been white at the beginning of
the week. Then he put on an old blue and red flannel shirt and, finally
over all this, he pulled on a pair of coveralls which covered him from his
ankles to his wrists and to his neck. He did not button the flannel shirt,
except at the bottom, and he snapped his coveralls only to his waist. It
was too hot here in the locker room to be fully dressed and he would wait
until he got underground to button up.

He sat on the bench near his basket and grabbed his rubber boots with
the steel toes. They were always a struggle to get on and sitting down was
necessary for the hard pull. Once on, they were laced and then he took
some black electrical tape from his basket and taped the legs of his
coveralls tightly to the outside of the boots as a safety measure. Some
men tucked their trousers inside their boots but John felt too much coal
dust slipped inside his boots that way.

Finally, John put on his green hard hat and strapped on his thick
leather miners' belt, with the brass metal name plate. Fastened to the
back of the belt was the self-rescuer, a pint-size metal container, holding
a mouth piece and a canister which contained chemicals to filter out
noxious gases. It was to be used in emergencies such as explosions or roof
falls or when dangerous gases were present and, under certain conditions,
it could keep John alive for perhaps an hour.

After pulling his empty basket to the ceiling and hooking the long
chain, John went into the lamp room area where some twenty other men were
putting on their miners' lamps. John went to the rack where the men's
lamps were being charged up and pulled his out of the little electrical
fixture. He removed his hard hat and slipped the lamp into the metal slot
on the front. He strapped the book-sized plastic-covered power pack to the
straps of his mining belt and then pushed his belt around so that the power
pack rested on his lower back. He fixed the electrical cable from his lamp
so it ran over the top of his hat and down his back to the power pack.

Fully dressed now, John went into the waiting room adjacent to the
cage and seeing Jack and Meatball sitting on a bench off to one side, he

walked over and sat down with them. These two men were in John's crew;
they were the "buggy runners" and each drove a shuttle car full of coal
from the back end of John's continuous miner, which cut the coal, to the
conveyor belt which took the coal from the mine. Jack and Meatball were in
their early 20's and were the two hot-shots on the crew. They joked a lot
with all the men, and meatball was an endless stream of silly chatter and
comment. They felt they were the best two buggy drivers in the mine, not
necessarily because they were the safest or most efficient but because they
could wheel the huge shuttle cars so rapidly along the dark tunnels and
around the dark corners of the mine. Jack had only sixteen months'
experience in the mine, starting right after his return from Viet Nam. He
was going to start college in the fall, although he had not told management
of his plans. Meatball had worked as a miner for six and a half years,
starting a month after high school. Meatball was married and had two sons.
His family lived in a trailer on the edge of the lot of his parent's home.
Jack, single, lived with his mother in Barnesboro and was saving his money
for college.

George Mikesic and Bill Perich joined them on the bench. George was
in his mid-fifties; Bill was sixty-two, and about to retire. He had forty-
six years in the mines, starting when he was fifteen as his father's mining
helper, or buddy. With his $150, per month miners' pension added to his
social security, he figured he could live quite comfortably. Also, he
thought he qualified for black lung compensation, and he was going to apply
immediately after he retired. George operated the roof bolter and Bill was
his helper. The two worked well together and shared a special camaraderie,

perhaps because they were among the oldest at the mine. Bill received a
friendly heckle from Meatball about the last time he had gotten laid.
George laughed. Bill said, "Screw you", smiled and then reached into his
bucket and pulled out some snuff which he offered around. He took a pinch
and placed it behind his lower lip and soon he was spitting into a paper
coffee cup he found on the bench.

        Corky was the crew's boss. He was a big heavy man of fifty--thick
waisted, thick-necked, with a powerful body. He gave the appearance of
being orderly and neat. He came into the waiting room and yelled through
the chatter from the conversation of the men from the other crews to John,
"Where's Slagle, the little bastard?" John raised his two hands up, palms
upward and fingers spread, to tell him he did not know. The crew smiled
and Meatball blurted out "He's home makin' it with his old lady" and then
he added, "If I had his old lady I'd be home too." The three older men sat
quietly and stared, as if they were trying to save their energy for the day
ahead. Richard Slagle had worked on the crew for only two months since his
graduation from high school. He was married now, to his high school
sweetheart, and he lived with his wife's folks. He had missed a good deal
of work already even though he had just started. The guys on the crew
figured he was just a kid and probably really did not need the money much.
They did not begrudge him his absences; besides, he was pleasant and John
found he worked very well as the miner operator's helper. He was quick and
he worked hard and he did not complain.

        Corky came back in with a new man, Andy Dunn. Before coming to the
mine, he had worked in construction driving a large bulldozer. He had been

at the mine for about four months doing general labor and he was moved each day from crew to crew. He did not enjoy this but he figured that in another eight months he would have his miner's papers and then he would bid to operate some machine, or perhaps he would go off and study to be a mine mechanic. Corky told John that Andy would be his helper today. John nodded. He had seen Andy around but had not met him. When Andy sat down beside him, John asked if he had been a miner's helper before. Andy said he had. John said simply, "Ain't bad, a lot of sit down time." Andy nodded but did not speak.

It was 7:50 a.m. The cage opened and the first crew of men coming off the hoot owl shift (midnight to 8 a.m.) hurried from the elevator. Most faces were black with coal dust and many showed the effects of extremely hard work: the coal dust was mixed with sweat and was plastered on their faces. Their clothes were black and damp, even wet, and their boots were covered with heavy chunks of mud from the coal dust and the powdered limestone spread by the miners to cover the exposed coal. John and his crew paid little attention to them but Meatball joked with one miner he knew, saying that if they had come out any earlier they may as well have stayed home. It was an old joke and John smiled as he usually did upon hearing it. The fellow who drove the same miner as John nodded gently as he walked by indicating that everything was O.K. and John, who understood this meaning, said nothing. George quickly learned from his counterpart that the bolter needed an extra long drive pod because they were working a high area and he turned and walked to the supply room to get one from the supply clerk.

Five times the large cage emptied the men from the night shift and as
it neared eight o'clock, the new crews began to assemble near the cage
door. Corky came along and stood near John. He had been talking to the
section foreman who had just come from the area in which they were working
and he learned what had transpired since his crew left sixteen hours and
two shifts before. He said nothing. Finally somebody said "Main C" and
Corky and John and the others and another complete crew stepped onto the
cage. The door was shut quickly and the miners snapped on their lamps.
The cage dropped 480 feet into the earth.

John left the cage and walked across a well-lit area and through a low
metal door that had been opened by the men ahead of him. He was now in the
mine, in a section known as the "low", since it was only forty two inches
high. The men walked along single file now, their heads bent forward,
their eyes to the ground. John's muscles were stiff and reluctant to start
supporting him in this awkward position and this short walk through the low
was difficult and soon John's body burst out into an itchy sweat. He hated
this feeling and could not adjust to it, even though he experienced it
almost daily. Finally they came to a "high" area where the motor ran and
John was able to stand upright again.

The mine was cool and there was a strong breeze from the huge exhaust
fans in this part of the mine. At first, John liked the feeling but he
knew that later in the day this pleasant coolness would turn to cold and if
he perspired at all he would become chilled. He slogged through the water
alongside the motor's tracks with about thirty other men--their lamps
throwing beams of light on the sides and bottom, their lunch buckets

swinging. This part of the mine was heavily used by both men and
locomotives and was regarded as safe. John gave no thought to the roof
conditions.

Quickly the group diminished in size as the work crews turned off to
the right, to enter B section, or to the left, to enter A section, and so
forth. Finally there was only John's crew and the other face crew of seven
which worked on the right side of the Main C section, directly parallel to
John's crew but some fifty yards apart. Both crews rode together on the
"man trip" into Main C and so they walked another quarter mile, until they
came to the end of the cut out high area, and were forced to step up into
the narrow 42 inch space where only the coal had been removed. They
struggled on, legs as straight as possible, and bent at the waist at right
angles as if they were a carpenter's square. If a man's legs were not
straight, he would be duck walking and he could not travel far. Straight
legs and a right angle bend at the waist was the only way to walk any
distance. John noticed that George had pulled a big hammer from his belt
and, holding its head, handle down, had created an extension for his arms,
and had converted his awkward two legged walk into an awkward three pointed
gait. John knew, however, that some of George's weight was now supported
by his arm and it was easier for George to travel.

After some hundred yards of struggling through the low, they came to a
set of narrow, temporary tracks. Here their long trip up to the mine face
would start. Most of the men were breathing heavily and sweating a little;
some knelt down on one knee. John climbed onto the low slung porta-bus and
banged the starter button with his thumb and the electrical motor turned on

easily. Seven more men climbed into the bus, four in the front section and
three in the back area with John. They lay flat on their sides, with their
legs and arms and lunch buckets tangled and mixed. Some men put on safety
glasses, others just half closed their eyes to protect themselves from the
dust and rock fragments which were going to be kicked up. "Ready?" John
yelled out but waited for no answers and they sped off over the bumpy
tracks through the narrow coal seam.

     After a quarter mile of travel, John slowed the vehicle to a stop.
The tracks went no further. The men quickly unloaded themselves and
struggled forward up to the face, another 100 yards or so. John turned
sideways and looked back into the dark where he had come from. He swung
the small boom which extended from the center of the portabus around to the
live electric wire to prepare for the return trip. The bus was put into
reverse and John went speeding back to get the remainder of the men.

     As the men came up to the area of the face, they stopped. The two
foremen went ahead, their safety lamps, commonly called bug lamps, in hand
to test for gas and to survey the work area. Corky went into C 'right' and
the other face crew foremen went into the left side of the face area. The
men sat and rested, and lunch buckets were opened. For some it was time
for a coffee break before work, and several men who had carried a thermos
with them poured themselves a quick cup; others ate a half a sandwich;
others just sat. There was some conversation between men on both crews,
but mostly the men within each crew sat together and talked among
themselves.

After a few minutes, the men started to move forward again. The
bosses had checked things out and now they could begin work. John who had
driven the porta-bus on the two man-trips met up with Andy who had come on
the first trip and they went up to the face and moved along a few headings
until they saw the water and electrical cables which led to the big
continuous miner which cut the coal. Corky was talking to Meatball who had
already driven his buggy up toward the miner. As John and Andy passed,
Corky outlined briefly what he wanted done. John could see for himself how
the crew could best proceed and was in agreement with Corky. It would not
be long before the miner would be finished in this particular heading and
then the forty-foot cutting monster would be pulled out and moved to the
left to cut a new heading. The roof bolter, operated by Bill and George,
would follow in after the miner to secure the top.

John and Andy reached the miner. They put their lunch buckets on the
machine and Andy put on a pair of gloves which he carried with him. John
mumbled about the outgoing crew leaving them dirty again since he felt the
miner itself was placed poorly in the heading for easy activity, but he did
not dwell on it. He told Andy to pull down a few props and throw them off
to the side and to get the canvas out of the way. He cautioned Andy to
watch and not get hurt, and also to watch out for Meatball and Jack because
of the carefree manner in which they drove their shuttle cars. As John
started the miner, a single headlight appeared behind him from around the
black corner of the seam and Jack's coal hauling buggy pulled up behind him
and his big machine. The miner was running well; the massive carbon steel
teeth on the spinning drum at the front seemed as if they were anxious to

begin, and John moved the machine forward into the coal seam. The loud, dull grinding noise of the teeth ripped the coal into the mid-section of the miner began; the noise would last the entire shift. Jack moved his buggy under the boom which extended from the back edge of the miner and from time to time John adjusted the boom's direction to keep the coal flowing smoothly onto the conveyor belt of Jack's buggy. Within a matter of minutes the buggy was full of some three tons of freshly cut coal, and so Jack stood and switched his seat to a new set of controls which now faced him away from coal face and out of the heading toward the route to the belt. He drove off and Meatball quickly wheeled his buggy in under John's boom and the cutting began again. And so it went. First Jack coming and then Meatball--the buggies always returning empty after unloading at the section's belt which eventually joined other belts to remove the coal the many miles from the mine.

Within two hours, this heading was finished. They had extended the front edge of John's continuous miner twenty feet beyond the last set of roof bolt supports which had been placed in the top to secure it and now John's head as he sat at the miner's control panel was beginning to extend into unsafe roof conditions. Also, it was illegal for the miner operators to endanger themselves by getting out in front of this last set of bolts. Corky came along and gave orders to move the big machine to begin a new heading. The waterhose which sprayed water over the cutting teeth was big and very heavy and so Meatball tied the hose to his buggy with a rope and then slowly backed away from the miner so that the hose would not be run over when the miner moved locations. Slowly, the tank tread wheels backed

the miner from the heading and then forward along the cross cut to the left
to begin a new heading, to cut more coal. Andy quickly went into the
abandoned heading and started setting up wooden props, with triangular cap
pieces wedged tightly on top and bottom, under the unsupported top in front
of the last line of roof bolts. With eight in place, he carefully made a
neat row of five props along one edge of the heading, about four feet from
the rib itself. On these props he hung the strong plastic sheets which
directed the air along the side walls and across the face as it was being
worked and which carried the dust-filled air away from the men and from the
mine itself.

This done, he moved along to catch up with John and the two buggy
runners who were now working the new heading. Soon Bill and George would
be coming along to bolt up the top and make the place safe for the next
time the miner was brought into this heading, perhaps during the next
shift. Andy's props would be knocked down one by one as Bill and George
moved their bolter closer and closer to the face itself. At least the
props which Andy had set would make things partially safe for the two men.

And so the work went like this until 3:20 p.m. Things had gone well
and there were no breakdowns of machinery. Their only real break from the
routine had been at noon time when they all had met on a pile of rock dust
bags to eat lunch together. Now it was time to leave. John and Andy
cleaned up the heading, with Andy shoveling loose coal onto the miner and
finally throwing handfuls of the inert limestone rock dust over the exposed
black coal. With the miner turned off, they made their way back to the end
of the tracks. There, as when they came to work, John made two man-trips

hauling the men. This time Corky left last. And so, the men traced their way out as they had entered. They arrived at the shaft and met the hundred other men who were leaving as well. It was only 3:45 so they stalled at the bottom of the cage a while, until finally the first twenty-five men boarded and were up and gone. John got on the third trip and soon he was squinting as his eyes adjusted to the increased light. The air smelled fresh and seemed warm, dry and very good. He felt liberated from the dampness and the confined spaces of the mine. He was happy that work was over.

His lamp was hung up and quickly he was putting his filthy clothes and gear into his basket. It was raised to the ceiling. John walked naked to his locker and grabbed a bar of soap and large wash cloth. He came back to the shower and scrubbed and pulled the soapy towel over himself until he thought he was clean. Then he walked to a mirror outside the shower to see if he had removed all of the sticky coal dust from his face. He had not and he still looked as if he had dark makeup outlining his eyes. He re-entered the shower area and scrubbed his face again.

At his locker, John dried and dressed quickly. He saw Meatball and Jack and Andy leaving the locker room to go to their cars but he said nothing. Old George came from the shower and he and John made some small talk as John combed his hair. Abruptly John shut his locker and told George he would see him tomorrow and in no time he was in his car and on his way home. He was thirsty and would have stopped for a beer as he occasionally did, but since he had told Catherine he might take her food shopping, he drove straight home to Bakerton. Things had gone well at work

but John did not give it much thought one way or the other. He was just
glad the day was over and was looking forward to a free evening.

I. INTRODUCTION

A. BACKGROUND OF THE STUDY

Coal miners, as an occupational type, comprise one of the most identifiable groups of working people in the United States. The image of the coal miner portrays a highly stereotyped quality in American culture. Popular belief portrays their work as dirty and difficult as well as very dangerous. The coal miner, himself, is looked upon as a man of strength, with great stamina, brave and fearless--a person surviving in a particularly cruel and unnatural environment by dint of brawn, muscle power, and sweat. He is thought to be uneducated, poor, exploited, and trapped into a way of life which in spite of his efforts he cannot escape. He lives, so it is thought, in a narrow isolated hollow in any number of Appalachian states. He exists, as if fixed in time--never changing--always the raggedy character, with blackened lined face and torn black clothes. He lives with his usually large family, in a bleak, squalid coal camp with its rows of look-alike old houses. The coal miner is considered a man to be pitied and, if possible, helped. What little boy boasts of his ambitions to be a coal miner? No one, it would seem, willingly becomes a coal miner if other choices and options are available.

1

There has been a great deal of research on the coal mining industry in the United States, both in anthracite and bituminous mining, but a review of this literature offers little help and understanding as to what a coal miner and his family are like. Robert Munn has published an annotated bibliography on the coal industry in America with 1928, listings but not a single published ethnographic account for northern Appalachia is included.[1] (There has been a small number of unpublished M.A. theses on various aspects of mining towns.) In addition, if one considers northern Appalachia to extend from the middle region of West Virginia northward through Pennsylvania and into southwestern New York state, very little has been written on life in the coal fields of these regions. In fact, the Appalachian Bibliography, published by the library of the University of West Virginia, lists 7632 references of which very few are concerned with coal mining in northern West Virginia or western Pennsylvania.[2] Archie Green, in his monumental work on folklore and folksongs of American coal miners, comments that the only ethnographic account of coal miners he is familiar with is the English ethnography, Coal Is Our Life: An Analysis of a Yorkshire Mining Community, by Norman Dennis, Fernando Henriques, and Clifford Slaughter.[3] However, a fine sociological work with emphasis on the personality and personality formation of miners of a southern Illinois mining town was produced by Herman R. Lantz, in People of Coal Town.[4] Only recently have two sociologists, Helen M. Lewis and Edward E. Knipe, using a combined sociological-anthropological approach, published a series of interesting articles dealing with work and family relationships in coal mining communities of Virginia.[5] In the area of the folklore of coal mining, George Korson has probably contributed as much ethnographic data as anyone through his writings.[6] His works, books, and recordings, are stored at King's College in Wilkes-Barre, Pennsylvania.

When one surveys the available literature concerning coal miners, it becomes evident that there is ample room for an anthropological study of western Pennsylvania coal miners. In response to this need, this research provides an ethnographic account of the lives of the coal miners in Cambria County, Pennsylvania. A practical consideration for this study is that it comes at a time when there is an increase in the demand for coal as an energy source and coal deposits do constitute some 88 percent of all known fuel resources in the United States. In light of the renewed and vital importance of the industry, such an ethnography is timely.[6]*

In addition to the need for a general ethnographic study of coal miners of Western Pennsylvania, the author wishes to place special emphasis on the need for a specific study of the coal miners' health situation. One cannot remotely understand what it means to be an underground miner without an awareness of the miners' occupational hazards, especially those conditions which lead to high incidences of illness and disease. This work was written in part to begin to reveal the nature of the relationship between coal mining and health and to develop suggestions that potentially could be useful in bringing about improvements in this problematic area.

As limited as the cultural research on northern Appalachian coal miners has been, there has been a sizeable research effort in the United States and England concerning the general question of coal miners' health.

While some of the medical commentary began as early as 1813, it was not
until the 1950's and the 1960's, particularly in the United States, that a
period of rather extensive research began. The concerns of this research
have generally been directed toward as examination of the respiratory
disease, coal workers' pneumoconiosis, or black lung disease as it is
called, with secondary efforts directed toward the study of emphysema and
other non-specific respiratory diseases. In addition, there has been work
of a biostatistical nature which demonstrates the mortality rates of U.S.
coal miners. Surprisingly, however, there is not a single article which
specifically concerns itself with the social and cultural factors involved
in the causes of coal miners' diseases. There has been no ethnographic
work which attempts to relate the fundamental questions of coal miners'
life styles, world views, attitudes and beliefs to the diseases from which
they suffer.

If the health picture including the morbidity and mortality rates of
the coal miner is ever to be understood, data to construct abstract
explanations must be available. In addition, the health situation among
coal miners cannot be sufficiently explained when research is limited to
the types of variables examined thus far. The need for solid ethnographic
work is clear--on its own terms and for the potential it may have in
explaining health and illness. The health of the coal miner in the United
States with a morbidity and mortality rate many, many times higher than
other citizens in this country demands the attention of medical and social
scientists alike.

There is also an attempt here to provide sociocultural materials from
which informed action can be taken to improve the health and working
conditions of the coal miner. In the final chapter, a number of simple
generalizations about coal miners are placed in a framework for
investigating coal miners' illnesses in the hope that these generalizations
can lead to positive action for the purpose of improving the health
situation of the coal miner.

B.   THE ETHNOGRAPHY OF COAL MINERS

The primary purpose of this study is to present an ethnographic
account of the lives of the coal miners in Cambria County, Pennsylvania.
The secondary purpose of this study is to consider the health and illness
picture from the broad perspective of the social and cultural factors
involved in illness and it is hoped that the information contained with
this work will lead to an improved understanding of research approaches
that can be used in establishing improved health care programs for miners.

The research is based on the assumption that the cultural changes that
occur among coal miners and their families are in large measure the result
of changes in the technology of underground bituminous coal mining. In
other words, technological changes have socio-cultural consequences.

It is a corollary to this assumption that, in spite of similar
technological influences on miners throughout the nation, coal miners from
Cambria County, Pennsylvania, still possess many unique cultural remnants

from their early histories and that only gradually are they moving to the
value orientation and world view of that of middle Americans.

In collecting information for this ethnography, data were gathered on
the basis of three working assumptions. First, the coal miners of Cambria
County, regardless of background (ethnic group, history of immigration,
etc.) represent, from a cultural point of view, a reasonably homogeneous
group of people. Similar experiences--immigration, work in the coal
industry, life in the coal towns--are believed to have produced a people of
very similar behavior, attitudes and outlooks.[6]**

Second, there are complex interactions between technology and the
social relationships of the people who use a particular technology.
Minimally, it is assumed that Harris in his The Rise of Anthropological
Theory is correct when he states, "...similar technologies applied to
similar environments tend to produce similar arrangements of labor or
production or distribution, and these in turn call forth similar kinds of
social groupings, which justify and coordinate their activities by means of
similar systems of values and beliefs,"[7] Arensberg and Kimball had stated
previously, "A particular shift in industrial technique becomes a
particular change in organization among persons of a specific community, to
be related at once to further, subsequent changes in other nonindustrial
patterns of organization among the same men in their lives outside of work
and in the same community."[8] And, finally, Lewis and Knipe, who themselves
have studied the relationships resulting from technological changes, state;
"If similar technologies produce like divisions of labor, social grouping,
values and beliefs, then a change in technology should produce changes in

the division of labor and the associated grouping, values and beliefs. Not
only would we expect changes to occur in man's work relationships which are
directly associated with technology but also in other networks of social
relationships of which he is a part. Thus, the impact of mechanization
extends to other areas of social life."[9] In short, what these three
authors assert is that the social relationships among miners and miners'
families have changed as the technology of mining has changed. The issue
remains, however, to document and describe these changes.

The third and final working assumption is that these technological
determinist positions alone would lead to an analytically incomplete
understanding of the modern coal miner. The coal miner must therefore be
viewed historically, with full recognition of the fact that the immigrant
coal miner and the rural American farmer of long term residence in the
region have unique culture histories. The early coal miners, while
influenced and shaped by the technology of their work, were not simply
passive recipients of this influence. Rather, the coal miners and the
culture of the coal miners, must be viewed along with the changes in
technology, and these changes must be viewed dynamically and as mutually
interacting.

In spite of these assumptions, there is no attempt here in this
revised presentation to make a rigorous analysis of culture change nor to
"prove" a sequence of causality, involving technological variables of some
type on the one hand and sociocultural variables on the other. Rather, the
broad view is that there is a complex set of relationships among such
phenomena as the technology of coal mining, the nature of work in the

mines, the number of people employed in mining, life in the coal towns, life outside of work, and the immigrant experience, which together have contributed to produce the peculiar qualities of the western Pennsylvania coal miner of today.

The chapters which follow demonstrate and document these relationships so that today's coal miner can be understood in an historical perspective. Those aspects of the coal miners' lives which have been selected for description represent those areas most influential in the molding process of the miner and essential for the broad understanding of the coal miner.

Chapter III describes life in the early coal towns. It illustrates the social atmosphere within the towns when the immigrants first came together and creates the initial context in which the coal miners are seen and from which the study begins. In the section on demographics, the mixing of the various ethnic groups and the patterns of emigration are presented. This pattern is re-emphasized in Chapter VIII, for it is argued that the pattern of emigration has contributed to the conservatism in the coal towns (people and new ideas rarely come in) and that the personality and world view of the first miners have persisted, at least partially, until today. In addition, the general health situation within the county is described both in terms of the health services available to the miner and in terms of the miners' morbidity and mortality rates.

Chapter IV describes the mines of the county. Since this work is about an occupational group, considerable emphasis has been given to the work environment of the miners. Effort has been made to show how a modern coal mine operates and what the miner himself does while working. The statistical data of this chapter illustrate and document the tremendous changes in underground coal mining and in the populations of the coal towns.

Chapter V describes the changes in coal mining over the past seventy years. It illustrated that as the technologies of mining changed (and improved) the social relationships among men while working changed; and with more efficient mining, less men were employed and finally less miners resided in the coal towns.

Chapter VI shifts from examining the actual mining itself to describing the social relationships within the mine. The work crew, in the context of the new large mines, is shown now as an important social institution. Attitudes to work and the relationship of the miners to their bosses is also described in the context of these large mines.

Chapter VII deals with the leisure time activities of the miners and describes their non-working activities as supporting their rural and provincial way of life.

In Chapter VIII the ideas presented in the preceding five chapters are brought to bear on an understanding of the miners' personality and world view. This attempts to clarify what today's miner, after as much as seven decades of work in the mines, is like. This not only provides another dimension to the miners' description but also some of the critical summary information used in the conclusions.

Chapter IX is the concluding chapter and draws from all the preceding chapters, especially from chapter VIII. The framework for investigating illness is put forward and the question of the miners' health is treated.

Conclusions are made on the basis of the general thematic approach of
viewing the miner in the social environment of his coal town with the
technology of his occupation changing constantly.

Finally, it should be noted that the reader will not find the bizarre
and strange within these chapters. Too often newsmen and writers of
limited experience in the coal fields have created a distorted and
emotionally charged portrait of the underground miner. This study attempts
to correct such misconceptions. The northern Appalachian coal miner is, as
we shall see, a well-adjusted member of American society and his
similarities to the rest of society far outnumber his differences.

C.   THE FRAMEWORK FOR INVESTIGATING ILLNESS

Disease, injury and death are universal facts of life in every human
society, but it is evident that these events do not occur randomly within
any human group or population. Studies indicate that there are patterns in
the rates of illness (morbidity) and death (mortality) within human groups.
In other words, there is a fundamental relationship between morbidity,
mortality and culture.

Anthropologists, sociologists and psychologists have made considerable
contributions to explaining the relationship between the existence of
disease and its possible causes in terms of social factors. These social
scientists with their special training and perspective have brought to
traditional medicine methods of relating modes of living, life styles,
values, attitudes, socialization processes, and social interaction patterns

to the types of illnesses from which a particular group of people suffer.
While the research efforts in this area have generally been descriptive in
nature, this remains a necessary step in establishing the social factors
involved in the causes of disease. E. Gartly Jaco has written: "Whether
or not social and behavioral conditions of human life will ever be fully
determined as sufficient or necessary, primary or secondary, immediate or
proximal, indigenous or exogenous causes of specific diseases in terms of
medical or non-medical models is still a moot question."[10] The fact
remains that there has been a beginning in relating social factors to
various forms of morbidity and mortality and the need to continue with
these attempts is clear.

If it is granted that biological and physical phenomena are
insufficient in themselves to explain rates of illness, then one is forced
to look at illness in a social context. This orientation takes into
consideration the association of a person with other human beings, and
acknowledges that these environments are sources of important events that
effect the human organism relative to illness. At this point of our
understanding, the relationships between physical, biological and social
factors are not clear and a detailed theory has yet to emerge. There are,
however, some patterns of interaction among these three factors, and there
is a need to expand upon current knowledge in order to begin to build a
solid theory of disease causation.

Essentially there are two approaches which can be used. The first is
to look at the etiological or so-called causal factors of illness and
death, and the second is to look at the patient's reactions to illness.

This particular study, as stated, does not establish causal relations
between culture and illness; but it has been influenced by the first
approach, the etiological approach, and the following ethnographic account
reveals those cultural factors essential for the full understanding of the
etiology of coal miners' diseases.

Central to this approach (discovering the effect of cultural, social
and psychological variables on the physiological processes leading to a
state of illness) is the problem of demonstrating causes. This is a thorny
problem and traditional approaches have been influenced by the thinking of
physicians who have sought simple explanations in terms of single or
specific causes. This mechanistic approach, assigning a direct cause to an
illness, has proved to be ineffective and divorced from the reality of the
human condition. Instead, the idea of multiple causation has proven to be
more efficacious in explaining the causes of illness. This approach
reflects reality more accurately, although it decreases the clarity of the
idea of cause. However, it is assumed to be the more reliable way to
explain causation since it is premised on the idea that illness is the
culmination of a complex series of forces, social as well as physical.
Edward Suchman has written, "If one's model of causality is limited to the
traditional mechanistic model of single causes, then socio-environmental
factors probably cannot be viewed as directly causing disease; they can
only influence, positively or negatively, the potential of the "real"
causal agent. If one accepts the concept of multiple causation, however,
socioenvironmental factors can be viewed as one of the direct causes of
diseases."[11] A working premise of this study is that explanations of the

causation of illness cannot be limited to single cause explanations in the final analysis.

In seeking explanations of multiple causation of illness and death, there are at least three broad research areas which can be examined. The first is the psychosomatic causes of illness, or those situations where the individual interacts in some fashion with his own environment to produce an emotional reaction which results in physiological change and possibly illness. These are the so-called psychosomatic illnesses. The second research area is that in which both psychological and social variables interact to facilitate the ability of actual physical disease agents to act in bringing about illness. The third area includes the life style, customs, family structure, work and the recreation patterns and how these bring the individual into actual contact with the disease agents or the objective causes of disease.

Each of these three broad research areas implies a research method of its own. In the first instance, the research technique is the clinical method. In the second area, both individual and group factors must be explored, and a large number of subjects examined in survey fashion. In the third area, there is emphasis placed on examining the individual's culture from a broad perspective and the research method requires an ethnographic account of the individual's social group.

While each of these research areas, and their related methodologies, is useful to an explanation of disease causation and warrants further exploration, it must be realized that each approach is founded on certain assumptions (and methodologies) which, when rigorously questioned, limit

the validity of any particular set of results. In the final analysis, it
is the researcher who must select the research strategy which offer some
hope of a solution or of yielding meaningful results. In this study, the
third area, that of exploring the socio-cultural factors involved in
diseases, has been utilized.

An investigation of coal miners using an ethnographic approach
presents the opportunity to gain some control of the relationship between
the socio-cultural and biochemical factors in disease causation. First,
there is strong clinical evidence of a relationship between high dust
levels in mines and various lung diseases. This demonstrated relationship
isolates some of the objective factors involved and provides the basis for
further investigation.[12] (Discussion of coal miners' morbidity and
mortality rates and the general "illness" picture for coal miners is in
Chapter III, Section 4a.) Second, isolating coal miners as a group helps
to narrow the problem and helps to make it manageable. In other words,
population groups that are somewhat culturally homogeneous are particularly
strategic groups to study in trying to establish causality of diseases.
And an occupational group (as opposed to more heterogeneous groupings such
as social class or "race") provides a particularly good and easily
definable grouping.

Although the social scientists and public health researchers who study
the role of socio-cultural factors in the etiology of disease have had
limited success in constructing an adequate sociological theory to explain
illness, there are useful and practical activities which researchers can
perform.[13] For example, it is useful to limit the field of inquiry and to

try to define the proper concepts with which to be concerned. This
activity can be considered as establishing a frame of reference in which to
construct an investigation.[14]   K. Bailey provides a convenient definition
and explanation of a frame of reference.[15]

> It is pre-theoretical in that it does not specify
> propositions, i.e., it does not state relationships
> between concepts, but merely a coherent body of
> concepts... The main advantage of a frame of reference
> is that it provides a context for the accumulation of
> research findings.

There are two advantages to establishing a frame of reference. The
first is that a frame of reference is exhaustive rather than narrow in its
scope, whereas theories are conceptually limited and often make the
accumulation of new scientific data difficult. A frame of reference also
provides the possibility of unifying data which would be considered
diverse. Third, a frame of reference often allows health action,
especially preventative action, to take place. For example, researchers
have planned and implemented preventative health programs with regard to
heart and lung disease by recognizing that emotionally stressful situations
and smoking behavior respectively contribute to causing these diseases.
The point is that public health action can be initiated even on the basis
of incomplete knowledge.[16]   Therefore, from a practical point of view, an
attempt to employ a frame of reference may be useful in helping coal
miners. From a theoretical point of view, if one admits to the paucity of
socio-cultural theory to explain illness and to the fact that coal miners'
illnesses have not been considered from a cultural perspective, there is
little real choice but to attempt to employ a frame of reference.[17]

It is to the ethnography of coal miners of Cambria County, Pennsylvania, that the frame of reference is applied. The ethnographic account of coal miners exists by itself and stands on its own merits, but it is also a body of material capable of being analyzed within a frame of reference.

D. SIGNIFICANCE OF A COAL MINERS' ETHNOGRAPHY

The significance of research of this type lies in three areas. First, as mentioned, there is a need for accurate ethnographic material on present day coal miners in the United States, particularly on deep coal miners in northern Appalachia. While there are books and articles on coal towns, a number of books on the labor history of coal miners, and some psychological studies of coal miners and coal communities, there is scanty ethnographic work. Also, there is no ethnographic account of miners actually at work underground. Rather, the accounts of coal miners appear to be written through interviews with coal miners and occasionally by a journalist who "toured" a mine. Second, research of this type holds the possibility of contributing to the theoretical body of knowledge that medical sociologists, social epidemiologists, and medical anthropologists have been struggling to build. Specifically, it may be possible to establish a frame of reference to explain the etiology of disease. There is in the United States at this time an increasing demand for the use of coal as a source of energy. While some of the coal will be gathered by strip mining (or surface mining), the great bulk of coal is more likely to be collected by

underground mining (the "ecology movement" and also formal declarations of
the United Mine Workers makes this quite probable). It appears that
increasing numbers of men will be employed as underground miners in the
foreseeable future. Any understanding of the processes of disease
causation among coal miners admits to the possibility that this knowledge
can be applied in some practical way to reduce both illness and
mortality.[18] Third, there is currently a movement in anthropology to study
people not as a territorial unit (or an ethnic unit) but rather dynamically
as a unit of process. While many possibilities exist (e.g. religious
groups, voluntary associations), occupational groups, in this case, coal
miners, provide a particularly good starting place in which to conduct a
study in a complex society. A man's work is one of the most significant
facts in his life.[19] There is evidence to indicate that in industrial
societies a man's primary social identity is based on occupation.[20]
Sociologists have conducted occupational studies on recent immigrants to
cities, on slum communities themselves, or on ethnic associations, but
these studies have often ignored groups with extended residence who have
already made a successful social adjustment, and therefore leave an
incomplete picture of a complex society.[21] Anthropologists since the mid-
1940's have also tended to limit their research efforts, ignoring both
occupational groups as well as people of long-term permanent residence.[22]
Research of this type would move anthropological inquiry into an area where
there is little information at this time. And, this type of information is
certainly necessary if anything more than a fragmented picture of culture
and society is ever to be achieved.

II. METHODOLOGY

This ethnography is exploratory since it describes an occupational group previously ignored by cultural anthropologists. I have attempted to achieve both comparability and comprehensiveness in the collection of data for this ethnography. By comparability I mean that the description of coal miners is expressed in terms which will permit comparison with other cultures or with other sub-cultures within the United States.

For the ethnographer, comprehensiveness means that data be gathered on a variety of topics representing a broad spectrum of customs and social institutions of a society. Second, those features peculiar to a society must be investigated and explained and the ethnography must not be simply limited to pre-determined categories. In order to contribute to the ethnographic record, the ethnographer must report that which appears distinctive and unique as well as the commonplace and then the ethnographer must explain the social context within which these distinctive features are found. In the case of this study, a good deal of effort has been directed toward those features which make coal miners unique and so the major subject areas discussed are the community, the work place, the miner's personality, and questions of health.

To some extent, the so-called common-denominator approach, in which the ethnographer collects data in the same areas as everyone else who went before him to insure at least some areas of comparability, has been minimized in this work because the assumptions, as expressed in the background section, were formulated clearly enough by the writer to shape and direct the data collection itself.

A further point about ethnography is in order. The basic ingredients of ethnography are generalizations about groups of behavior which occur with regularity. In a sense, a generalization within an ethnography is an expression of a pattern of behavior (or a pattern statement) and it is far more than just a simple descriptive account. It is rather a statistical account, a statement of probability, which has been determined by the observer to be correct on the basis of empirical observations or statements from informants.

The ethnography involves a descriptive summary of the customary practices of a group of people. It is derived from thousands of these generalizations, each having varying degrees of validity, and is based on different amounts of observation and the frequency of occurrence. In the final analysis, accuracy depends upon the skill of the observer who makes the generalization through inference and with judgement. As Levi-Strauss has stated, "The anthropologist attempts in description to enlarge a specific experience to the dimensions of a more general one."[1] Implicit within this ethnography, as within all ethnographies, is the question of the validity of the inferences, since, as a function of organizing and writing, there has been a move from the data to generalization. While there is a growing concern within some areas of the discipline of anthropology for improved data collection itself to insure more accurately written ethnographies (in a sense implying an end to holistic ethnographies), there also exists a strongly humanistic approach to ethnographic writing. This work tends toward the latter of these approaches, and while the possibility of distortion cannot be denied, it is felt that the clarity of the assumptions held and the questions asked about the coal miners insures a high degree of validity within the ethnography.

This research began in 1973. Prior to this time, I had simply engaged in informal conversations with coal miners about their actual working conditions. The stories of men 500 feet below the earth in seams of coal sometimes as narrow as 24 inches picking coal with a small hand pick and shoveling 10-15 tons of coal per day into coal cars seemed beyond human capabilities. What began as simple curiosity gradually developed into a formal research effort, dealing with the life experience that these men and their families experienced after coming to this part of the New World. From these discussions, I learned about their labor history and the difficult times these people often encountered when strikes were lost or the demand for coal diminished. The coal towns themselves, with row after row of nearly identical houses, depicted a life style for the coal miner and his family which seemed unpleasant and was certainly strange to me. As my knowledge and interest grew, I realized that here was a unique group of people which could be studied systematically.

In delimiting the population for this study, I have directly
considered only coal miners. Other people naturally have had considerable
effects on the dynamics of the coal miners' lives--the wives, children and
neighbors of the coal miners--but the ethnography describes actively
working miners, as they live in 1973-75. Although the information
collected from retired miners is essential for understanding the modern
miner, this thesis is not directly about their lives--only inasmuch as
their past actions have helped to shape the present.[2]

The study deals with actively working underground bituminous coal
miners from Cambria County, Pennsylvania. The geographical boundary
facilitates the collection of certain statistical data and demographic
information and identifies the location of the study. Conclusions drawn in
this study apply, therefore, directly to the miners of Cambria County,
though obviously many inferences may be extended to miners in surrounding
counties.

Cambria County is in six Pennsylvania State Coal Districts, Districts
17, 18, 19, 20, 21, 24, and strip mine district 42. From an analysis of
each district, the total number of persons engaged in mining, either
administrators, technical employees, or working miners, is 4,149 men for
1973, the last year for which figures have been compiled. The number of
miners actually working underground in 1973 was 3,562. (Arriving at this
figure required certain assumptions which will be discussed in Chapter IV,
The Mines.) More specifically, 3,562 persons were engaged in deep or
underground mining, 204 in strip mining, 29 in refuse mining, and 354 were
engaged in tipple and preparation work.[3] Supporting these figures, the

United Mine Workers of America indicated on December 1, 1972, a total membership of active and retired miners in Cambria County of approximately 8700 men.[4]

In addition, all national and local trends for which statistics are available show steady increases in the number of men employed as miners from 1969 through 1971.[5] It is probably safe to assume that this trend exists in Cambria County as well; and so, combining all the information available and allowing for moderate increases, there are approximately 4,300 persons actively working in the coal mining industry and 5,000 retired miners in Cambria County in 1974.

The total number of mining operations actively in operation in Cambria County in 1973 is officially listed as fifty-three.[6] (See Chapter IV, Mines, for a more complete explanation.)

The research includes a non-probability sample (where the sampling has not been random and statistical calculations cannot be made) of coal miners studied.[7] This was necessitated by the fact that employment by the researcher as a coal miner took place only at one mine, and as a consequence, the research on the working conditions within the mine (summer, 1973) was conducted at only one location. Knowledge of the broader aspects of coal miners' lives--their personality, their family life, their towns, and in fact, their culture has been gathered throughout the county. Interviews took place whenever and wherever the opportunities presented themselves and flexibility in this exploratory study has been part of the approach to gathering information.

It should be emphasized again that the study is not a community study if by community is meant some sort of territorially defined area. The use of a county is simply to place the location of the study and to help develop close approximations of the number of miners and the population density of the active and retired miners within the area of the county.

The problem of over-generalization, of abstracting too much from the data, deserves comment especially when part of the methodology is the participant-observation approach. Margaret Mead has pointed to the fact that the anthropologist tries while doing research to establish the norm or the cultural pattern itself of the social group being studied. This differs, she has argued, from the approach of the sociologist who is generally sampling to determine the extent of variation within a pattern. This allows the anthropologist an opportunity to construct the pattern by using a small number of non-rigorously sampled cases.[8]

This study is of a group of men who share an occupation.[9] Formerly, the miners also shared a common residence--the coal towns; but with steady employment, increased earning power, and better transportation, the coal miner has become more mobile and often resides some distance from his place of work. Although it was necessary at one time for coal miners to live in coal towns, many no longer live near their place of employment.

Some of the major strengths of this study are my observations which were made possible through my employment as a coal miner during the summer of 1973. My work as an apprentice miner began just after the customary miners' vacation in the first week in July and continued for seven weeks into August.[10] I was employed at the Greenwich Collieries Company, North

Mine, which is a subsidiary of the Pennsylvania Power and Light Company. The location of the mine entrance was in Indiana County just north of Barnesboro, Pennsylvania, and the business offices were located in Ebensburg, Pennsylvania, which is the county seat of Cambria County. (See Chapter IV, Mines)

The work experience began with job interviews by the company personnel officers, a physical examination, a three day training session by the safety officials of the mine on various mining techniques, including safety and first aid instruction, and finally work as a general laborer at various jobs within the mine (standard 8 hours/day, 40 hours/week).

In addition, my place of residence for the seven week period was at the Susquehanna Hotel in Garman, Pennsylvania, in northern Cambria County. This afforded close association with the miners in a non-working situation, since many of them lived and socialized at this small hotel. The miners who resided at or frequented this hotel were not necessarily from Cambria County, just as the miners who worked at the Greenwich Collieries mines were basically from a tri-county area--Cambria, Indiana, and Clearfield Counties. A return trip was made to the northern Cambria County area the following summer and residence was again taken up at the Susquehanna Hotel for three weeks. This offered a chance to review the actual working conditions and mining operations and to review the work of the previous year for accuracy of detail.

Some social scientists feel that the participant-observation approach of the anthropologist can be a troublesome technique for gathering information, especially when one is working in one's own culture. It is

felt that one is too close to the people being studied, and matters of
interest are apt to be overlooked or misinterpreted. On the other hand,
one gains advantage by sharing a common language and so one is able to
quickly learn the special coal mining jargon. In addition, the preparation
prior to fieldwork can be rather extensive thus making the time spent in
the field useful from the first moment one arrives.

In addition to participant observation, a number of other methods were
employed. These included an oral history project on the labor history of
the area conducted in part by university students, extensive interviewing
of key informants, and some extensive discussions on coal mining literature
by three colleagues who were raised in coal mining communities of the area.

The research project on the labor history of the coal miners of the
county was begun in the Spring of 1974. This was an oral history project,
and the initial goal of gathering 150 tape recorded interviews of
approximately 1.5 hours duration each was achieved finally during the
Summer of 1974. This project was continued into the Fall of 1974, now
exclusively through the use of student interviewers, and the number of
taped interviews was increased to approximately 300 tape recordings by the
end of the year. Through these tapes, an attempt has been made to
construct in a general way the sequences and issues involved in the labor
history of the coal industry of Cambria County. It was felt that a
thorough knowledge of the events since 1922, which was the year of a major
coal strike in the area and the oldest major labor event which large
numbers of old retired miners could recall, was essential to a
comprehensive understanding of the coal miners.[10*]

The initial part of this historical study was conducted by thirty-two college students from the University of Pittsburgh at Johnstown during May and June of 1974. Each student was to locate five coal miners and to question these men in detail about certain specific events in the labor history of the area which they as students had studied. In addition, the students explored any aspects of the miners' lives which seemed interesting and which the miners were willing to discuss. If a particular man appeared to have an insight on an issue which the interviewer considered to be extraordinary, a further, more extensive interview was conducted. On a second occasion when student interviews were used to collect tape recordings, the students themselves were taking a course on coal mining and coal miners. The students were therefore given ample opportunities to become sensitive to the general nature of the research project. In this study, the seventeen student interviewers were residents of the area and seven of the students were from coal mining families and this made the interviews and tapes particularly useful.

With guideline questions to serve as an outline, the students were left to their own devices in contacting and interviewing the coal miners. (See Appendix A, Interview Guidelines, for copy of the guideline questions) These contacts were facilitated by the fact that coal miners were often relatives of the student interviewers and benefits appear to have been gained because these men and women talked more openly and freely than they would have if interviewed by strangers. The students conducted the actual making of the tapes in any manner they felt was comfortable for the miner-interviewees. For instance, the retired miners sometimes were given the

list of guideline questions to read in advance of the taping sessions; at
other times, long hours were spent in general conversation and later the
taping was done; finally, some taping was done directly with no previous
discussion concerning the nature of the questions.[11]*

In addition to the interviews with coal miners, a special effort has
been made to interview and record the wives of the coal miners. It has
been found that the wives of the miners frequently have special insight
into the nature of the social relationships in the coal towns, especially
of those relationships during the formative periods, 1910 to 1930.

In my role as participant observer, I simply went to work as would any
miner trying to earn a living. If questioned, I did not deny my research
activities, although I never volunteered this information without being
asked. To a very few men, I was a college professor, but to most, I was
just a new miner, learning a new occupation. To upper level management I
was a researcher, but to the foremen, I was simply one of the their crew of
miners. An interesting aspect of the miners' perception of me was this
very difference in their awareness of my real purpose - most never
indicated any knowledge of my real intent. In a few instances, I was
initially received with curiosity, but when it was understood that my
objective was to learn what coal miners did for a living first hand, I was
hospitably accepted. In fact, almost all of the miners thought it only
sensible to work as a coal miner if one wanted to understand the industry--
a position, incidentally, questioned by some academic colleagues of mine.

While living as a part of the mining community, I tried to maintain as
low a profile as possible. To the coal miners who frequented the hotel in

which I resided, I was known as someone researching coal miners. Since I was also known to be working in a local mine, I was generally treated in a friendly manner and my questions were answered politely, and, I believe, thoroughly and honestly.

Of prime importance to me in gaining an understanding of the personalities of the miners themselves were two men who were the sons of the coal miners, who were raised in coal mining towns, who were educated through Master's Degrees, and who were working in administrative capacities at the University of Pittsburgh at Johnstown. These two men, both raised in the local area, understood and respected my interest in learning about their lives and the early lives of their parents and proved extremely helpful in reconstructing a picture of life in the coal towns. One of these men proved to be most useful as a source of information, since his perceptions and objectivity provided me with a set of baseline data from which to derive questions and upon which to build a framework for a great deal of this study.

The final set of selective interviews which I used to sharpen my perceptions involved three faculty members of the University of Pittsburgh at Johnstown who were raised in the Cambria County area. Two were raised in coal towns and one was raised simply within the area of the county. The three people read Lantz's People of Coal Town.[12] While this book is about coal miners in southern Illinois and not western Pennsylvania, it provides many parallels between the situation of coal miner immigrants, both the English speakers and the non-English speakers of Illinois, and the situation found in Cambria County, Pennsylvania. This book laid the basis

for discussion and comparison by means of which these three men were able
to examine their own experiences and to sharpen my insights. By carefully
reviewing the book with each of them separately, I was able to acquire
types of information which would ordinarily have taken far longer to
uncover.

The view of women and family life comes mostly from the statements of
the miners' wives themselves and from the knowledge gained from the student
interviews in the miners' homes. The fact that information on the coal
miners' wives and children was obtained only from these sources is an
admitted limitation of this study.

The principle of holism has typically guided the nature of the field
work undertaken by anthropologists. In small societies with observable
geographical boundaries and relatively self-contained economic and
political organizations, it is possible to conduct a reasonably
comprehensive study of an entire society. However, a truly holistic study
of a dispersed occupational group like coal miners is not possible.
Rather, the opportunities open to me during field-work have led to the
emphasis on mine workers as an occupational group. It is, in fact, heavily
oriented toward men at work and toward their social relationships primarily
as they are shaped and influenced by their occupation and the technological
change which have taken place within that occupation.

Finally, the study of coal miners of Cambria County was initiated with
only an intuitively held set of assumptions in mind and undoubtedly with
some unconsciously held meta-cultural view of the lives of miners. When I
went to work as a coal miner, I had no expressly preconceived theories or

hypotheses. Although I had fear of the dangers, visions of the darkness, and reservations about the heavy work ahead, I felt that my starting place should be the employment line, and that I would later integrate my experience with what others had written. This is how I proceeded.

III. COAL MINING TOWNS

A. SETTING

1. Cambria County, Pennsylvania*

a. Location. Cambria County is in the southwest central portion of the State of Pennsylvania. It is surrounded by Clearfield County to the North, Blair County to the East, Bedford County to the Southeast, Somerset County to the South, Westmoreland County in the Southwest and Indiana County to the West. The county encompasses 695 square miles of land and has one urbanized area--the Johnstown region--which is located in the southwest corner of the county.[1] (See Appendix B, map of Cambria County)

b. Climate. Cambria County lies in the middle latitude area of the North American continental region at approximate coordinates of 40° 30' north latitude and 78° 50' longitude. The climate particular to Cambria County

---

*   A new book on Johnstown which deals with many of these topics has recently been published. See Johnstown: The Story Of A Unique Valley. Ed. Karl Berger

is a humid mesothermal one, characterized by ample annual rainfall, with warm to hot summers. A freeze-free season of 140-150 days is average for this climate and occurs between May and early October.

Temperatures vary from 29° F low month average temperature to a 72° F high month average, and extended periods from these extremes are rare occurrences.[2]

Cambria County's location places it in a climate between the polar continental air masses to the north and the maritime continental tropical air masses to the south and southeast. Therefore, contrasting air masses and severe frontal activity are not uncommon and are the sources of periodic, highly changeable weather situations.[3]

c. Topography. There are two generalized physical features of Cambria County. The northern one-fifth of the county is within an area known as the Pittsburgh Plateau section and extends from the northeastern section of the county westward throughout much of the state. The elevation on the plateau is from 1500 to 2000 feet, and rises gently from northeast to southwest.[4]

The Allegheny Mountains section covers the remaining four-fifths of the county. This section is characterized by fairly sharp rises and falls in altitude, so that ranges of 800 feet in altitude to almost 3000 feet occur over fairly short distances. This causes numerous valleys which, while providing impressive scenery, make the building of roads and railroads difficult and serve as barriers for the movement of men and machinery.[5]

The land forms in the county are directly related to the synclinal and anticlinal geologic structure underlying it. There is a general northeast-southwest orientation to the ridges and valleys in most of the county; however, in the north these ridges and valleys become rolling. The highest mountain ridge is in the southern part of the county and rises to 3000 feet.

d. Soils. The most extensive geologic soil formations in the county are the Conemaugh formation and the Allegheny formation. In addition, there are four other small formations in the eastern and western areas of the county--Pottsville, Mauch, Chunk, and Pocono formations.

The Conemaugh formation is roughly 600 feet in thickness and consists of alternative beds of sandstone, shale and clay shale with thin beds of coal (See Appendix C, Geological Map of Cambria County). The Allegheny formation is approximately 300 feet in thickness and is known for its valuable beds of coal. There are seven minable coal beds with sequences of sandstone, shale and clay shale mixed between them.

Cambria County's economic orientation was caused by two primary production materials: iron ore and bituminous coal. Iron ore has ceased to be economically minable in the area and consequently is no longer a primary production resource. Bituminous coal still dominates the local scene as a source of energy to the local steel mills and to an ever increasing number of electric generating plants in the region. Other minerals in abundance include fire clay, limestone, sand and building stone.[6]

e. Water Supply. Cambria County lies in part to two major drainage
basins. In the northern part of the county, the Susquehanna River drains
40% of the county and the other 60% of the county is drained by the
Conemaugh River and its tributaries which are part of the Ohio River Basin.

Precipitation, in the form of rain or snow, is the source of the
water supply and is abundant and variably distributed annually. The
average rainfall is 42 to 48 inches; however, dry spells during the summer
are not uncommon.[7] It is felt that drainage problems will begin to occur
as industrial development alters the state of the natural forest and
vegetable cover. In addition, water pollution from mine acid water run off
is a considerable problem, and because of the extensive coal mining within
the region, the drilling of deep wells proves unreliable as well. It is
estimated, in fact, that ninety percent of the potential surface water
within the county has been severely polluted by this mine acid drainage.[8]

2. Early History and Economic Activities of the Area

Cambria County appears to have been first settled by Native Americans,
among them the Old Delaware and Shawnee. There are written reports of
Indian villages in 1781 at the confluence of the Stonycreek and Conemaugh
Rivers on the present location of the City of Johnstown.[9] The first
Europeans to settle in the area were present in the county, although in
small numbers, by 1758, since there is evidence of the use of Forbes Road
by early settlers. Forbes Road, while it did not actually enter Cambria
County, went through the neighboring counties to the south and was the
first major thoroughfare linking the people of Cambria County with Eastern

cities and with Fort Pitt of Pittsburgh to the west. Prior to 1764 and the

signing of the Fort Stanwix treaty by various representatives of the

British Crown, the Governor of New Jersey, Commissioners from Pennsylvania,

and a delegation from Virginia with chiefs from the Seneca, Shawnee and

Delaware tribes, the area of Cambria County and, in fact, much of western

Pennsylvania was a dangerous place to live. While threats from Indians did

not completely abate even by the late 1770's, the first permanent

settlement of any size within the county was in 1778, when Michael McGuire,

a Catholic Army Captain from Maryland, built a settlement on the headwaters

of the Clearfield Creek, which soon attracted hundreds of fellow

Marylanders. In 1793, Joseph Johns, a Swiss Mennonite, came from Berks

County in Pennsylvania and settled on the Stonycreek in the area of

Johnstown with a group of Amish Mennonites. In 1795, a settlement at

Beula, near the present city of Ebensburg, was settled by the Reverend

Morgan John Rhees. He was apparently a rather militant Baptist Minister

who had left Wales for reasons of religious disagreement, and he found this

settlement in the hopes that it would become the county seat. German

settlers, under the leadership of a Peter Lemke, were able to establish a

permanent community in the area of the present day Carrolltown in northern

Cambria County in 1796. Finally, Welsh settlers were able to establish an

enduring colony in 1796 in the area of Ebensburg, the present county seat.

(Cambria is derived from the Welsh word for Wales, Cymri or Gymur.) This

ultimately lead to the abandonment of Beula.

    Cambria County proved generally to have unfavorable soil for

horticulture or the raising of livestock. Clearing of the many steep hills

and valleys was often difficult and the grasses did not make good hay for
the animals. However, the forests produced other benefits and yielded
large numbers of game animals, maple sugar syrup, and later, fine orchards.
The beginnings of the steel industry in the Johnstown area took place in
1809, when John Holliday constructed the Cambria Forge on the Stonycreek
River. This event was to shape in many ways the growth of the county.
Until the time of the Civil War, a number of forges, furnaces and factories
existed in the Johnstown area for short periods of time, until finally in
1852 the Cambria Iron Company was organized. By the close of the Civil
War, this iron works, whose principal productions were iron rails, was
perhaps the largest in the nation. The properties of this company were
transferred to the Cambria Steel Company at the end of the nineteenth
century, a second time to the Midvale Steel and Ordinancy Company and
finally there were merged in 1923, with the Bethlehem Steel Company.

The adoption of the Bessemer process for making steel and the
subsequent refinements in this process led to the abandonment of the local
Cambria County iron ore because of its high sulfur content. Fortunately,
railways in Pennsylvania were growing during this period and provided the
means for transportation of the necessary iron ores from the Lake Superior
region to the Johnstown steel mills. The coal industry in the area
initially grew as a result of the need to supply the fuel for the growing
steel industry, and it can be safely stated that many of the small
communities of Cambria County owe their existence to the coal industry.
(The coal fields of Cambria County, however, supplied more than just the
Johnstown steel mills; coal was exported from the region too.)

Population grew steadily within the county as a result of the influences of the steel and coal industries. For example, there were 7076 people in the county in 1830, and twenty years later the population was 17,773 persons. By 1940, the population had grown to 213,459 although by 1972 the population declined to 186,785. Since World War II, the county has undergone a period of economic and population decline. The reasons for this are varied but are generally attributable to a decreased reliance on coal (a situation which has begun to change in the past six years), to improved technology requiring less labor, and probably to changes in the national transportation patterns involving a greater use of trucks rather than trains (Cambria County's hilly topography does not readily lend itself to industries relying on truck transportation). The county's economic expansion of the late 1880's and early 1990's, based as it was on coal as a fuel source for markets in the United States and for the local steel industry, has not responded especially well to fluctuations in the economy at large. Only in recent years has the coal industry shown increases in the number of men employed and tons of coal produced per year. Extreme specialization and a lack of diversification characterize the county's economy.

a. The Coal Industry. Coal mines were opened in the South Fork area of Cambria County in the 1800's and in the northern areas around Barnesbro and Patton in the 1870's. Then, in the 1890's, the Blacklick coal fields were opened followed by the large operations of the Berwind-White Coal Mining Company in the Windber area on the northern border of Somerset County.

Finally, in the mid-1910's the Maryland Coal Company developed shafts in the Beaverdale and St. Michael areas.[10]

In 1918, it was estimated that the coal mines within a forty mile radius of Johnstown had produced 60,000,000 tons of coal in one year which was one-tenth of the coal produced nationally. This was the peak amount ever produced in Cambria County throughout its entire history of coal mining.

Since then, the coal industry has undergone a slow but steady decline not only in tons of coal produced but also in the number of coal miners employed in the county. The coal industry suffered from a number of conditions, most of which were external to the operators and miners of the county. Briefly, railroads in different parts of the county were competing for business by offering coal operators in other sections of the county lower rates for haulage; various classes and grades of coal were subjected to changes in freight rates which proved unfavorable to local coal operators; there was a rapid development of new coal fields; and finally, bickering between union and non-union operations created a somewhat unstable economic situation. The result of these developments was the beginning of a steady decline within the local coal industry.

b.   Other Economic Activities. As indicated, the economic orientation of Cambria County has been almost exclusively determined by its rich deposits of coal and, to a lesser extent, iron ore. At the turn of the century, Cambria County had a boom in the economy with rapid growth in both the steel and iron industries. Since that time, there has been little real diversification in employment and, in fact, technological improvements in

these industries have, in effect, tended to reduce employment. In
addition, there has been a steady decline in the use of coal as a major
fuel source. The net result of these factors, including increased
mechanization, has been an emigration of people and a subsequent population
decline for several decades.[11]

Since the county's basic economic structure depends on heavy
industries which do not reveal a growth potential of any significance, it
appears that as long as the economy remains dominated by heavy
manufacturing, the future potential for increased employment and
significant economic expansion is not good. Furthermore, the present
economic structure is extremely sensitive to changes in the national
economy. For increased stability of the economy and for economic growth,
Cambria County needs to attract new and diversified industries.[12]

The county's leading industry is manufacturing; in 1970 there were 167
industrial manufacturing plants, producing about 1.25 percent of the total
state's output (in value), and twenty-two establishments exporting goods
and products valued at $6.3 million.[13]

Agriculturally, the county is principally a potato and livestock area.
In December, 1970, there were 910 farms which derived $2.1 million from
potatoes and $5.6 million from livestock.[14]

The third major economic activity is bituminous coal mining and in
1970 Cambria County ranked fifth in Pennsylvania in the amount of coal
produced in the twenty-six bituminous coal producing counties. Natural gas
is also found in the county and approximately two percent of the state's
natural gas was produced in Cambria County in 1970.[15]

Johnstown is the county's only city and is the center of manufacturing
activity. It has sixty-four manufacturing establishments and in 1971
provided jobs for 16,127 persons or 83.1 percent of the county's
employment.[16] However, an analysis of the employment trends within Cambria
County between 1960 and 1970 reveals the general pattern of emigration from
the City of Johnstown. Fewer people were employed in the city in 1970 than
in 1960, whereas there was an increase in the numbers employed in the
suburban areas and the remainder of the county.[17]

In summary, the economic picture for Johnstown is stable and shows
some signs of growth. However, the economic basis within the county must
be diversified to provide stability to the economy and to check the out-
migration of people from the county.

3. Demographics

a. Population at the Turn of the Century. At the turn of the century and
for the next twenty years, the population of Cambria County was basically
composed of three elements: Americans of long residence who no longer
claimed any ethnic identity other than being an American; immigrants of the
middle period, the mid-nineteenth century, who were originally mostly
German, then Italian, followed by Irish who were sometimes referred to as
"Scotch-Irish"; and finally the recent immigrants who were newly arrived
from Europe, mostly from Eastern Europe.[18]

The problem of characterizing the nature of the population in the
Cambria County area for the first twenty years of this century, the peak
period of coal production, is not a simple task since there are many

problems concerning definition of ethnic identify. The information
contained herein is meant only to be suggestive of the nature of the
population in Cambria County during the time in question.

John E. Gable in his 1926 publication, History of Cambria County,
Pennsylvania, indicates the early population figures.

CHART I

Population Figures for Cambria County

Year	Population[19]	Percentage Increase for Years[20] in Question	
1850	17,773		
1860	29,155		
1870	36,369		
1880	46,811		
1890	66,376	1890-1900	57.9 percent
1900	104,847	1900-1910	58.5 percent
1910	166,331	1910-1920	19.1 percent
1920	197,839		
1940	213,459		
1970	186,785		

In 1920, as stated, the county had a total population of 197,839 and
38,538 of these people claimed to be European immigrants, or foreign born
whites as the census lists them. The available figures are as follows:

CHART II

Foreign Born Persons, Cambria County, 1920[21]

Austria	7949	Yugo-Slavia	1430
Canada	148	Lithuania	390
Czecho-Slovakia	3272	Poland	6213
England	2200	Rumania	39
France	405	Russia	1498
Germany	2443	Scotland	791
Greece	165	Sweden	289
Hungary	3839	Switzerland	53
Ireland	627	Syria	309
Italy	5104	Wales	573

All Other Countries   802

The following figures are available for immigration into the state of Pennsylvania:

CHART III
Some Immigration Figures for the Commonwealth of Pennsylvania[22]

Years	Number of Immigrants Arriving
1901-1905	226,007
1906-1910	259,979
1911-1915	273,473
1917-1918	16,470
1918-1919	11,257

Finally, for the year 1921, the total number of mining companies engaged in bituminous coal production in western Pennsylvania was 1,236. The total number of employees was 174,489, and these are divided into "Americans," 72,285 and "Foreigners," 102,204.[23] For a more local picture of the nationalities of miners, the following figures are available from Berwind-White Co. for the years January 1, 1922, and January 1, 1923. These figures were prepared for the Pennsylvania State Mine Inspectors' reports. The Berwind-White Company had mines in both Cambria County and Somerset County to the south. In one sense, these figures may more accurately reflect the ethnic composition in the southern areas of the county, rather than being applicable to the whole county.

CHART IV

Employees by National Origin

Berwind-White Coal Company[24]

	Jan. 1 1922	Jan. 1 1923		Jan. 1 1922	Jan. 1 1923
American	411	507	Scandinavian	6	3
Slavish	753	275	Spanish	23	90
Polish	495	264	Belgian	1	2
Hungarian	545	358	Serb	0	3
Italian	415	179	Croat	15	7
Germany	37	40	Lithuanian	40	20
Scotch	25	17	Greek	2	17
Austrian	35	13	Mexican	6	15
Welsh	6	7	Porto Rican (sic)	0	1
French	3	1	Macedonian	1	2
English	23	20	Turk	0	1
Irish	4	9	Bulgarian	1	1
Rumanian	47	24	Canadian	0	1
			Totals (26)	2894	1877

The above figures, as given by Blankenhorn, are verbatim copies of the state's mining records. They include, therefore, some expressions denoting nationality which are not in use today, or which are confusing in today's terminology. For instance, the term Slavish is no longer in wide use. At the time of the report, it presumably referred to people from Slovakia (today a part of Czechoslovakia). The term is somewhat confusing, since among the English-speaking communities the expression tended to apply to Eastern Europeans in general. Interestingly, there are few Scots, Welsh, Irish, and English miners listed in these reports. This is probably because their immigration took place at an earlier time and because these men, with the advantage of speaking English, now classified themselves as American, whereas non-English speakers assimilated more slowly and still considered themselves to be of their original nationality. Finally, these figures and those of Pennsylvania in general indicate that in the mines of

Pennsylvania forty percent were "Americans" and sixty percent were "Foreigners."[25]

b. Current Population. The Census of Population indicates that in 1970 Cambria County, Pennsylvania had a population of 186,785, a decline of 8.1% from 1960. The percentage of people classified as living in an urban setting in 1970 was 58.9 percent compared to 41.1 percent in a rural setting. The projections for the population in 1975 were for a continuing decline, and it was estimated that only 180,203 persons would reside in the county. This trend in population decline may have been reversed or at least abated somewhat with the increased demand for coal in the area.[26]

The population is primarily located in the south-western area of the county, around and including the City of Johnstown, which itself had a population of 42,476 in 1970. In addition, the City of Johnstown, when classified as a Standard Metropolitan Statistical Area (SMSA), had a 1970 population of 262,822 persons.[27] This SMSA includes not only a number of boroughs and townships which surround Johnstown itself but also some boroughs and townships in northern Somerset County which lie to the south of Johnstown. If the areas immediately surrounding the City of Johnstown are ignored, the remainder of the county has a very low population density. Only three boroughs have a population greater than four thousand people and less than five thousand. In addition, there are only four townships not immediately contiguous with Johnstown with populations greater than three thousand persons and less than seven thousand. A trip through the county supports this impression for most of the area is woodland or farmland with occasional small trading centers or small coal towns.[28]

4. Health Delivery Services

Cambria County is relatively rich in medical care resources, but these tend to be concentrated in the Johnstown area. Johnstown has three major hospitals: Lee Hospital, Conemaugh Valley Memorial Hospital, and Mercy Hospital. There is another comprehensive hospital in the borough of Windber, Windber Hospital, which is located in northern Somerset County, some fifteen miles to the southeast of Johnstown itself. In addition to these three large general hospitals, Cambria County has Miners Hospital of Northern Cambria County, a 145 bed, fully accredited hospital, in the borough of Spangler in the northern part of the county. There is also a small hospital, perhaps more correctly termed a private clinic, in Colver, known as Colver Hospital (and until recently known locally as Dr. Martin's hospital after the single physician who operated it) which served for emergency and obstetrical care. In the eastern area of northern Cambria County, there are no hospital facilities, and the people from this area appear to be serviced by hospitals in Altoona and Phillipsburg in neighboring Blair and Clearfield counties respectively. In addition to these hospital facilities there are offices maintained by private practice physicians which can supply some limited emergency care and diagnostic treatment.

The number and location of physicians in the Cambria County area reflects the pattern which the location of the hospitals implies. The United Mine Workers of America's Health and Retirement Funds indicate that seventy percent of the county's primary care physicians, who are specialists in internal medicine, pediatrics, obstetrics-gynecology and family practice are located within the Johnstown are in the extreme south of the county.[29] Furthermore, it is clear from the information available on physicians within the county, that the vast majority of specialists are located within the Johnstown area. Mr. Eli Cvijanovich, a hospital administrator at the Lee Hospital in Johnstown, suggests that U.S. Census figures which list 163 physicians within Cambria County in 1970, are high, and gives the following information for December, 1973:

CHART V

Active Physicians in Cambria County, Pennsylvania, 1973[30]

Primary Care Physicians
      General Practitioners   40
      Internists   9
      OB/GYN   15
      Pediatrician   5

Specialists
      General Surgeons   15
      Neurologists   3
      Orthopedic Surgeons   5
      Urologists   4
      Otolaryngologists   4
      Radiologists   9
      Anesthesiologists   6
      Pathologists   9
                                    113

The discrepancies in the two figures may have been due to a decline in the number of physicians caused by retirement or relocation of a medical practice. This seems unlikely, however, since there is general agreement among hospital administrators within the area that the number of physicians is increasing. The discrepancy is perhaps more attributable to the data collection process of the U.S. Census, and no discrimination is made for physicians who reside, and primarily practice, outside the county but who practice occasionally within the county.

There are two basic but related health delivery problems within Cambria County. The first is that there is a shortage of primary care physicians. The second is the problem of the distribution of physicians. The Comprehensive Health Planning Association of Western Pennsylvania gives the following figures for the four primary care specialties:

CHART VI

Physician/Population Ratios[31]

	Optimal[a] Ratios	1973 Pa.[b] Ratios	1974 Cambria-[c] Somerset Ratios
Family Practice	1:2000	1:3875	1:4620
Internal Medicine	1:5000	1:4657	1:23,942
Pediatrics	1:10,000	1:12,909	1:65,841
OB/GYN	1:11,000	1:10,838	1:23,942

Furthermore, the Comprehensive Health Planning Association indicates that by 1980 Cambria County will be in need of 41.1 additional physician equivalents.[32], [33]

The second problem--that of the geographical distribution of physicians--impacts strongly and immediately on the coal miners and their families. Simply stated, most of the coal miners live in the rural areas of the county where there are few physicians and few or no medical facilities. The United Mine Workers of American through the Health and Retirement Funds lists 21,250 persons as of September, 1973, who are beneficiaries of the various health programs which exist for miners and their families.[34] As of March, 1975, this figure has risen to approximately 24,000 because of the increased types of eligibility for various categories of persons previously ineligible (particularly benefits to widows).[35]

There is a highly complex set of regulations guiding the Health and Retirement Funds in serving the coal miners and their families. It is not the task of this work to outline these services except in a general way. Simply, the Health and Retirement Funds, one of the most comprehensive health plans in the United States, pay for complete and total health care expenses to physicians and hospitals for an active or fully retired miner (twenty years of work; at least 55 years of age; five years of work after 1946) and his wife and dependents. The eligibility rule on dependents is complex but essentially it means that all children up to the age of nineteen years of age are covered as well as some other relatives, e.g. an aged parent, if dependency can be demonstrated. Miners must go to physicians approved by the fund. Most primary care, including visits to doctors' offices, and all specialist care will be paid for. In addition, there are no limits on the total cost of treatment or the length of time for which payments will continue. Oral surgery is paid for, but not general dentistry. Hospital costs, nursing home costs and pharmaceutical costs are all covered. Further, the fund dispenses the monthly pension payments for the miners. The amounts paid to the men are determined through the U.M.W.A. contracts with the National Coal Association which represents the coal mine owners, or the coal company in national contracts. Basically, the contracts are negotiated according to the number of tons of coal produced at mines unionized by the U.M.W.A. For each ton of coal

produced, an amount of money (currently $1.50 per ton) is sent to the
Health and Retirement Funds for its expenses. Within this contract also is
the negotiated pension payment.

Finally, the Health and Retirement Funds concerns itself with
additional health matters pertaining to the coal miner. The fund sponsors
health research, publishes findings, and lobbies for improved health safety
standards. Within the various districts of the U.M.W.A., the fund actually
services the miners and their families as day to day problems occur, and
can, for instance, put miners in touch with various types of medical
specialists throughout the country if the need is demonstrated. In
addition, the fund seeks to improve health conditions by physician manpower
recruitment and through assistance to hospitals. In a very direct way, the
fund is interested in all aspects of the coal miner's life pertaining to
health.

While the health care plan is certainly adequate in its intention to
provide medical care to miners, its success is significantly impeded by the
unequal distribution of physicians within Cambria County. About 4000, or
13 percent, of the county's population (estimated in 1975 at approximately
187,000 plus) qualify for the benefits of the Health and Retirement
Funds.[36] As mentioned, these include coal miners themselves and retired
coal miners and their dependents. Only about ten percent of the
beneficiaries live in the Johnstown area, where seventy percent of the
physicians are; the rest are scattered throughout the rural areas, with
almost one quarter living north of Route 22 (see map No. 2). In this area,
north of Route 22, there are only ten physicians--one general surgeon and

nine general practitioners, seven of whom are over fifty years of age.[37]
All specialists except the surgeon come on a visiting basis from outside
the county. This area, especially in the extreme north, has more active
bituminous coal miners than any area in Pennsylvania other than the
Uniontown area in the southeast area of the state. And this northern
Cambria County area as been designated a critical manpower shortage area by
the National Health Service Corps.[38]

     The problems of available services generally include availability to
specialty and primary medical care as well as emergency medical service in
all areas of the county except in Johnstown. This is an especially
important health issue for coal miners since there are so many accidents
taking place and emergency care is constantly needed (see Chapter V for a
discussion of accidents and accident rates).

     There are serious shortcomings in related health matters. There are
few organized water supplies or sewage treatment systems. The water
systems, where they do exist, are not fluoridated. There is no county
health department, and consequently there is no systematic program for
childhood immunization. For retired miners and their wives, there is an
acute shortage of nursing home care, and the Health and Retirement Funds
indicate that many people seek nursing homes outside the county.

     In summary, it appears that the coal miner and his dependents are
being offered one of the most complete and comprehensive health plans in
the United States, but a health plan which cannot deliver good health. The
miner works in a highly dangerous industry with a high rate of accidents
and disease, and the miner and his dependents generally reside in areas

lacking in sufficient numbers of hospital facilities, physicians and emergency treatment centers. For the coal miners of Cambria County, the general health care picture, in spite of the best efforts of the Health and Retirement Funds, cannot be considered a good one.[38]*

a. Morbidity and Mortality. The health of the coal miner has long been a concern of physicians and public health workers who have practiced in the coal fields of the United States, England, and Wales. Much of the research effort has been directed to questions of respiratory disorders in miners and former miners, with particular emphasis being placed on the specific role that coal dust plays in the etiology of the coal miners' respiratory problems. While the early studies attempted in the United States focused on the effects of silica dust on the lungs, it was gradually discovered, as the British began to realize in the time period 1935 to 1942, that there was little silica in coal dust. It became clear that coal dust itself, consisting predominantly of carbon, could produce pneumoconiotic changes in the lungs.[39] In spite of these early discoveries, extensive research was not conducted by the U.S. Public Health Service until January, 1963, when a research team designed a field survey in the Appalachian Bituminous coal fields.[40] This survey attempted to determine the prevalence and nature of respiratory disorders among miners, retired miners, and non-miners who lived in the area of the coal fields. In addition, respiratory conditions in miners' wives were examined and, finally, the survey was extended to two communities where both mining and non-mining occupations existed.

In Pennsylvania, two early studies began to indicate the high rates of
pneumoconiosis among coal miners. From 1959 to 1961, a roentgenologic
study of 16,000 coal miners was conducted among active bituminous miners of
central and western Pennsylvania.[41] The evidence showed that of the 4,200
working bituminous miners, 29 percent had roentgenographic evidence of
pneumoconiosis. Likewise, 11 percent of 8,200 bituminous coal miners in
western Pennsylvania showed similar evidence. In addition, Henry Doyle
indicates a correlation between age and prevalence of pneumoconiosis. In
reviewing the evidence from Pennsylvania, Doyle cites the following facts.
In central Pennsylvania, only 16 percent of working miners under age 45
(299) had roentgenographic evidence of pneumoconiosis, whereas 41 percent
of those in the age group 45 to 64 (926) had pneumoconiosis. In western
Pennsylvania, 4 percent of 3,425 working miners over 45 years of age, and
29 percent of 1,939 retired miners had pneumoconiosis.[42]

At this time, bio-statistical studies by Enterline focused on
mortality rates of various categories and demonstrated that among coal
miners death rates are nearly twice as high as those of other working age
adult males (actually, of any other large identifiable male occupational
group) in the United States, and that there are excessive morbidity rates
for a great number of disease categories (e.g. malignant neoplasms,
coronary heart disease, other heart and articulatory disease, respiratory
disease and tuberculosis, cirrhosis of the liver, digestive disease, motor
vehicle accidents and other accidents, homicide and suicide.)[43] Among
Enterline's conclusions is the firm suggestion that the excess in mortality
rates among coal miners cannot be explained by respiratory diseases and

accidents, which are conditions naturally recognized as being related to
the hazards of coal mining. In fact, when death due to these causes is
eliminated, the mortality rates for coal miners still remain about 1.5
times the death rates for all working males.[44]

These studies are significant, if not conclusive, with respect to the
high morbidity and mortality rates. It is clear that the health situation
for the coal miner has been proven to be serious. The coal miner works in
an industry full of risks from accidents as well as from the subtle
environmental dangers (e.g. dust) which kill him at a rate two times faster
than other men in this country. And there is no observable basis for an
assumption that the situation in Cambria County differs significantly from
these figures which have been gathered from a wider geographical area.

B.   LIFE IN THE COAL TOWNS

1.   The Early 1900's

Nestled beside huge black slag heaps of discarded coal and rock, the
coal towns of Cambria County bear a lasting witness to the industry which
brought them into existence. The tall cylindrical tipples, the boarded up
mining offices, the unused bath houses, and the rusting remnants of
machinery, invite the student of coal miners to return to consider these
reflections of life gone by. A form of living that appears so unique must
certainly still be affecting the coal miner of today, and must be
considered in the social evolution of the modern day coal miner.

The coal towns of Cambria County, which began to appear in the early 1880's, were built for the purpose of housing coal miners and their families close to their place of work. Since walking was their only means of transportation, living close to one's work place was necessary. As was mentioned in section 3a, Population at the Turn of Century, the miners were immigrants from Europe and possessed little wealth. Because of their poor economic situation, they needed this housing which the company provided.

By and large, the miner arrived with a very small amount of money and some clothes. If he was married, he often had children as well, and he and his wife may have possessed several heirlooms or small pieces of furniture but little else. Transportation from Europe was too costly.

The actual houses were built by the company and rented to the miners on a monthly basis. The rent, which was not high, was usually deducted directly from the miners' wages. All the houses as well as the land surrounding the town and the mine were owned by the company. There were no privately owned houses. This ownership of the houses provided a mechanism for control of the miners by the company since any miners who were outspoken and critical of the company could simply be evicted. Privately owned stores, bars and social clubs were not allowed on the mining property. Today, establishments such as these can generally be seen on the fringes of the former mining property. On the company property, nothing was allowed except what the company owned although sometimes, if the town was large enough, a church or two was found. Besides the houses, mining offices and the various buildings associated with the underground operation, there usually could be found a company-owned store, known appropriately as the "company store," which supplied a full range of goods to the miner--mining equipment, foodstuffs, household needs, clothing and so forth. In Cambria County, it appears the miner was not forced to buy at the company store, but the ease of doing so, especially when he had little access to transportation, resulted in his shopping at these stores. Miners were extended easy credit by these company stores, and the money which the miner owed was simply withdrawn automatically from his wages at payday. Stories abound about families who were continually in debt and who received no money, but only a negative wage statement.[45]

The physical construction of the towns varies throughout the county, and the architecture of the houses even today varies noticeably between towns as well as within sections of towns. The general design of the towns reveals the obvious constraints of topography and physical setting, whether it was a narrow valley or an open flat plateau area. Given these differences, however, the coal towns do share many similarities and are today very easily recognized as coal towns. Generally the towns were constructed in straight neat rows of houses, with houses facing onto a road from each side. The roads within the towns were almost always perfectly parallel, four to six in number, and were connected to one another by perimeter roads usually forming a huge rectangle of houses. Finally, one additional road led out from the coal town to a main county or township road. In tiny coal towns, or where the topography was particularly steep, the homes were simply constructed on either side of a short distance of winding road. Settlements of this nature usually had fewer than ten houses on each side of the road and the mine associated with such a town was

likewise usually small. It is probably incorrect to refer to these strings
of roadside houses as towns since they were so small but they did display
the same features of company ownership and association with a coal mine as
the homes in the larger coal mining towns.

Even today, these houses are locally referred to as mining houses,
although the companies no longer own them. Beginning in the early 1930's,
during the depression, when mechanization was expanding, the coal companies
sold homes to whomever would buy them. (The number of coal miners was
constantly diminishing and the company would have empty homes if they were
not sold.) It appears that it was almost exclusively coal miners who
bought these houses.

Throughout the county, two basic types of houses were constructed--
single houses in which one family occupied a whole house and double houses
in which two families each occupied one-half of the house, each family
having a first and second floor on one side. Within each category, there
was a fairly wide variety of construction designs, but generally the houses
were made of wood, had two stories, with four to six rooms (or four to six
rooms in each half house) and had porches front and back.[46] Originally,
all the homes had outdoor sanitation in the back, a situation which existed
in some of the towns until the middle and late 1950's. Indoor plumbing for
sinks was not found in some houses until as late as the 1920's and water
was obtained from a common faucet or well. The rooms were small, the
construction was cheap, the walls were generally thin and the insulation
was poor. Usually the houses had furnaces in the basements with registers
to transmit the heat through the floors, but some houses only had stoves in

the kitchen. Bathing was done in a large tub in the kitchen, and in the
early days when there were no bath houses, the miners came home dirty and
bathed in the kitchen. It is said that one of the wives' important duties
was to have hot water ready for their husbands' baths.

Only working coal miners and their families lied in the coal towns as
a general rule. The populations of these towns were a mixture of various
nationality groups from western, eastern and southern Europe, as well as
the United States. The people in the latter group were most often
"American" farmers who had changed their occupation to mining.

In the earliest days of the coal towns, the English speaking
immigrants constituted a majority of the residents. The term "Johnny
Bulls" is still used today, especially by the non-English speakers, to
refer to this group.[47] Within the group, the early immigrant Welsh coal
miners and some Scots miners, because of their past underground coal mining
experience and their facility with English, were able to secure for
themselves the supervisory positions as foremen and superintendents in the
mines. These positions of relative privilege and authority were passed
along to other English speakers, or to men who were most like the original
men of authority and position. There is some suggestive evidence,
furthermore, to indicate that the Irish, who were Catholics, suffered job
discrimination, at least in terms of supervisory positions, well into the
late 1920's and early 1930's.

The cultural and religious differences among these immigrant peoples
played a significant role in determining the nature of life in these towns.
Although the eastern Europeans and the southern Europeans arrived later in

the region, they were still among the first residents of many coal towns,
especially if the towns were built after 1890 or even after 1900. The
experiences, past histories, and motives of these people appear to have
been sufficiently different from those of the English speakers to have
resulted in a social climate within these towns which is best characterized
with such terms as suspicion, prejudice, friction, and a general lack of
social harmony or solidarity. The eastern Europeans and southern Europeans
were sufficiently different in language, customs, habits or culture from
the western Europeans to elicit feelings of prejudice which have been
observed in many ethnic neighborhoods within the United States.
Furthermore, this general atmosphere of prejudice and suspicion existed
within these larger geographical classifications, so that, for instance,
Pollocks (Polish) and Croats (Croatians) or Dagos (Italian) and Hunkies
(generally any eastern Europeans) were equally suspicious of each other.
The fact that these people lived together within the isolated setting of
the coal towns, instead of within large ethnic neighborhoods as in many
urban areas appears to have aggravated the suspicions, at least in the
initial experience, and hindered the growth of a feeling of acceptance and
understanding among the various groups.

The ethnocentric views of the immigrants can be explained in part by
the fact that many of these people came from rural farming societies (the
term "peasant societies" might even be applied) and that they lacked the
sophistication and experience to deal with people of a different culture.
Living in such a setting as the coal town, and living with people who were
so different from what he had known, the immigrant seemed to react with a

feeling of distrust and suspicion, not only of those outside his social group, but within as well. And it was within this basic social milieu that the coal towns began.

a. The Social Atmosphere. The social atmosphere of the coal towns in the early days grew out of the mixing of peoples of very divergent cultural backgrounds. It was a situation where many new immigrants were forced to live with people of different nationalities. Social tensions which resulted from this were aggravated even more by the harsh economic realities which often pitted one man against another and one family against another. It is a contention of this study that an awareness of this feature of the early coal town is necessary for understanding the coal miner today.

Even today the early social atmosphere of the coal town is reflected in some organizations of the town. Throughout the county, it is not uncommon to find two or three Catholic churches within the area of a small town, each associated with a different nationality group.[48] A great number of the social and drinking clubs of long standing are nationality based and it is not uncommon to see a privately owned barroom located beside two or more nationality clubs at the edge of a coal town as a reminder of the initial social and religious segregation of the early coal towns. (see chapter VII for more on leisure and recreation)

There is some evidence suggesting that many of the eastern Europeans did not desire to settle permanently in the United States. They sought economic security and money rather than personal or religious or political freedom, and planned to return home to Europe with the financial means to

buy land.⁴⁹* Such intentions would naturally diminish their desire to
assimilate into the culture of their new country. On the other hand, it
clearly was not the goal of the English speaking immigrants to remain
isolated and different--rather, they assimilated quite rapidly to a new way
of life here in the United States. This difference in goals appears to
have heightened the already existing cultural differences between the
"Johnny Bulls" and the "Hunkies." The eastern European, saving his money
regularly in the hopes of returning home to Europe, lived his life
differently from his English speaking neighbor. He spent little money on
clothing for his children, furniture for his home, or entertainment. To
the Johnny Bulls, the Hunky appeared down-troddened and his children
appeared raggedy and unkempt. Even his appearance became for the English
speaker a further source of curiosity and prejudice and magnified the many
other social differences that existed between them.

   The eastern Europeans were unaccustomed to the western Europeans'
ideas of individual rights, personal freedom and democracy. The English-
speaking miners had much experience with unions and formalized management-
worker relations while the eastern and southern Europeans had none.
Therefore, in labor activities, the eastern and southern European was a
reluctant and timid follower, often failing to provide the solidarity
demanded by the more militant English speaking leaders. (Today, U.M.W.A.
union leadership comes from all nationalities. However, John Mitchell,
John L. Lewis, Anthony "Tony" Boyle and Arnold Miller do reflect the
'Anglo-Saxon' leadership bias of the U.M.W.A.) These attitudes only served
to widen the gap between the English and non-English speaking miners.

Ironically, it was the luke-warm unionist eastern Europeans who were able to better withstand the strikes and walkouts since they had the accumulated savings which could carry them through strike periods.

To the English speakers, the eastern and southern European, with his desire to save and his general appearance of frugality, appeared to be too easily controlled by management. They appeared at once opportunistic, as if they would do anything for personal gain, and submissive, since they appeared to be totally receptive to any orders which the bosses issued. These different approaches to work and to their relationship with management created further antagonisms between the various ethnic groups and enhanced the isolation between the groups.[50]

These feelings of prejudice and discrimination often manifested themselves in the spatial living arrangements of the town's residents. Certain streets, or certain sections of small towns, would often be inhabited by only one ethnic group, with the "Johnny Bulls" and the "Hunkies" constituting a major division. This physical segregation of people only mirrored the social distance between the groups. For instance, in a small town, two or three Cub Scout Packs may have existed for different ethnic groups of similarly aged young boys on three neighboring streets. Socializing after work, or among the wives and children of miners, generally took place within one's own nationality group and among one's immediate neighbors.

It appears, furthermore, that it was the women of these towns who most rigidly adhered to these rather strict social patterns. The miners themselves worked with men of different nationalities and were forced to

interact with them. They had to learn eventually to get along together,
although admittedly their interactions outside of work were initially
minimal. The women, however, remained at home and found themselves in a
more difficult situation than their husbands because they had little
opportunity to interact with others outside their own social sphere, or
nationality group, and they had little time for socializing. Interviews
done today suggest that it was the women, since they carried the primary
responsibility for their children's socialization, who were able to
consistently instill and propagate these prejudices.

There were considerably large numbers of single men in these towns in
the early days. This appears to have led to, or at least reinforced, a
pattern of heavy drinking, rowdiness and a general emphasis on rugged manly
activities among young bachelors who had little else to do. Fighting
appears to have been commonplace, and the ability to use one's fists and to
defend one's own rights was often required. (Police departments were
generally quite some distance from these towns, and personal aggressive
action was a common means of resolving disputes.) The somewhat violent
atmosphere of the towns required one to personally legislate his own rights
and soon the idea of being rugged and tough became a matter of pride. (The
heavy emphasis placed on high school football and other sports then and
today is but one reflection of this attitude.)

On the other hand, organized crime, such as gambling and prostitution,
never developed. In many ways, the towns were not "wide open" places, but
in fact were quite puritanical, straight-laced and conservative, with
men's, women's and children's roles carefully defined. A man's family was

always of prime importance to the coal miner, and he worked very hard to support his family as best he could. Many had come from small isolated villages in Europe. They could be described as provincial people, emphasizing family life, and they displayed a resistance to change. It is within this pattern that the miner maintained his masculine image - the stern and authoritative father and husband. Interestingly, the miners drank far less heavily than reputation would have it. They were hard working family men, first and foremost, and the pattern of going out and drinking nightly was beyond their economic means and their physical stamina. However, the miners often drank heavily on the night before a day off or on payday, and it was not uncommon to see men staggering through the towns on such nights. But the pattern of heavy regular drinking for the vast majority of miners was rare.

The physical layout of the towns, if they were at all sizeable, usually had a special section set aside for foremen and other "Bosses." These houses were generally larger and of more sturdy construction than the regular mining houses and had considerably more land around them and they clearly, they set off the bosses from the working miners. The owners, superintendents, and high company officials generally did not reside within these coal towns. Even today, within the various trading centers and commercial areas of the county are found the elegant homes of the so-called coal barons and their manager-representatives.

The miners and their families were of course subject to external economic conditions which were beyond their control. Naturally there were periods of relative prosperity and periods of distress. The general economy of the nation had a great and an immediate effect on them as the demand for coal rose and fell in close relationship to the nation's general prosperity. After World War I, during the so-called Great Depression and after World War II, there were difficult times. Factors, such as competition from other fuel sources and the increased mechanization of their industry, made their economic picture unstable and often bleak. It was commonplace for men to work steadily for a few months and then to find themselves out of work because their company lost a contract. When the demand for coal was reduced, the men would have to start working on a two or three day a week basis. It was also frequent for men not to know if they would work from day to day, and they would simply have to wait in the morning for the sound of a whistle at the mine to inform them that work was resumed. In addition, wildcat strikes over minor grievances were frequent and the miners occasionally walked off the job for two or three days at a time. This general economic instability, coupled with tense social conditions, as the various nationality groups mixed, produced a complex atmosphere in the towns which led people to be fearful of others and to be cynical and distrustful of people's motives. People learned to watch other men carefully and sought out the real motives behind a man's actions. People learned that watching out for oneself was necessary and that other men too would be scheming to protect their own positions.

As a consequence the people tended to withdraw into themselves or their family. One did not fully make known one's position on issues to others unless one knew the other person intimately; in fact, even emotional expressions of happiness or displeasure were controlled, so as not to give impressions which might be used against oneself. In addition, people tended to be competitive, although often subtly, and to be very individualistic. Success was calculated in terms of one's own personal success rather than that of the group.[51]

In spite of this, the coal miner and his family were able to join together at times with others and to work collectively to build themselves a better life. The coal miner learned that the pragmatic course of action called for unity and a collective struggle.[52] Union activities stand out as the major expression of the miners' unity, and, while there remains much to be learned about the unionization process within the area, union activities played a major role in socializing the miners to a new world view whereby men regarded themselves as workers with rights to reasonable wages and working conditions. Slowly, over the past seventy years, especially with the coming of second and third generations, the social climate of the coal towns has changed. As the towns evolved, people of diverse cultural background learned to live with each other more easily.

2. The Coal Towns Today

Today the houses of the coal towns are still providing residence for many people and they are considered by their inhabitants to be enjoyable places to live. With private ownership of houses, the coal towns took on a new appearance as the miners put more effort into maintaining their own homes and so most of the houses today have been renovated and are well kept. One notices added-on rooms, enclosed porches, aluminum siding and brightly colored paint. Occasionally, houses with two owners, living side

by side will have separate color schemes, or will be renovated with new
windows and siding on one side while the other half remains as originally
constructed. Some homes have small swimming pools, two car garages,
elaborate patios and well manicured lawns. While the indelible marks of a
coal town cannot be entirely eradicated, the houses do reflect a
significant degree of individual pride and satisfaction which are found
among today's inhabitants. It can be stated with certainty that people
enjoy living in these coal towns and that the dwellings are considered
acceptable places to reside. Many of the small towns have even grown
slightly in size so that additional new modern homes or trailers are now
mixed in with the former mining houses.

It is interesting that the present inhabitants of these towns are
generally the sons and daughters of the original inhabitants. The
demographic patterns and the migration patterns have yet to be worked out
for these towns but the general picture which emerges is a simple one. A
majority of the young people move away for the purpose of gaining
employment, but there still remains behind a population of young people who
marry and take up residence in the now privately owned "company houses."

This pattern lends itself to maintaining a conservative atmosphere
because new ideas and new life styles from the outside are rarely brought
in by outsiders. It is a rare event when "strangers" or people who are not
from the coal town or a neighboring coal town move into one of these towns.
If asked, people can vividly recall the arrival time, housing location, and
length of stay of outside people who have come and gone. One woman,
commenting on new neighbors, could describe in detail the toys that the new

neighbor's children had since they were so different from the type of toys
of the children in her town. Clearly, the lack of stimulation from outside
the community has meant that the attitudes, social views and personality
configurations which were a part of the lives of the early miners and their
families has been maintained to a remarkable degree. It is true that some
features of the social milieu have been modified, but the life in the towns
is highly resistent to change.

Large numbers of people have been forced to leave these towns from
time to time to seek employment. For example, in the northern part of the
county in the 1950's when the demand for coal diminished greatly and many
miners were unemployed, people simply left the area for industrial jobs in
Pittsburgh, Buffalo and Cleveland. Most interesting is that many people
returned to the area and to mining when the opportunity presented itself.
Related to this general pattern of returning after living elsewhere is the
custom of the frequent and extended visit. Many former residents from
these coal towns drive considerable distances from urban areas like
Pittsburgh on a regular basis to spend weekends or vacations with their
families within these towns. In addition, substantial numbers of men work
for large construction companies which require them to work away from home
for months at a time. Their families reside safely in these towns near
neighbors and relatives and the men travel great distances for extended
weekends at home. This practice, it must be argued, has helped to reduce
the social isolation of the coal town from the larger society.

The most significant change in the coal towns has resulted from the
changes in employment patterns in the mines. The coal mining industry has

changed dramatically. No longer can mining be done on a small or moderate
scale, employing small numbers of miners. Rather, mining is almost
exclusively done on a large scale, with individual mines often employing
seven or eight hundred men. In addition, the technology has become so
sophisticated that modern mining requires even fewer men and man hours of
labor for each ton of coal produced and there has been a steady decline in
the number of coal miners in the county since 1918 (Chapter V traces these
trends in considerable detail). The result of these changes is that only a
few men in the coal towns today are now actively working underground as
coal miners, and they travel by automobile great distances to the large
modern mines which no longer require mining towns to be built near them.

The men in these coal towns work in a variety of occupations within
the county; many in the southern areas of the county now work in steel
mills. With the advent of the widespread use of automobiles and of
improved roads, employment opportunities have opened up. While the coal
miners still reside in these towns, and the tradition of sons following
their fathers into the mines still exists, the vast majority of the town's
residents are not miners. In addition, many women in these towns now have
employment of one type or other, often in the garment industry, which arose
in the county in the early 1950's when many coal miners were unemployed.
(Furthermore, in the early 1960's, the public schools in the rural areas
have developed large regional school districts which bring students out
from the narrow geographical location of the small coal towns.) These
changes in the employment patterns have led to a variety of new experiences
with different types of people, and have resulted in a clear shift in

attitude, outlook and life style toward that of middle America. The coal

towns exist today as communities well integrated into the society at large.

The residents of these towns work away from their homes but choose the

familiar surroundings of the coal town for its peaceful and quiet

environment. There they find a sense of security in belonging to a group

which shares the same outlooks and legacies from the early coal mining

days.

IV. MINES

A. STATISTICS ON MINES OF THE COUNTY

There are very few small independently operated coal mines because it
has been difficult for the small mine owner to maintain the safety and
environmental standards which the Federal government, through the Federal
Occupational Safety and Health Administration, has imposed in 1966 and
1969.[1]   This has resulted in the closing of many "house" mines, or
somewhat smaller independent mines, and in the selling of many of these
mines to the larger corporations.[2]   Consequently, the mining is dominated
by large corporations which have developed mining on a very large scale.

In Cambria County, there were twenty-four underground bituminous coal
mines in operation in 1972, and twenty-nine strip permits which allowed
strip or surface mining to take place. Sixteen of these mines were large,
employing hundreds of men. The remaining mines were small, employing
between one and forty-five men. Four large corporations owned all the
large mines with the exception of one operation, and this mine employed
only seventy-three miners. In fact, all the large corporations operated
more than one mine, with the Bethlehem Mining Corporation operating six
mines and the Barnes and Tucker Company operating four mines. In total,

70

these four large corporations employed 3,659 persons while smaller mines
employed 123 persons. In addition, there were nine cleaning plants,
formerly known as tipples, which served to clean and prepare the coal
before shipment. The men in the cleaning plants were considered to be coal
miners although they work above the ground.[3]

In 1973, there occurred a slight, but obvious, trend toward the
expansion of all types of activities related to coal production.
Additional cleaning plants opened and two companies began operations to
separate the coal from the rock in the huge slag piles, locally known as
boney piles. This reclamation activity reflects the high price of coal per
ton. It is now economically worthwhile to separate and sell this coal
which was once considered worthless. The number of strip permits also
increased from twenty-nine to thirty-three.[4] As indicated earlier
(Chapter II), the number of persons engaged in coal mining in Cambria
County was 4,149 in 1973. Strip mining activity utilized 204 persons, and
29 persons were engaged in refuse work. (All strip miners and men who work
reclaiming coal from refuse piles are union members although they may never
have had any experience underground. They are basically operators of earth
moving equipment.) The number of persons considered as employees in deep
or underground mining activities is listed as 3,562.[5] Of this number, a
small percentage are supervisory or technical personnel. Without specific
figures from all twenty-four underground mines in the county, it is
difficult to know exactly how many men are actually working coal miners.
The Greenwich Collieries Company, which is a large mining corporation in
the area, lists as of August, 1974, the following employment figures: 975

total employees of which 27 are administrators, 160 are considered
technical and supervisory (foremen and mine superintendents, etc.) and 788
are members of the United Mine Workers of America, or are working miners.[6]
Approximately 19-20% of the employees are not working as miners.
Therefore, it is probably safe to assume that there are approximately 3000
persons who are actual working underground miners in 1973-74. The total
production of coal within the county also increased between the years 1972
to 1973 to 6,891,222 tons.

Appendix D, Mines in Cambria County, gives some brief statistics on
the underground mines in Cambria County during 1972 and 1973. Cambria
County is in Pennsylvania Mine Inspection Districts 17, 18, 19, 20, 21, 24,
and 42.[7]   (Districts 42, which spatially overlaps all the other districts,
is a strip mining district.) It should be noted that the mining districts
shown in Appendix D contain other mines beside these listed, but these have
not been included since they are outside the geographical area of Cambria
County. Although the portals, or physical entrances, to the Greenwich
Collieries mines are located within Indiana County, some two miles from the
Cambria County boundary line, it is included in Appendix D since the
headquarters and business offices are located in the borough of Ebensburg
within Cambria County.

B. THE PHYSICAL LAYOUT, TECHNOLOGY, AND OTHER CONDITIONS

The technology of mining which the large corporations employ is very similar. From conversations with miners and technical employees who have worked in mines throughout the county, it is evident that there is substantial similarity in the equipment used within the mines, the strategy or method of actually developing the mines, and the design and construction of the mines. There appears to be no significant difference within the large mines in the work duties that the men actually perform or in the organization of the work crews themselves.

Some basic geological and environmental variations within the earth itself are sometimes responsible for slight physical differences in the construction of the mines. The miners therefore say that some mines have "high" coal and some have "low" coal. In "high" coal mines, the seam of coal is thick and after the coal is removed, the vacant area which remains, that is, the height from the bottom (floor) to the top (ceiling), allows the coal miner to stand upright. In Cambria County, most of the mines are low, and the seam of coal which is mined is from 3'6" to 4'0" in thickness. There are some mines, however, where the coal is over 5' in thickness.[8]

Two other important physical conditions in the mines are the humidity (water vapor) and the condition of the top. These conditions, however, do not fundamentally alter the basic activities of the miners or the mine's construction. Furthermore, some mines of the county are gaseous and some are non-gaseous. This methane gas is colorless, odorless, and highly explosive, and is a constant concern for the miners.

For descriptive purposes, an account of one modern coal mine has been included. The information was collected from the work experience of the author as he worked as a coal miner during the summer, 1973. The corporation which owned the mine, as indicated in chapter II, was the Greenwich Collieries Company with offices in Ebensburg, Pennsylvania. This company was a wholly owned subsidiary of the Pennsylvania Power and Light company. The mine was part of a two mine complex which was opened in 1969 and 1970 for the purpose of supplying coal to the parent company for generating electricity for its customers' use in eastern Pennsylvania.

The Greenwich Collieries Company mines (known locally as GREENWITCH) are located about five miles north of Barnesboro, Pennsylvania. At present, there are two separate mines with one centralized area for the processing and cleaning of the coal and the handling of supplies. The original mine is referred to as the South Mine No. 2. The portal, or entrance, to the mine is located in Greenwich, Pennsylvania. The other mine, developed a year later, is known as Greenwich No. 1, or the North Mine, and while the portal of this mine is also located in Greenwich, Pennsylvania, a matter of a few hundred yards from the portal of the south mine, the shaft by which the men enter the mine is approximately three miles directly north (about six miles driving distance) of the South Mine. (Mine No. 1 and Mine No. 2 are separate mines and are not connected underground.) The coal coming from each mine on large conveyor belts feeds into one common cleaning plant. This design simply allows one centralized place for the cleaning equipment and the railroad tracks and is more efficient than two separate areas.

A modern cleaning plant is a series of large buildings, five to seven stories high, designed to separate rock from the coal, so that when the cleaned coal finally reaches the trains there remains only small pieces of fine coal dust. The rock which is separated is put off to the side in huge piles, known as slag heaps, or boney piles.

Cleaning plants of the past were known as tipples, and they were simple in design. They were large, tall buildings, shaped like large cylinders, some fifty to sixty feet in height and some twenty feet in diameter and resembled in many ways a sturdy concrete silo. Coal was poured into the top of the tipple either from conveyor belts coming directly from a mine or from trucks which hauled the coal to the tipple. The coal itself was sifted down through the tipple through a series of smaller and smaller wire "gradients" or screens so that the pieces of coal themselves become increasingly smaller and cleaner. Rock (known as boney) which was attached to much of the coal was separated and, as with modern cleaning plants, was deposited in slag heaps.

The coal at the Greenwich Collieries Mines is being removed from a 42 inch seam of coal some 480 feet below the earth's surface in a bed of coal known as Lower Freeport.[9] The distance below the surface naturally varies since the top surface may be hilly. A seam of coal is in a plane with a thickness of, for example, 3.5 feet extending in all directions. Therefore, once the miners reach a particular seam, they potentially have the ability to pursue the coal in any of the 360° of the plane.[10] The miners at both the North and South mine are working in the same seam of

coal but never come in contact with each other underground since the two
mines are not connected.

The purpose of coal mining is to remove as much coal as possible in a
highly efficient way and to sell this coal for the largest profit possible.
While there are some constraints under which this is done--the safety and
health of the miner, the environmental impact, the external market
conditions and the labor-management relations, -- coal mining remains a
profit seeking industry through the direct sale of coal. The activities
within the mine are directly oriented to achieving high productivity and
the construction of a mine reflects this.

The North Mine was approximately four miles in length from the point
above ground where vehicles first enter the mine to the forward or front
edge of the mine. This forward edge is known as the "face", and it is at
the face that the actual cutting of the coal takes place. The width of the
mine varies considerably but could generally be considered about two miles
in width.[11]

The mine is composed of a vast labyrinth of tunnels, known variously
as headings, entries, and haulage ways. These are simply the tunnels or
underground corridors of the mine and are carefully designed to be of
nearly constant width and height, although they vary in length within the
particular section of the mine in question. An entry or entry way and a
heading are tunnels of a particular section of a mine and are the height of
the coal seam and of uniform width. Basically, a heading or an entry runs
along the long axis of any one section of the mine. The tunnels which run
along the short axis, or at right angles to a heading, are known as

crosscuts. (See diagram below) In general conversation, the term heading,

or headin', is used most frequently and it appears that this term is

reserved for those tunnels at the face where the work activity is taking

place. These headings are dead-ends, although they are constantly growing

in length as the cutting moves the mine forward. In any one section of a

mine, there will be a central tunnel through which air is moved up to the

work area. This is referred to as the air course, although the term

haulage way is sometimes used in casual conversation.

Ideally, the entries are uniform within the mine--all twenty feet in

width--and, except for special haulageways, are the height of the coal

seam. Some entries extend the full length of the mine, or a section of the

mine, while others are shorter and cut across the longer entries. These

shorter passageways which are cut or "driven" from one entry to a parallel

entry are known as crosscuts and are found in the mine approximately every

ninety feet. The mine, as diagramed below, therefore takes on a

checkerboard pattern.

DIAGRAM I

Design of A Modern Underground Bituminous Coal Mine

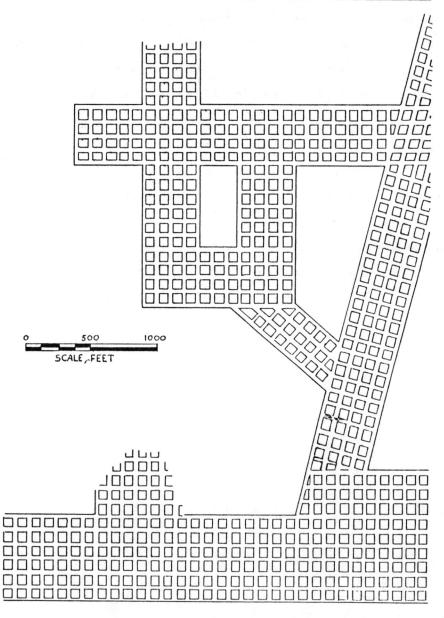

0   500   1000

SCALE, FEET

The squares in the diagram represent the areas where the coal has not been removed. These areas are known as "stumps" or "pillars." The unshaded areas around the squares represent the area from which the coal has been removed. The height or thickness in these unshaded areas is 42 inches in the North Mine which is the height of the coal seam. Although it would be preferable for the miners if they could work in an area with a height greater than 42 inches, it is too difficult and expensive for the modern machinery to dig out the rock above or below the seam of coal. Bituminous coal is soft when compared to the rock that surrounds it and cutting rock is very slow and costly work.

There are a few haulageways in the North Mine where the rock has been cut away. These haulageways are the tunnels which lead to the various working sections of the mine. It is in these haulageways that much of the transportation of men and materials takes place, and it makes transportation far easier when the entries are high. One of these haulageways is known as the main haulageway and contains a set of railroad tracks on which a motor, or locomotive, pulling flat railroad cars of various descriptions moves supplies in and out of the mine. The main haulageway, about eight feet high, is the only high place within the mine.[12] It is constantly being expanded in length as the mine grows and becomes longer and this allows the locomotive which pulls supplies into the mine to get closer to the work areas. The other haulageways which contain tracks are not cut out as yet and vehicles known as portabuses are used to transport men in these areas.

All machinery within the mine is powered by either electricity or batteries.[13]   Large electric cables carrying some 20,000 volts enter the mine through the main haulageway or through special holes drilled directly down through the earth and run to the center of the mine where they are linked to smaller electrical lines with distributions to the various sections of the mine.   Throughout the mine are large transformers for converting the current and for relaying the electric power to the various machines.

In addition, electrical power is used to supply the motor (locomotive) and a variety of smaller transportation vehicles which move the men themselves.   Throughout the main transportation routes where these vehicles travel, large copper cables are suspended from the top.   A boom, much like those found on trolley cars, extends from these vehicles to this electrical wire and the men are very cautious when working near it or passing under it.

The following is a representation of a typical section of the North Mine:

DIAGRAM II

Section of A Modern Underground Bituminous Coal Mine

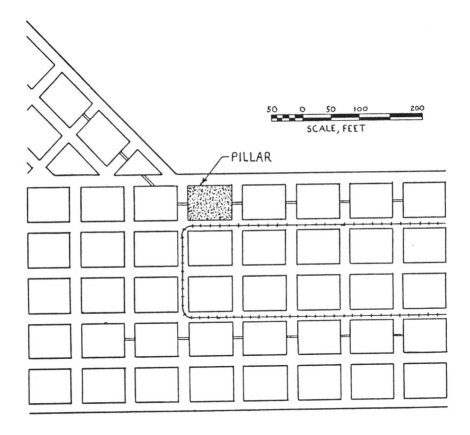

The mine as represented has a number of sections, each of which is lettered and numbered according to a well planned scheme.

The mine is generally unlighted although in a very few places where there is a possibility of danger, especially from an electrical outlet, there may be a red warning light or a white light for better illumination. It is the light on the miners' helmets which provides the illumination necessary for work. These lights are attached to the front of the helmet and are powered by a battery device which is hung from a belt on the miner's waist. A flexible cable runs from the back part of the light, or, as it is sometimes referred to, the lamp, along the top of the helmet and down the back of the miner to the power pack.

The mine is damp and in some areas there are large pools of water from underground springs which have been uncovered in the course of the mining operation. These pools of water create many hazards for the miner and the machines. It is difficult to move the heavy equipment through the water, and more seriously, the deep water can damage the electrical parts within the machines. Therefore, continuous efforts are made to pump the unwanted water from the mine.

The machine which cuts the coal at the face, known as the continuous miner, is supplied with water as well. Large water hoses run alongside the large electrical cables which supply power to the continuous miner. Water is sprayed out of the miner over the coal as it is being cut in order to reduce the amount of coal dust which is put into the air.

The machines themselves are subject to the harsh, damp environmental conditions. Generally, it is considered better to have a machine running as much as possible so that the heat of the motor will keep it dry and reduce the corrosive effects of the environment.[14]

The temperature in the mine is fairly constant throughout the year, about 40°F., although it varies slightly with the extremes of the seasons. Since the mine is damp and the temperature cool, the mine is chilly and the miners must dress appropriately. Generally, a miner wears a full set of thermal underwear and a one piece pair of coveralls such as those that a mechanic might wear. The coveralls are useful in reducing the amount of coal dust and dirt which can get inside a man's clothing. Wearing a shirt and trousers could be dangerous since they might get caught in the machinery. Rubber boots with steel toes are also worn with pants or coveralls tucked inside them or the pant legs are taped with black electrical tape to the sides of the boots for safety.

The mine is ventilated by large fans which pull air out of the mine and the overall effect is that fresh air comes into the mine from the outside to replace this evacuated air. The ventilation system itself is well planned and serves two important functions.[15] First, fresh, clean air is brought into the mine for the working miners to breath. Second, the moving air pushes out the dangerous methane gas which can collect in the mine.[16] The effect is that a draft of air is pulled throughout the mine so that air is eventually directed over the working face, the area where the miners are cutting coal. This moving air removes the dust which is produced by the cutting action of the miner or other machines and carries this dust away from the face area. From the health standpoint, this is essential in keeping the miners relatively free from dust. In the event that the ventilation system breaks down or the air becomes misdirected and is no longer flowing over the working face, the air becomes completely dust filled in a matter of minutes and the miners can no longer breath deeply or see well. In such a situation the miners quickly put on respirators which they keep with them and attention is immediately given to correcting the situation.

There is great attention paid to the ventilation system within the mine and a considerable amount of man hours each day are directed to the related problems of ventilation, dangerous gases, and dust control. The air which is pulled into the mine is directed by the use of large sheets of plastic canvas which completely fill the space between the top and the bottom. The air moves along carefully planned and designated headings (called air courses, or main airways) up to the face area where the men are working.[17]   The plastic canvas, nailed to wooden posts, or props, which themselves have been inserted between the top and the bottom, directs the flow of air along the sides of the headings so the air, after miles of travel in the mine, eventually reaches the dusty face. The returning air then carries the dust out by moving along designated headings called returns, areas where men are not working. Finally, this air exits from the mine. The following two diagrams illustrate the general air control process. The second illustration displays split air ventilation, which prevents air from being carried from one working place to another.

DIAGRAM III

General Mine Ventilation Process

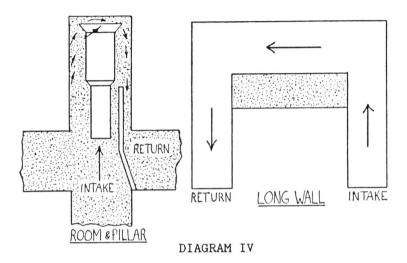

ROOM & PILLAR

DIAGRAM IV

Split Air Ventilation

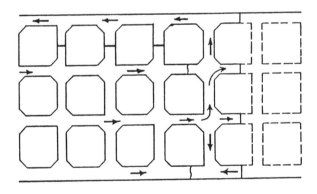

The movement of dust (coal dust from the coal seam itself and rock dust from the rock cut from above and from below the coal seam) results in a gentle wind carrying dust particles throughout the mine. This dust eventually settles on all surfaces in the mine but it is in the return air passages where the largest build up of coal dust takes place and so these locations are potentially the most dangerous in terms of explosion or fire.

As an attempt to reduce the volatility of the coal dust, a fine powdered limestone dust, called rock dust, is thrown on the top, the bottom, and the ribs (or sides) of the headings. The miners take fifty pound bags of this ground limestone and distribute them along the return air returns, it could be for miles of distance, and then one or two miners are assigned the task of scattering the dust on all surfaces. This dusting is done periodically to reduce the chances of explosion and as the mine expands the surfaces to be continuously rock dusted increase as well.[18]

To reduce the problem of inhaling this limestone dust while distributing it, the coal miners usually work backward, moving into the wind so the rock dust blows away from them: some of the miners were observed wearing respirators while performing this task.

When the miners leave their work area at the end of a work shift, the last activity performed is the rock dusting of all the newly exposed surfaces.

There is a considerable effort made to keep the mine clean and free of debris. The strong paper bags which held the rock dust are collected by the miners and removed. Wooden props or roof bolts or any type of materials, for reasons of economy and safety, are stacked along the sides of the headings in neat piles which make them easily retrievable. It is company policy that all waxed paper or tin foil used to wrap the food which the miners have brought into the mine for lunch be put back into the lunch buckets and be carried out of the mine. In addition, food is not to be thrown away within the mine because there are many rats which live within the mine and it is felt that rats are a source of disease and a potential cause of accidents.

Since the miners urinate and defecate in the mine and spit out snuff and chewing gum, and drop food on the ground, a small population of rats could probably survive in any event and miners delight in telling stories of rats jumping out at them or over them. A small body of mythology has grown up about rats and some men claim that the rats can sense danger--a falling roof or an explosion--and so, if rats are seen running, it is a signal that the miners should run too. It turns out that rats, at least for some men, are actually considered good to have around the mine.

The conditions which have been described in this section are basic for mines within the area, whether large or small. The description of the physical layout and technology, however, is limited to the larger mines.

1. The Top

The top or roof of a coal mine must be supported or it will eventually collapse or cave in. Consequently, two of the major tasks in the mine are roof control, or holding up the roof, and rib control or maintaining the vertical sides of the mine so that they will not collapse inward. Rib

control is important because the pillars of coal which are not removed
support the great weight from the earth above and the pressure on these
pillars occasionally causes the sides to be pushed into the headings.
Miners are advised not to sit against the rib, although few seem to follow
the advice.

The Greenwich mine has an approved roof support plan which has been
submitted to the U. S. Bureau of Mines and to the Department of
Environmental Resources, Office of Mines and Land Protection, of the
Commonwealth of Pennsylvania.

The top can be supported in two ways. The first method is through the
use of wooden props, or logs, which have been wedged between the top and
bottom. (The mine purchases thousands of these props from local lumber
mills).[19]   The miner takes a prop and stands it up vertically, then
inserts "cap pieces", triangular wedges of wood, on the top of the vertical
wooden prop. Depending on the exact height of the mine and the length of
the particular prop, one or two cap pieces may need to be hammered into
place by the miner until the prop fits snugly. This supports the roof by
pushing from the bottom upward. Although this method is effective, in the
North Mine it is used only for temporary roof support.

The second type of roof support, and the one employed throughout the
Greenwich mine, and generally in modern mines today, is roof bolting. With
this method, holes are drilled into the top itself and long steel rods or
bolts are inserted into the holes and screwed into the roof. A steel
expansion piece on the top end of the bolt having been inserted into the
bored hole is drilled or twisted until it spreads out or expands to anchor

the bolt in place in the firm rock. The principle of roof bolting differs from the method of employing props for no longer is the top pushed up from the bottom but rather it is held up or pulled up from a position from within the roof itself.

The horizontal distance across any entry or heading is twenty feet, except when human error causes the miner operator to remove slightly more width than called for. Four roof bolts are inserted into the top, spaced four feet from each other, and the two end bolts are placed four feet from either rib, or side. When the bolts are placed into the top, a long metal piece of either steel or aluminum, twelve feet long, and a foot in width, is placed against the roof itself. This metal piece, known as a channel, provides a continuous line of support between the four bolts and in the event of a roof-fall or cave-in links the four bolts together. Each set or row of four roof bolts and the metal channel are placed at a distance of no greater than four feet from the channel on either side of it. In other words, the parallel rows of bolts are set four feet apart.

Roof bolting is done in all areas of the mine. In addition, if the top appears dangerous, further roof support is added. Generally, large iron rails, the type used on regular railroad train tracks, are dragged up to the dangerous location in the mine and are fitted tightly against the top. The rails are lifted by the men, with the aid of jacks, up against the top and wooden props are placed under each end of the rails. Using their judgement as to the severity of the roof conditions, the miners place the rails along the entire distance which is thought to be dangerous. The rails are generally spaced every three feet.

The miners have an expression which can be misleading to the non-miner when roof conditions are discussed. The miner will refer to the "top coming down" which implies to the non-miner that the top is actually falling. The miner means that the top may be coming down soon--it could be in an instant, or a month, or a year later--but that at this given moment it merely shows the subtle signs that it is 'working' or moving and that it will come down. The experienced miner with a carefully trained eye for danger can identify cracks, slips and faults in the top, which give evidence that the rock is slipping and will eventually fall. A "pot" in a roof indicates a small circular crack in the top. Inside this circle, the rock is not attached to the other rock in the top and so a "pot", resembling a large bolder, can fall at any time. Kettles are essentially large pots and are more dangerous because they are larger and heavier and are more difficult to spot. A 'heavy roof" is an expression used by the miners to describe a roof which is slowly sagging and may eventually collapse. In all these situations, there is no guarantee when the top will fall, but since all signal danger, the miners go into action to help keep the top up. (See Chapter VI, Section A, for more on the miners' approach to roof support.)

When the top comes down or falls or caves, it does not necessarily mean that huge pieces of rock are going to fall. Rather, any piece of rock of any size can fall the 42 inches to the bottom. There is usually no loud wrenching sound but simply, without warning, the rock descends. The size of the rock may vary in size from a small boulder to an extremely large piece of rock three or four feet thick, and finally to something as large as six feet by ten feet in its dimensions.

The miners claim there is less danger in places where the top is known to be falling because here the miners take an action and apply their considerable skill to supporting the roof. The real danger exists in areas of "good" roof where no trouble is expected, for here insufficient supports may have been employed and the top falls down without warning potentially harming a miner or some machinery.

There is another situation in which the mine caves in disastrously, and there is nothing that can support it. This occurs when the mine "vaults out" and huge amounts of rock above the level of the top, perhaps to a distance of twenty or thirty feet in height, will crash down. Miners say that nothing, even roof bolts reinforced with iron rails, will support a roof in this condition. An example of this is a "clay vein," a situation in which the mass of fallen rock is geologically separate from the basic shale located over the coal seam. Naturally, this is a most dangerous situation which is difficult to stop once it begins and the miners take extreme caution in areas where these conditions are suspected.

In certain circumstances during the mining operation, the miners consciously seek to have the top fall. (See Chapter VI, Section A, Miners.) For instance, when a vast area of coal is removed, as when a pillar or stump of coal is removed, practically no support remains to hold up the top, and the downward pressure from the earth's great weight can cause a massive and sudden cave-in. In this dangerous situation, the miners prefer that the top cave-in systemically and with some regularity

after they have vacated the area so that the pressure is relieved. If the
top should fail to come down naturally, they may even dynamite it to jar
the top and make it fall.

The pressure from the weight of the earth can also have the effect of
forcing the bottom up by pushing through the remaining pillars of coal.
While an infrequent occurrence, this can be very dangerous since there is
no mechanism to keep the bottom down.

Roof support, by whatever method, reflects one of the basic principles
of the mine's construction. It is planned by mining engineers and
specifically directed by surveyors who come regularly into the mine to see
that the headings and crosscuts are following the prescribed, pre-planned
routes. Even if there is a dangerous roof condition a heading is continued
as planned and the area is not ignored nor are alternative headings
constructed. It is essential that the developing mine be constructed as
designed because the ventilation system, the transportation routes and
conveyor belt systems are integrated physical systems and are engineered
within the mine in a very specific way. No important disruption of the
master plan of the mine is permitted and so a thorough knowledge of roof
conditions and the ability to deal with dangerous conditions are
fundamental not only to the miners' safety but to the entire mining process
itself.

2. The Belt

Basic to the complex process of gathering coal is the problem of
transporting the thousands of tons of coal which must be moved through the

mine. The goal in transporting coal is to get it out of the mine to the
cleaning facilities and eventually to a central storage pile where derricks
at some later time can load it onto trains for further transport. In the
large mines, the coal is moved on large conveyor belts which collect the
coal near the working face and then transport it continuously through a
complex system of belts to some designated end point.

In the North Mine, the conveyor belt system is a series of rapidly
moving belts traveling some five-hundred feet per minute, with the smaller
belts coming from the more isolated sections of the mine emptying into
increasingly wider and more centrally located belts. The belt systems are
powered by electricity with each section of belt having its own power
source and its own separate electrical switching system, known as the
Jabco, which when pulled in emergency situations stops all the belts in the
mine.

In some of the mines in the area, the miners ride on the belts at a
reduced speed in order to get to their work places or to leave the mines
after work. This is generally considered a dangerous way to travel in the
mine and the Greenwich Collieries Company had a policy which forbade this
practice. As the belt moves from the areas near the face where the coal is
being cut, the belts themselves become progressively larger so that the
last few sections of the belt which exit from the mine are fifty-four
inches across. Here, the belt, itself, is tilted into a concave shape by
the top set of rollers so that the coal stays in the center of the belt as
it moves. When the belt circulates back and returns, it is flattened out
by running along a bottom set of rollers.

The belt system must be cleaned regularly by the miners because as the belt is returning (it is now on the bottom of the steel structure which supports the belt and the rollers) fine pieces of damp coal dust are pulled from the belt in the process of running over the bottom layers of rollers. Over a period of weeks the fine coal dust builds up into increasingly larger piles and these piles eventually rub against the belt and rollers and can cause serious trouble.

Periodically, the miners must work their way along the many belt ways and clean away these piles of dust. Usually two men work together, each taking a position on opposite sides of the belt in order to be able to reach the dust in the center. This is heavy and dangerous work since the miner is working in cramped conditions, some 3.5 feet in height, and the rapidly moving belt with its spinning rollers could easily injure a man. The coal dust itself adds to the problem as it is very dense and heavy since it is thoroughly mixed with water. The shovels which the men use are short-handled, some twenty inches across, and when full can weigh as much as forty pounds. For the miner, this heavy lifting from a position on his knees frequently leads to fatigue and it is not uncommon for the men to mistakenly touch their shovels to the edge of the belt and have it ripped from their hands by the rapidly moving belt. Caution must be exercised at all times when performing the task of 'cleaning belt' since clothing or a finger might be caught between a roller and the belt with disastrous consequences.

To complicate the problem, the damp coal often sticks to the shovel itself, and the miner must extend the shovel over the moving belt using a great deal of physical effort and tap it against the top to knock off the coal.

Some miners are called beltmen; it is their job to inspect and maintain the belt system, and so they patrol the beltways, lubricating the rollers and checking on the electrical and emergency systems. In addition, they inform the general foremen of the areas in need of cleaning so that laborers will be assigned to the job.

Since a modern coal mine can operate only if its conveyor belt system is functioning properly, constant attention is given to the maintenance of the belt system as well as to its design and location.

V. CHANGES IN MINING AND MINING TECHNOLOGY

    The first systematic mining of coal in the United States took place
near Richmond, Virginia, 1750, by Negro slaves. The bituminous coal was
used by blacksmiths to make cannon balls for the Continental artillery.[1]
The first large scale coal mining operations began in the anthracite fields
of eastern Pennsylvania in the latter part of the eighteenth century. By
1803, boatloads were being sent to Philadelphia by the Lehigh Coal Mine
Company and, by 1829, four canals had been completed to allow for a rapidly
expanding market in the use of coal for heating homes.[2]

    In western Pennsylvania, bituminous coal was first collected from
outcroppings of coal in the Pittsburgh area, and by 1790, 30,000 tons were
being produced yearly.[3] As glass and iron factories grew, so did the coal
production in the area, and this production was further increased by the
Civil War and by industrial expansion in northern cities in the years after
the war. Between 1890 and 1900, annual coal production of both bituminous
and anthracite increased from 160 million tons to about 270 million tons
while the number of men employed in mining increased from approximately
326,000 to 448,000 men.[4] From 1900 to 1910, the coal production increased
further to 500 million tons and the number of coal miners employed
nationally rose to 725,000.[5] From 1920 to 1972, the United States has

produced with great consistency 500,000,000 tons to 600,000,000 tons of
bituminous coal per year, with slight reductions during the depression
years and again during the 1950's when the use of oil as an energy source
was rapidly expanding. Over this fifty year period, the number of men
employed in bituminous mining shows a steady downward trend from 639,547
men employed in 1920 to 140,140 employed in 1971.[6]   Pennsylvania's
bituminous coal industry reveals the same patterns with regard to the
employment of men and tonnage produced. But from 1968-1972, with an
increase in the demand for coal, there has been a slight increase in the
number of men employed, with 16,878 underground bituminous miners employed
in 1968 and 19,444 miners employed in 1972.[7]

The changes in mining and mining technology relevant to this
discussion occurred in three 'stages' during the period from the turn of
the century to the present, and these stages are marked by increased
mechanization in the technology of coal mining. As a rough index of these
technological changes, one may consider the period from 1900 to the 1920's
as the stage when men were handloaders and the technology was crude and
quite simple, involving the use of a pick, shovel, a few explosives and a
great deal of muscle power to collect as much coal as possible. From the
1920's until after World War II, so called conventional mining techniques
which basically employed the limited use of machinery for the collection
and transportation of coal were introduced. This conventional mining still
required a great deal of physical effort by the miners because even though
the coal was dynamited from the coal seam it still had to be shoveled into
coal cars or onto the loaders which transported the coal from the mine.

During the 1940's increased technological advances led to what is known as continuous mining. In Cambria County, the mines did not adopt these technologies on a large scale until the late 1950's and mid-1960's, although they were becoming available to the coal mining industry immediately after World War II. With continuous mining, the goal is to have the coal move without interruption and so the cutting and the transporting of the coal are a continuous non-stop operation in which a machine, known as the continuous miner, cuts the coal and at the same time loads it onto the various types of shuttle cars or shuttle buggies which then haul it to conveyor belts for removal from the mine. There is, in theory, little actual physical labor associated with the removal of the coal itself since the machines do all the cutting and the transportation and the miners become machine operators when they are not working on matters of safety and ventilation.

CHART VII

Percentage of Total Underground Tonnage Mined by Each Method[8]

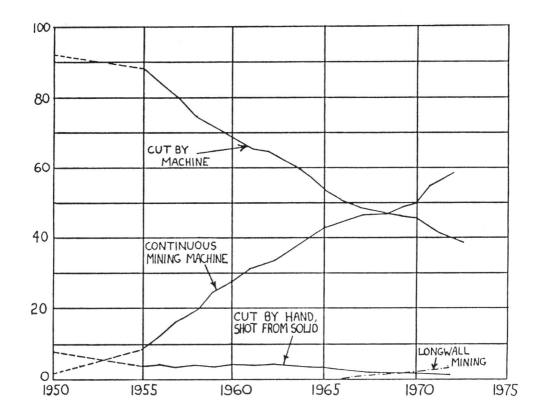

It should be noted that even today the three basic approaches to mining, as well as the newly introduced longwall method of mining, are still in use. As of 1972, 58.7 percent of American coal production made use of continuous mining, 37.4 percent used various types of conventional mining, 2.6 percent the longwall method, and 1.3 percent the so-called handloading method. Generally, a mine employs only one of these mining methods although the large modern mines which use continuous mining are sometimes undergoing a slow conversion to the longwall method. Small 'house' mines employing one to ten men use various combinations of machines but the type of mining must still be classified as conventional mining.[9]

The net effect of these changes in technology has been a steady and dramatic increase in tons of coal produced per man per day, at least until recently. A fair estimate of a miner's production using handloading techniques in underground bituminous coal mines was about 3.9 or 4 tons per man per day in 1920.[10]   By the early 1940's, with conventional mining techniques, this figure had increased to about 4.9 tons of coal produced per man per day. With the advent of continuous mining techniques, the average output per man per day in underground bituminous coal mines has risen to approximately 12 tons per man-day.[11]

A.   HANDLOADING

The handloading approach to coal mining demanded an extreme physical effort on the part of the miners since this method required the miners to shovel and move all the coal themselves. The miners worked in pairs known as buddies and were paid piecework or only for the coal that they removed from the mine.[12]   This meant that the miner worked as rapidly as possible and it was not uncommon for a man to go to work early, before the formal start of the work shift or even by himself on Sunday afternoons, to prepare his work place for the next working day. At the turn of the century, most miners worked about ten hours per day, although they remained in the mines well over eleven hours per day.[13]   One miner's comment was: "We went to work in the dark and came home in the dark and it was dark in the mine."[14] The need to work rapidly and continuously is demonstrated in the story of the miner who ate his dessert in the morning as he rode in on the "man trip" to his work place and after the day was over ate his sandwich as he rode out. While at his work place, there simply was little or no time for eating, only for working.

At this time, the miners had to purchase all their own equipment for work--oil for their lamps, picks, a tamping bar, shovels, drills, powder, and fuses: they even had to pay to have their picks sharpened, and the companies made deductions directly from their wages for the service. John Brophy offers the following figures to illustrate the costs to the miners shortly after the turn of the century. A twenty-five pound metal keg of black powder cost him $1.50 to $1.75 and lasted about two weeks. Fifty cents would purchase a gallon of lard oil to use in the lamps on the caps. Sharpening picks and augers every pay day or so cost fifty cents. The cost of the checkweighman who represented the miners when the coal was weighed was about one ton of coal per man semi-monthly. Doctors fees were subtracted at a flat rate of seventy-five cents a month for a single man, and a dollar per family. Brophy estimates that, if the mines were operating regularly, the miners received about twenty to thirty dollars semi-monthly. (He assumes the miners got forty to fifty cents per ton for four to five tons per shift and worked about twenty to twenty-four days per month.)[15]

Handloaders practiced what was known as the room and pillar method of mining. Each pair of buddies was given their own room, actually a heading, to work themselves, and the amount of coal that they collected was entirely the result of their own efforts. They would blast the coal from the face and shovel it into coal cars which were provided for them by the company.

The physical construction of a section of the mine containing rooms and pillars was basically as follows:

DIAGRAM V

Room and Pillar Mining, Circa 1900[16]

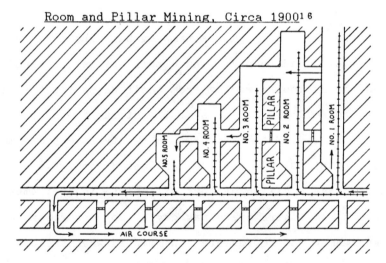

By the turn of the century, some mines were beginning to use electric motors to haul out the coal, but only mules appear to have been used in the Cambria County area.[17]

The "company men" at the turn of the century performed a number of tasks which supported the working miners. Tracklayers or trackmen were

responsible for laying and maintaining track from outside the mine up to
the point of the track switches which went into the rooms where the miners
worked. Company men were responsible for timbering (maintaining the roof)
all the areas of the mine which were not actually being worked on by a pair
of miners. Company men were also the general maintenance men in the mines,
taking care of the ventilation problems and the problems of flooding, etc.
The man specifically in charge of testing for gas before the start of a
work shift was known as a fire boss. He was the company man responsible
for closing the sections of the mine he determined to be gaseous and
dangerous, and occasionally he was given the dangerous job of purposefully
exploding pockets of trapped gas to get rid of it. The men who handled the
mules and coalcars were responsible for the transportation of the coal and
they were also company men. Boys, often ten to fourteen years old, known
as trappers, worked in many area mines, opening and closing trap doors for
mule-drawn coal cars as they moved from one section of the mine to another.
It is estimated that at the turn of the century approximately one fifth of
the total employees at a mine were company men.[18]

Usually the first task of the two buddies when they came into their
work place, or their own room, was to make the undercut: that is, they
removed a wedge of coal from the bottom of the coal seam for a horizontal
distance of about three or four feet into the coal seam and at a vertical
thickness or height of about a foot. After this, holes were drilled some
four of five feet into the coal seam above the undercut and filled with a
charge of black powder. The holes were then filled with dirt, or tamped,

and the powder was soon ignited and the coal was blown downward and forward.

The process of making the undercut was a physically tedious and demanding one since it required the miner to lie on his side and cut out the coal with a small hand pick. In all interviews with older coal miners, there is constant reference to the extreme physical difficulty of this particular task and there is little doubt that it was brutal work. In addition, this work was dangerous since the coal seam could collapse onto the miner as he reached beneath it in the process of cutting it out.

The blasting of the coal was done by the miners themselves, so it was the ordinary coal miners or the tonnage men who handled the explosives. In the earliest days, the miners simply ignited a primitive fuse known as a squib which, as it burned, shot forward like a small rocket into the hole containing the explosives. After igniting the squib, the miner would run from the room into the main haulage way or at least to some safe distance away from the face. If there was a misfire and the powder failed to explode, the miners were frequently forced to leave work or at least suspend work for a long interval. The fear was that a remaining spark could ignite the powder as the men approached the face and this was a highly dangerous situation. With further developments, explosives were ignited by a battery powered source and since long wires were used, the men could remain a safe distance from the face at the time of the explosion.

The following diagram represents a diagram of these basic mining techniques:

DIAGRAM VI

Early Mining Techniques for Blasting Coal[19]

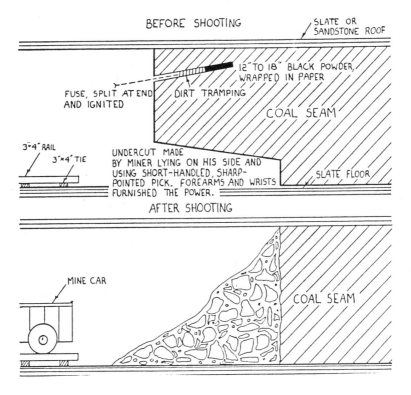

After the coal was shot down and all the coal dust and dynamite dust had settled, the two buddies returned to the room to load their coal cars. This too was backbreaking labor with the two buddies working on their knees and shoveling as much coal as they possibly could. After filling a coal car, they would push it out into the main haulage way where the young boys who were working as company men would bring along the mules and pull the cars from the mine.

The older miners of today often reminisce about the miners of the past who had such great strength and stamina. Stories still abound about how strong various individuals were and how much coal they could load during a work shift. To load fifteen or sixteen tons of coal was considered an extraordinary feat, and one that was done infrequently, although many men claim to have loaded that amount from time to time. Two buddies claimed to have loaded 36 tons on one shift, and one man told me that he loaded 21 tons by himself one time! (Of course, these large amounts of coal were collected during the period of conventional mining when machines did the undercutting and the transportation was quite mechanized and there was more time for shoveling.) Miners claim that a considerable amount of skill was required to handle a large number four shovel and that shoveling coal for hours on end required a certain rhythm and dexterity to minimize wasted motion and effort. John Brophy claims that at the turn of the century four or five tons a day was an average expected amount of coal collected on a work shift.[20]

Loading the coal was not simply a matter of the effort of the miner for if the blasting of the coal from the seam was imperfect in some way, then the miner simply did not have as much coal to shovel as he might be able to handle. Moreover, there were many necessary tasks to do besides the actual loading of coal. The workplace had to be kept safe and a great deal of time was devoted to moving props around in order to keep the top safe and to laying tracks within the rooms which incidentally, were usually constructed on a slight slope with the low point at the entrance near the main haulageway. This allowed water to run from the rooms and the filled coal cars could be more easily pushed to the main tracks. The coal cars were extremely heavy, even the unfilled ones, and pushing them was exhausting work for the miners and men could seriously injure their backs while straining to move them.

One of the worst problems was the problem of "dirty coal." In this situation, the actual coal seam in which the miners were working deteriorated in quality so that the coal was mixed with a high percentage of rock or slate, or in some rare instances the coal seams may have thinned out almost to the point of disappearing. The two buddies were obliged to continue to work their room and remove this dirty coal, in effect working for free, since they were not credited with producing coal. This situation might last for several days until the miners worked their way through to a new part of the seam where the coal was good again or until the miners were allowed to develop a new room.

The miners would inadvertently collect some unwanted rock or boney as it is called when they shoveled the coal since the blasting itself would inevitably bring some rock down from the top. In filling the cars, some rock would become mixed in and when the coal was weighed and credited to the proper miner, a strong protest was apt to be made by the company officials, resulting in the miner being docked for some percentage of the coal he had obtained. Within reason, rock was supposed to be separated from the coal and thrown into a waste pile known as the gob pile, or the gob, and not to be removed from the mine.[21] (The gob is also the part of the mine where the top has fallen, usually because the miners allowed it to fall, and is, therefore, an area of unsupported roof and fallen rock.)

The men would place a small circular metal disk, known as a check, on the coal car after it was loaded. Each check had a number for each miner stamped on it and the miner was credited with the coal when it was brought from the mine.

There are many tales of men not receiving proper credit for the coal they dug. On occasion, it appeared to the miners that when the coal was collected and company officials credited the men, arbitrary decisions about weight were frequently made by company officials. The problem, so the miners claim, was that if the coal cars were not heaping with coal, or if there was boney in the coal, a company official would simply assign an arbitrary and small tonnage to the car. To overcome such problems, the miners in one of the first actions as organized labor, contractually established the position known as the checkweighman to work alongside the company's weight boss to make certain each man received proper credit for his efforts. The checkweighman was paid by the miners themselves at a percentage of each man's tonnage.

The mules which pulled the coal cars lived in the mines year round and only on rare occasions left the mines. In the summer they were sometimes brought out to graze and it is claimed, perhaps fancifully, that they could barely see from having lived so long in the darkness. Room were constructed in the mines to serve as stables for the mules and some men and boys specialized in caring for them.

The time period, 1900-1910, was the most hazardous and dangerous in the history of American mining. The average number of fatalities from explosions per year for 1901-10 was 391.[22] In the 1901-1910 period, there were 111 major explosions and the total number of deaths from gas and dust explosions for these years was 3,912.[23] It should be noted that the rate of increase in disasters was disproportionately larger than the increase in the number of mines in use, the amount of coal produced, or the number of men employed when compared with the preceding ten year period.[24]

During this time, the safety conditions for the miners were exceedingly lax. One result of these many tragedies, however, was the establishment on July 1, 1910, of the United States Bureau of Mines whose specific charge was the "investigation of the methods of mining, especially in relation to the safety of miners.[25] Improvement came about gradually and by 1920 the figures, while far from satisfactory, reveal that the rates of fatalities and explosions had been reduced by about 50 percent. The following chart shows this trend.

CHART VIII

Tonnage, Man-Shifts, Explosions, and Resulting Fatalities in Coal Mines
of the United States, by 5 year periods, 1890-1955.[26]

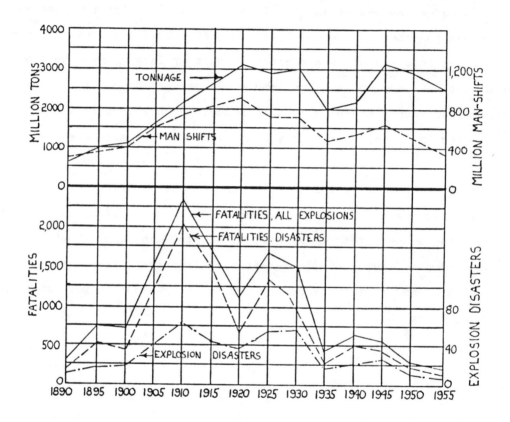

Early reports from the U.S. Bureau of Mines clearly show the great
dangers under which the miners worked. Among the conditions responsible
for the danger were poor or inadequate ventilation, negligence in testing
for gas, use of open lights in gaseous mines, failure to remove dust

accumulation and to keep the dust wet, and the use of black powder and overloaded holes (too much explosives.)[27]   Interviews indicate that similar conditions existed in Cambria County.

The miners dressed somewhat as they do today, warmly and in old clothes.   They wore leather boots instead of steel-toed rubber boots.   The hard helmets and battery powered lights worn on today's helmets did not exist at this time, nor did the closed carbide lights of the next period. Instead, the miners wore open flame cap lamps pinned to the front of their cloth caps.   These lamps were basically nothing more than small tea-pot shaped lamps, some three inches in height, containing lard oil, and with a wick coming out of the spout.   The open flame was a serious cause of thousands of mine explosions in the United States.[28]   Although electric lights began to replace open lights around 1915, by 1940, only fifty-three percent of underground miners used closed electric lamps.[29]   Instead they used the closed carbide lamp which burns carbide.[30]   From interviews with retired miners it appears that in the Cambria County area the percentage of men still using carbide lights in 1940 was even higher than the national percentage.

Miners smoked pipes in mines at this time.   Cigars were too expensive and cigarettes were regarded as effeminate.   Although laws in various states began to appear after 1910 forbidding the practice of striking matches and smoking in mines, it remained a common practice even up to 1940.

The use of the open flame lamps and pipes for smoking, coupled with the particular methods of using explosives (mostly black powder) in 1910,

resulted in the highest rates of accidental explosions in American coal
history. These percentages have, however, steadily declined to the point
where explosions in mines are now a rare thing.[31]

In addition to the constant danger, there were many other sources of
discomfort as well. The miners were extremely dirty when they finished
work and there were no bathhouses in which they could change their dirty
work clothes and wash themselves. Instead, the men walked home, black
faced and covered with the sticky black dust, exuding the odor of
perspiration and of the coal itself. Mercifully, the men usually did not
have more than a mile or two to walk since the coal towns were located near
the mine entrances. At home, they would remove their clothes in the small
kitchen of the mining house and bath there in a huge tub of hot water which
their wives would have ready for them.

In summary then, just how is the handloader, the working coal miner of
the not too distant past, to be described? Carter Goodrich described him
in 1925 as a nearly independent worker, a sort of private entrepreneur,
working with very little supervision, and earning a living based almost
entirely on his own personal efforts. Carter Goodrich wrote of the
handloader, "The miner is an isolated piece worker on a rough sort of craft
work, who sees his boss less than once a day."[32]   But this view of the
miner of this period is not complete enough. For while it is true that the
miner was substantially an independent worker--his own boss--and that he
made many decisions independently about gathering and moving coal, he was
still bound to his fellow workers. Careless or selfish or dangerous
actions of a miner could result in the injury or death of the others and so

cooperation among the miners was a necessity. The miners simply could not tolerate a man who was not safety conscious and a man who did not work and act in a safe way was shown strong disapproval. At any sign of danger a man had to warn the others, and if any miner was in trouble, a man was required to offer his aid.   If a pair of buddies needed assistance in lifting or pushing something heavy, aid was expected and it was given without question. And so there are two contrasting themes. On the one hand, the coal miner was highly individualistic and independent while at the same time he was a member of a closely knit social group operating in a highly dangerous environment where cooperation and interdependence of action were necessities for his survival and the group's survival.

B.   CONVENTIONAL MINING

In conventional mining, machines were used to perform many of the tasks which were formerly done by hand. The introduction of machines into American mining took place in a small number of progressive mines as long ago as 1870, with the introduction, among other mechanical conveniences, of Horace Brown's Monitor Coal Cutters and compressed air driven mechanical picks.[33]   McAlister Coleman estimates that by World War I 18,000 cutting machines were in operation on fifty-six percent of the coal mines.[34] Furthermore, he states that nearly ninety percent of the coal mined by the time of the publication of his book in 1943 was machine cut.[35]   These estimates are consistent with the figures published by the National Coal

Association which reports that in 1950 91.4 percent of coal mined was cut by machines or by conventional mining.

Since conventional mining spans nearly a century, the changes in technology even within this type of mining have been considerable. The machinery used has been developed by a large number of manufacturers and even today the National Coal Association lists nineteen large companies as equipment suppliers and associate members.[36] These types of machines obviously vary in specific design from manufacturer to manufacturer, but the approach to collection and transportation of coal is basically the same.

There were two basic but separate aspects to conventional mining: the cutting phase and the coal removal phase. The cutting phase was accomplished by machines which either fully cut and removed the coal from the coal seam or, at the least, made the undercut which had formerly been done by hand. If the mechanization was limited to the undercut, as when mechanization first came into being, the mechanical drills were employed because it was still necessary to blast or shoot down the coal. Sometimes additional vertical cuts, known as center cuts, were made by mechanical saws in the middle of the coal seam. This allowed one half of the seam to be shot at a time and was a safer procedure than exploding the entire face which required large amounts of powder. A third approach was used in a limited way and required an overcut to be made along the top of the coal seam. These three approaches to mechanically cutting the coal seam changed from time to time as new cutters were developed and they all saved the miner a great deal of time and effort. Their shortcoming was that they still required the coal to be dynamited and that left the coal lying in piles on the bottom.

The second part of the job, the coal removal phase, again meant new technologies for the collection and removal of the coal. While coal was originally hauled by mules, electricity was quickly applied to the task of pulling the coal from the mines after it had been placed in large coal cars. The two most common techniques used in the Cambria County area were the electric locomotive and the use of long steel cables which simply pulled coal cars from inside the mine out to the tipple. Later, conveyor belt systems were introduced in some of the country's most modern mines with some of the belts extending to the area of the face where the men could load coal somewhat directly onto the belts. These belts in turn loaded onto cross belts and finally onto the "mother" belt which took the coal from the mine.[37]   In most mines with conveyor belts, electrically driven shuttle cars carried the coal from the face to the belt itself (see chapter VI, section B for an account of miners using shuttle cars in modern mines).

In Cambria County, however, coal cars were used exclusively until the 1950's when conveyor belt systems first appeared. Some progressive mines also used mechanical loaders to gather up the shot down coal and to place it into coal cars or onto conveyor belts but this was a later development in this area of the country.

In the most modern mines within the region in the 1930's and 1940's, the mining process was broken down into three sequential but separate steps. These were: the cutting phase, in which the coal was cut, drilled

and blasted; the gathering phase, in which the coal was placed in coal cars
or on conveyor belts; and the transportation phase, in which the coal was
removed from the mine. While all of these could be accomplished with
varying degrees of efficiency with machines, the vast majority of the mines
did not involve the mechanization of all three phases. It was the second
phase, where the coal was gathered up, which resisted technological
advances most stubbornly and the miners were still required to shovel, or
handload the coal. In fact, most miners were still tonnage men receiving
wages on the basis of the tons of coal collected until the middle and late
1940's. The critical link missing in this basically mechanized operation
was a heavy loading machine, or the scraper loader, which was capable of
moving into the face area and gathering up the shot coal and then relaying
this coal to the cars without interruption.

This changing technology is reflected in the 1941 contract agreement
between the United Mine Workers of America and the coal operators of the
states of Pennsylvania, Michigan, Ohio, Maryland, West Virginia, Virginia,
Northern Tennessee and eastern areas of Kentucky.[38]   This agreement
included District 2 of the U.M.W.A. of which Cambria County was a part.
The miners worked seven hours per day at their work places (travel into and
out of the mine and lunch periods were not included in the seven hour work
time). There were wage provisions for miners doing piecework and also for
those miners earning an hourly wage (Schedule A and Schedule B
respectively, of the agreement). In western Pennsylvania, for example, the
tonnage rates were: pick mining, thick vein, $1.05 per ton; machine
loading, thick vein, $ .83 per ton; cutting shortwall machine, thick vein,

$ .11 per ton.   Reflected in these three rates are three separate
technologies, the first being the old handloading technology and the latter
two pertaining to cutting machines, of which the last one was a reasonably
quick and efficient way of getting coal.   For miners working by the hour,
the following are representative wages: cutting and loading machine
operators, $1.28 per hour or $9.00 per day; face men $1.11 per hour or
$7.80 per day; operator helper $1.13 per hour or $7.96 per day.[39]   In the
classification of general day labor (these men were not connected primarily
with producing coal), the following are representative of wages: motormen
and shuttle car operators, $1.02 per hour or $7.16 per day; trackmen and
timbermen, $1.00 per hour or $7.00 per day; unclassified inside laborers,
$ .73 per hour or $6.76 per day.[40]

In Cambria County, tonnage rates were abandoned by the late 1940's.
The U.M.W.A. had won by that time what was known as "portal-to-portal" pay,
whereby the miners were paid on the basis of an eight hour day and were
paid from the time they entered the mine to the time when they came out--
eating time and travel time being included within the eight hours.   With
portal to portal pay, all tonnage piecework disappeared and all miners were
paid on an hourly basis with wage differentials (rates) existing between
job classifications.[41]   The miner was no longer a pieceworker.   In mines
in the area which were not under union contract, however, tonnage work
continued to exist for a time.

Toward the end of the period when some miners still did piecework in
Cambria County, an extremely hard working miner with the good fortune to be
working in a seam of coal that was easy to work, with good height and a

minimum of roof support problems, could count on earning as much as one hundred dollars for a week's effort and perhaps as much as $4500 for a year's work. Older, less ambitious, or less fortunate men, may have earned $3500 for the year. Older miners today claim that in the middle and late 1940's, the miner considered himself to have been making big wages and that relative to other groups of working people in the area the coal miner was financially very well off.

The conventional phase of coal mining produced a mixed but improving record for safety in terms of explosions, disasters and fatalities. Since 1920, the rate and the absolute number in all three areas has been declining, but so too has the number of miners themselves been declining since about 1920 when mechanization was increased significantly. There was a slight rise in serious accidents between 1925 and 1930, which the Bureau of Mines was at a loss to explain, and again, in the 1940-45 period, when employment increased in the mines nationally.[42]

This improvement of the safety record appears to be related to stricter federal and state laws and the efforts of the U.S. Bureau of Mines, since throughout this period a great deal of experimentation and testing was being done to reduce the high fatality disaster rates. New equipment and new approaches to mining were introduced. Among these were the introduction of far safer explosives, black powder being used less and less; improved ventilation systems, with split air ventilation; larger fans; automatic warning signals; regular checks on the air flow; watering of the areas where the coal was being cut; and finally the practice of rock dusting.[43]

Finally in 1941, Public Law 49, the Coal Mines Inspection and Investigation Act, empowered the Secretary of the Interior, acting through the Federal Bureau of Mines, to make inspections and investigations of the health and safety conditions of coal mines.[44]   No authority was given under this law, however, for the enforcement of safety standards. On July 16, 1952, Public Law 552, known as the Federal Coal Mine Safety Act, was enacted and this law empowered federal inspectors to require compliance with mine safety provisions.[45]   This law is comprehensive and has led to highly increased safety standards and has obviously reduced the rates of disaster, explosion and fatality.[46]

The technological changes associated with conventional mining have resulted in significant changes in the basic work organization of the mines. Much of the new technology required the men to work in groups or crews of men with pairs of men performing specific and limited aspects of the job. For instance, two men might be working on the coal cutting machine, two might be on a loading machine and two might be doing some timbering work. In addition, the miner no longer worked in isolation and for the most part his wages were no longer directly related to his own personal effort. Now, each part of the work effort was intimately tied to the actions of the others within the crew. Helen M. Lewis and Edward M. Knipe have studied this change in work relationships in some detail and offer some insight into the changes in the dynamics of the work crew. They claim that the miners no longer determined the pace of the work but rather that the pace was determined by the group itself or by the machines, and the miner was now forced to respond directly to his fellow workers.

Secondly, they claim that there grew a sense of solidarity and interdependence among the miners and this is a fundamental change from the situation that existed among the "independent" handloader.

It is clear that conventional mining did mean a shift in work organization. Further implications of this change in organization will be discussed in Chapter VI.

C.   CONTINUOUS MINING

Continuous mining is the latest mining technique to be in widespread use in Cambria County and is found in all the large modern mines in the county. To a limited extent, a newer technology, known as the longwall method, is found in some mines but at the time of this writing it accounts for only a small fraction of the coal produced (2.6 percent nationally in 1972). In Cambria County, only a small percentage of the coal is produced from handloading or conventional mining (see Chapter IV, section A, where it is demonstrated that practically all mines are large modern operations).

This section contains only limited comments on continuous mining because this has been adequately done in Chapter IV, The Mines, in section B on the physical construction and technology of the modern mines and in Chapter VI, The Work, sections A and B.

With continuous mining techniques, the coal is cut from the face and moves almost continuously from the place of the cutting itself to a storage location outside the mine. This represents a major technological improvement over conventional mining where there is a break in the flow of the coal. The previous approaches to mining have always involved a series of discrete and separate operations, e.g. cutting, gathering, transporting, and each operation was an activity unto itself. Continuous mining, by way of contrast, is one continual operation and the coal in principle does not stop moving after it is cut.

The key to continuous mining was the development of the continuous miner, or the continuous mining machine. This large, flat machine, some thirty-five feet long, has a spinning drum on the front end which contains the sharp carbide "teeth" which dig into the coal seam and rip or cut the coal down onto a pan under the drum. Large mechanical arms scoop the cut coal into the center of the miner and the coal is conveyed by belt through the machine until it moves onto a boom-like extension which itself contains a conveyor belt. From this boom, the coal is loaded onto shuttle cars which in turn transport it to large conveyor belts which quickly move the coal from the mine. The coal is moving almost continually if all goes well although there are brief stops in the flow as a full shuttle car moves away from the belts and an empty car carefully moves in under the boom of the continuous miner. (As described here the system works effectively and efficiently, but there are occasional problems with mechanical failures.) In addition, the continuous miner itself must be moved frequently to new locations or entries and this is a slow process in which coal production stops.

While the technology of continuous mining was an improvement over that of the conventional types, both technologies shared the work arrangement whereby the miners did not work alone or even in pairs but rather they were

organized in work crews of five or six men. It should be emphasized that
the work crew for the modern miner is the basic unit with which he
identifies while at work and so the work of the modern miner can best be
understood in terms of the work crew.

The sophisticated machinery employed in the underground coal mining
industry has not resulted in a greater output of coal per man per day.
Stricter safety laws (Coal Mine Safety Act Amendments of 1966, Coal Mine
Health and Safety Act of 1969, and the Occupational Safety and Health Act
of 1970) it appears have caused a decline in output, especially since 1969
when the Coal Mine Health and Safety Act became quite strict. In the
absence of these laws, the output presumably would have continued to
increase steadily as it had been doing for some time because new machines
clearly do remove the burden of the heavy work from the men.[48]   In a sense
what has happened is that the potentially greater output of coal which
could have resulted from these technological improvements has been
exchanged or sacrificed for improvements in the health and safety
conditions within the mines.

VI. WORK

A. MINERS

The National Bituminous Coal Wage Agreement of 1971 lists twenty-nine
separate job classifications for men working underground in deep coal
mines. These twenty-nine categories are further grouped into six wage
grades. (See Appendix E, Data for Wage Classifications, for the job
classification and wage grades for underground, strip and auger miners, and
preparation plant workers, and a summary of the Principle General Pay
Provisions.) The rationale for dividing the jobs into six wage grades is
based on the skill involved in the performance of a job and on the hazards
to health associated with a job.

In addition to these categories and grades, the men can also be
grouped by work activities. Within the mine, the miners engage in four
basic types of operations. The first is the activities of the production
crews or the face crews. It is the task of these men to actually produce
or cut the coal and to move this coal along to the conveyor belts. At the
Greenwich Collieries Mines, this group consists of six workers and a
section foreman. The six workers are the continuous miner operator, roof
bolter, two shuttle car operators, and two less skilled laborers to help
the machine operators on the miner and on the bolter.

123

The second group of men transports the vast amount of supplies from outside the mine to the miners located at the face. The motormen who drive the locomotive, or motor, and the operators of large battery powered transport machines known as kerseys, are within this category of worker.

The third category of worker is involved with maintenance, particularly machine maintenance. The harsh conditions of the mine make the breakdown of equipment a common occurrence and electrical cables are frequently pulled loose from the machinery or driven over and cut. Mechanics, welders, and mechanics' helpers are the men in this group.

The fourth category of worker performs more of the technical tasks. A beltman, for example, maintains the conveyor belt during a typical work shift, making certain that all the rollers over which the belt travels are well lubricated and that the electrical equipment is in working order. Trackmen lay track for the locomotive. Bratticemen construct walls in the cross-cuts to insure that the air travels in the correct pattern and masons perform many jobs, one of the most common of which is the building of overheads or enclosed cinder block passageways to move air. A pumper's function is to pump water out of places where it has accumulated. Most of these specialized jobs are coveted by the miners since the work tends to be less repetitious than production work and because many of these men only work the daylight (8:00 a.m. to 4:00 p.m.) shift. Unlike some of the other jobs, these skilled positions demand a good deal of personal decision making and imagination from the miner and add to the job satisfaction.

The remainder of the jobs listed in Appendix E are not found in modern mines but rather in mines with older technologies.

Although the work of the miner is rarely monotonous, the work of the six men on the production crew involves the greatest amount of routine found within the mines. The job of each man on the crew is essentially the same from day to day, although judgments must regularly be made by each man for good coal production. The section foreman is responsible for the activities of the crew and for outlining the approach to work, but individual miners are constantly called upon to make decisions. For instance, roof bolters may place extra roof bolts into the top because in their judgement this is needed for safety, or shuttle car operators may at their own discretion deposit wooden posts at locations near the work area in anticipation of their future need. In addition, the miners must be constantly on the lookout for bad roof conditions and must take appropriate action if danger is perceived.

The distance at which the miners work from the foremen is often considerable. The physical construction of the headings and crosscuts since they surround the large rectangular pillars of coal leaves the workers with little awareness of the location of the foreman. The result is that the miner cannot rely on the foreman to make decisions for him in most circumstances. This appears to be a benefit for the miner since autonomy in making decisions gives him some control of his work and a genuine sense of job satisfaction. Safety and production depend on the individual miner's ability and initiative and the miners rarely complain of boredom, since even on the production crews where the work is most routine, the miner must be aware and thinking.

The United Mine Workers of America as a matter of policy have
established through their union contracts with the operators a situation in
which there is no incentive pay. This policy was instituted since
incentive pay leads to hurrying, and haste to complete a job can lead to
accidents. At the Greenwich Collieries Mines, however, the production
crews are given one small incentive. If a crew is able to deliver 150
shuttle cars of coal (approximately 400-600 tons) onto the conveyor belt
during a work shift, each of the six men on the crew is allowed to collect
one case of beer of his choice from a local beer distributor. This little
incentive further serves to break up the daily routine for the crews.[1]

The miners are happier with themselves when they are able to get large
amounts of coal. While getting 150 shuttle cars of coal is a rare event,
it is remembered with pleasure. There is a real sense of satisfaction when
the crew produces large amounts of coal--90 to 100 shuttle cars or more--
but at the same time there is no shame or embarrassment if only small
amounts are obtained. The shuttle car operators record the number of
shuttle car trips by putting chalk marks on the side of their car, and they
are usually asked by the crew members how they did for the day as they
leave to go home.

It is worth noting that the miners have a sense of honesty and pride
in their work as evidenced in part by their desire to get as much coal as
possible. In addition, the miners generally make an effort to protect the
machinery, making certain that it is properly oiled or lubricated and not
abused. Rarely does the situation occur where the lack of attention to
some detail on the machinery results in a breakdown in the equipment.

With regard to safety, most miners are noticeably conscientious. If
loose rock is seen hanging from the top, the miners immediately make an
effort to remove the hazard so that it will not fall at some later time.
Often this is easily done and involves no more than grabbing the rock and
pulling it down, although at other times the miner may have to use a large
hammer or steel rod to pry or beat the rock so that it will snap off and
fall. The attention to roof conditions is not something that preoccupies
the miners, but if there is a potentially dangerous condition, the miners
take time to correct the situation. Many of the miners carry hammers in
their belts and from time to time they hit the top solidly with the hammer
and listen for a soft or hollow sound indicating that the rock is not
solidly attached and that the roof is poor and likely to fall.

In general, situations considered dangerous by the miners are acted
upon quickly and prevention of accidents is an important part of their
routine. For instance, small pieces of wire, which are commonly used in
the mines to suspend water or electrical lines occasionally get lost and
end up lying on the bottom, a situation which could cause a man to trip and
possibly fall into moving machinery. Such a situation would not be
ignored and the wires are quickly picked up and rolled into small bundles
because the miners take safety very seriously and they do not need to be
told by a boss to take an action.

New miners are required to work for one year at the face of the mine
alongside an experienced miner, and it is through this process that the
skill of recognizing dangerous roof conditions is passed on from the
experienced miner to the novice.[2]   Not all men possess equal skill in

being able to hear or interpret the ring in the hammer head as it hits the top, for it is really an artistic ability to interpret the sound; but the obvious hollow "thud" of a loose piece of rock is enough to keep even beginners hitting the top and detecting obviously unsafe conditions.[3]

The miners do not work under conditions of anxiety and fear.[4] Rather, they have a respect for the dangers of the mine and take positive actions to keep their work place safe. Although they work in extremely dangerous conditions, they appear to deal very well with this danger both psychologically and emotionally because it seems they possess the ability to actively control their environment. It is said by the miners that some men simply do not have the ability to work in the confined spaces of the mine, and, whether it is fear of cave-ins, or explosions or some form of claustrophobia, they soon quit working. As a result, this leaves men without these strongly developed fears.

In observing miners at work or at rest underground, one can only have the impression that they have very little or no fear. In a social setting, after work, one would never hear any mention of fear, although there might be brief mention of a particularly dangerous situation that a man was working in on a particular day. When miners are questioned directly about their fears while at work, there is usually a muted expression of some sort such as, "I suppose most men have some fear", or as one retired man expressed it, "Nobody seemed to fear. Most times it was the wives who had fear that their husbands wouldn't come home." But, there is very little verbal evidence to indicate fear. (My own experience was one in which I went from an initial position of nearly complete terror to a feeling, after just several days, of little concern for the dangers at work.)

In studies of the perceptions of danger in underground coal mining (as noted previously, an occupation which has the highest accident and fatality rate for which statistics are kept in the United States), it would probably be expected that coal miners would perceive their occupation as being more dangerous than other occupations. Lewis and Knipe studied coal miners in nine mines in Virginia with the use of questionnaires and interviews and found that only 21 percent of the miners stated that they felt mining to be more dangerous than other occupations, while 63 percent felt it was equally dangerous, and 6 percent felt it was less dangerous.[5]

While it is claimed that coal miners do not generally perceive their occupation as particularly dangerous, they do have very accurate perceptions about the most dangerous aspects of mining. For instance, great concern is expressed about the dangers of roof falls (cave-ins) and, since 63 percent of coal mine fatalities nationally were caused by roof falls at the time of the study, it was felt that their perceptions were quite accurate.[6]

Some clinical psychologists disagree with the sociological findings of Lewis and Knipe, as well as with my observations and experience. Their general claim is that the miners do in fact have latent fears which remain as unconscious sources of tension and often reveal themselves in personality traits, such as the appearance of being physically and mentally exhausted. The miners, it is claimed, repress their anxieties about the hazards (falling rock, explosions, high dust levels) soon after beginning work. While they may not appear to be suffering, they do struggle with a subliminal or latent tension state. (It should be noted that the causes of mental illness among miners are not only attributed to the stresses of working in a mine but also are attributed to changes in the social groupings within the mine and to social and economic conditions outside the mine.)

Lewis and Knipe, while stating that coal miners basically do not regard their occupations as dangerous, present some confusing and contradictory comments in their findings. They write that coal miners reflect the general phenomenon of persons who work in dangerous environments in that they tend to sublimate any expression of fear. They also argue that the miner accepts the danger of his work as a payment of sorts which is exchanged for the image of a rugged, highly masculine man which he portrays to those who do not work underground, such as family, women, and friends.[7] Implicit in these arguments is the idea that in some psychological way the miners are in fact afraid, although this fear is never expressed.

If there are deep psychological tensions or fears within him, the miner is very successful at concealing them. It is my contention that the miner is actually much less fearful than Lewis and Knipe suggest. There are several legitimate and, I think, convincing explanations for the lack of fear in the miner. Most importantly, the coal miners' knowledge of roof conditions allows a reasonable degree of control and therefore of safety. In addition to hitting the roof and listening to the sound which gives clues about the conditions of the roof, some miners feel the roof with

their fingertips as they strike the roof with a hammer because the
vibrations give additional evidence of good or poor conditions.
Experienced miners, in addition, can visually spot slips and faults in the
top which indicate danger.

The basic strategy of the miners is to take positive action to control
their environment and to reduce the danger. The setting of wooden posts,
the roof bolting activities, the constant testing for gas, and the frequent
tapping of the roof are only the overt manifestations of this positive
action. To observe the miners in a situation where a recognized dangerous
condition exists makes it clear that it is their ability to recognize
danger and to take positive action to control the environment that keeps
him safe and serves as the basis for reducing his fears.

Moving heavy iron rails under a falling roof requires a certain degree
of boldness on the miner's part, but this boldness is never reckless. The
miners proceed deliberately and with confidence, but they never hurry. In
a sense, they balance their skills against the dangers and proceed on the
path where caution and confidence seem to meet. Their knowledge of the
danger is critical to this process. To be sure, there are extreme
conditions when no amount of human effort will stop the roof from vaulting
out and falling but in such conditions the miners must wait for the roof-
fall to take place before acting. In most situations, however, they do
take action.

The miners themselves say that generally there is not much danger if
they are aware of bad roof or of gaseous conditions. Instead, accidents
occur when men become over-confident of the roof conditions for it is then

that the coincidental occurrence of a falling roof with a man under it takes place. Caution, awareness and constant suspicion of the roof assures them that their positive action will keep things safe: over-confidence can result in a lack of action and this is when accidents occur.

The data on fatal accidents appear to support this theory on coal miners' attitudes toward fear. In Pennsylvania, in 1971, there were 32 fatalities for 26,549 coal mine employees, and in 1972, there were 19 fatalities for 25,627 employees.[8]   In Cambria County, there was one fatality due to a roof fall in 1971.[9]   In 1972, Cambria County experienced two fatalities from roof falls.[10]   In 1973, there were 17 fatal accidents in the bituminous coal fields in Pennsylvania for 26,772 workers, or 0.64 fatalities per 1000 employees.[11]   An analysis of the mine inspector's reports with regard to these fatalities is enlightening. When one examines the fatal accident reports for the year 1972 in bituminous mines in the state of Pennsylvania, the number of accidents which resulted from basic human error is significant. Of nineteen fatalities, nine deaths appear to have been clearly cases of human error. The miner was too close to a moving machine or was driving a machine recklessly. The ten other fatalities appear to have been those which occurred through a combination of fate and human error. As one mine inspector expressed it after reviewing a fatality, "The responsibility for these accidents must be charged to the hazards of the industry as the victim was experienced and considered to be a safety-conscious man."[12]   While appearing to be matters of fate or coincidence and while difficult to prevent, these accidents do involve a certain human element since vigilance and positive action in constantly rechecking posts or tapping the top increase one's knowledge of conditions and presumably reduces accidents even of the highly unpredictable kind.

Whether one considers national, or Pennsylvania or Cambria County statistics, the number of fatalities of coal miners has been reduced steadily, if not dramatically, over the past fifty years. (See Appendix F for industry figures and Appendix G for Pennsylvania figures.) In 1972, there were 19 fatalities in Pennsylvania or .74 fatalities per 1000 employees. Roof falls accounted for the largest number of these fatal accidents with transportation related accidents, which imply human error, being second in frequency. More precisely, there were eight deaths from roof falls and five from transportation related causes.[13] In 1971, this trend was slightly reversed when nine deaths resulted from transportation accidents.[14] The evidence, while admittedly limited, indicates that fully one-half of the accidents in modern mining result from roof falls, or cave-ins, and that an aggressive or positive approach to safety is required in all mining situations.

Gaseous conditions are not a constant concern to the miners but the operators of machines and the section foremen carry safety flame lamps, referred to as bug lights, for testing purposes. Periodically, the foremen do test for gas and the machine operators who work at the face are supposed to check for gas about every twenty minutes. These tests are infrequently made; instead, operators appeared to test only two or three times per work shift, and occasionally not at all. The Greenwich Collieries mines have recently been reclassified as gaseous mines after a small gas explosion gave definitive evidence of the presence of gas.[14]*

The attitudes of the miners toward work is generally positive. Nearly all the men questioned said it is the best job in the area, at least from the standpoint of wages. For young men of 18 or 19 years of age, with high school diplomas or less, the chance to earn over $10,000 per year is considered a great opportunity. For more experienced men with higher hourly rates, the ability to earn $14,000 to $16,000 per year is considered desirable. Since coal mining is the only major industry in the area of northern Cambria County, the miners as a group are the largest wage earners in the area.[15] In addition, the cost of living in the area is low by standards of the northern United States, or even when compared to the City of Johnstown forty miles to the south. Housing costs, whether rented or bought, are low, and entertainment and recreation cost are low as well.

Besides desirable wages relative to those of other workers in the area, the work itself is also appealing to the miners. A constant response to questions about coal mining as a life's job is, "It gets into your blood," or "We have dirt in our blood." There are a number of factors which contribute to this feeling.

As mentioned, the general lack of a boring work routine along with the chances for personal decision making helps to make coal mining appealing. The miners today know that the work is no longer as physically difficult as the mining which was done in the past when the men hand-loaded the coal and were paid on a piecework basis. Many men are now machine operators of one sort or another and not simply laborers working with hand tools. The eight hour work day extends from the time the miners step on the elevator or cage to go underground until they "come out". This "portal to portal" pay has dramatically changed the actual work time of the miners since it now includes all the travel time up to the work area from the time they first enter the mine.[16] It is not uncommon for forty minutes to pass before the miners actually get to work and for the miners to leave their work places thirty minutes before the end of the work shift so that only about six and one-half hours actual work remain. This is perceived as short working hours by the miners.

While all these factors contribute to the perception of coal mining as an appealing job, it is the social relations within the work crews which add the critical element to the enjoyment of the job. The men of a work crew form not only the basic work unit, but also, and more importantly for the miner, the basic social unit of the work environment. The men who work together generally get along very well in a social sense and, while the men may not socialize together after work, they have an obviously close social bond while at work. On many of the production crews, joking and playful heckling are constantly going on among the men who, in addition to displaying a genuine interest in the outside activities of one another, obviously get along very well while at work.

1. Work Crew

It is essential in understanding the work of the coal miner that the individual miner be seen not only in terms of his actual work activity but also in the broader context of the mining town. Chapter III dealt in part

with the coal towns of the miner and illustrated the changes which have
taken place in these towns as a response to changes in the coal industry
within the region. It was pointed out that the changes in mining have
resulted in fewer men being employed in the coal mining industry and that
now the majority of the coal towns have very few working miners residing
within them. Therefore, when a man goes to work in a large modern mine, he
is apt to be working mostly with strangers rather than with his neighbors
as in times past.

The technological changes in coal mining, as described in Chapter V,
have been substantial and have generally resulted in greater efficiencies
per miner per unit time. In addition, the technological improvements have
meant a change in the work organization of the miners from rather
individualistic pursuits to highly organized teams of men working in crews
with each man performing only one aspect of the total job. The work crew
has become more than just a new type of work arrangement for the miner: it
is for the miner the primary social unit within the large modern mine with
which the miner identifies. As indicated, the camaraderie among the men of
a work crew, whether it is on a production crew at the face or on a crew of
mechanics is most important but this friendship does not extend outside to
different crews, even though an individual crew member may have friends
outside of his own crew.

The importance of the work crews as a social unit within the mine
cannot be overestimated. This, in a simple way, is the basic unit, and
perhaps the only unit, with which the miner identifies in the modern coal
mine. In addition, the choice of an employer matters very little to the

individual coal miner who is a member of the United Mine Workers of America, since wages, retirement, and health benefits are set with minor variations within union districts or by national labor contracts.

The main offices of the management of the mine are located some twenty miles from the mine itself and the upper level management rarely comes into the mine. For the miner, management is represented by the section foreman with whom he works on a day to day basis and, as will be shown in section B, "The Supervisory Personnel", these foremen are miners themselves and their relationship to the men cannot be characterized strictly by the terms of "worker" versus "manager". In fact, the section foremen themselves are an important part of the work crew. Their actions, since they have authority to order the men to do certain tasks, are important to the harmony of the crew, and if the work crew is considered a social unit, these men are integral parts of this social unit. And so, from the miners' viewpoint, the section foreman represents the management for the most part in only a legalistic or formal sense. The management appears distant from the majority of the miners, and the miner does not, as mentioned, identify strongly with the company. Rarely does he feel that he owes the company any particular loyalty.

This attitude, it should be pointed out, is shared by the foreman as well. They too are coal miners first and foremost, and if a better job opportunity presents itself at another mine or with another company they would make their decision to seek the new position without a feeling of disloyalty to their current employer. For the section foremen, the men of the work crew, with whom he spends eight hours of every work day in essential isolation, are very important in terms of social identity and social interactions as well.

Many of the men arrive twenty or thirty minutes before the crews actually descend down the cage and they smoke or chew snuff and talk and joke together. This sitting as a group has the added practical advantage that the men will be together as a crew when they enter the mine and travel on to their work place. The "man-trip" as it is called can be miles in distance and since there are only one or two trips made to transport the production crews into any section they must travel as a group.

Two crews basically take the same man trip to the face in any one section of the mine. It is clear that while the relationships between the men of the two crews are cordial and men will make jokes with men on the other crew, the relationships are still distant and do not show the warmth found within one's own crew.

Other types of workers, particularly if they work in crews or on gangs, display social relations similar to those of the production crews. They joke with one another, take an interest in each other's non-working activities, and usually give some indication that they enjoy working together. These men, however, are more apt to be moving throughout the waiting room before work and to be chatting with other men, since many of them move throughout the mine while working and therefore have a wider network of social relationships than production men. To some extent, these men help to bridge the work crews, as do those few individuals who happen to know men on other crews, and this helps to create a simple network among all the men where information can be exchanged.

Outside the small network of comrades who work together, there is a surprisingly small amount of interaction among the men on a shift. This is a distinct difference from the social conditions which miners claim existed formerly within the coal mining industry of the area. The fact that the number of coal miners within the county has declined from 20,708 in 1940 to approximately 4,088 in 1973, certainly gives evidence that the community of the miner has changed dramatically.[17] In addition, many of the men now drive considerable distances to work: one man at Greenwich Collieries drives sixty-five miles to get to work and many men drive forty-five miles from the Johnstown area. After work, many miners do not socialize or even come in contact with each other since they must commute long distances to their townships and boroughs. The result, in contrast to former times, is that many of the men are strangers outside of work, and, at best casual acquaintances while at work. Once again the social significance of the work crew to the individual is emphasized since it is only within this small group that the miner has comfortable relationships.

With the private ownership of homes in the coal towns, this pattern has been further exaggerated. Now a man can live in one town near a particular mining operation and work at another mine some distance away. In other words, the miner is independent of his employer when choosing a place to reside.

While working, various categories of men move throughout the mine to perform their work duties. Occasionally, it is necessary for a miner to ask for help from another man or group of men not actually assigned to work with him. For example, a mason may need the help of two or three men to lift heavy iron rails into place. According to the miners, in former times help would never be refused to any man. In the mine today, however, this is not always the situation. Men who are basically strangers to each other will sometimes refuse to help another man. If the men are spread out, the darkness of the mine can provide a miner with a screen of anonymity whereby he can be reasonably certain that he will not be recognized if he refuses to help other men. For instance, mechanics often complain that when they are sent to a section of a mine to repair a machine the machine's operator will not offer assistance but will simply sit and watch the mechanic work.

A change in the traditional wage structure is another cause in the growing impersonality and the decreased sense of community among the miners. It is evident today that in contrast to wage practices of the past, some categories of workers are beginning to make significantly more money per hour than other workers. Using the three year interval, 1971 to 1973, for a comparison of wages across the various grades, one notices that there is a greater proportional increase in wages at the higher grades than with the lower ones and so the gap between upper and lower ranges is widening. (See Appendix E) This is a change in the wage structure which has existed since conventional mining techniques were introduced and it contributes greatly to the differences, both economic and social, among the men.

For the men on the production crew, the differences in hourly wages do not seem to produce resentment. Here relationships are cordial and friendly and the men take an interest in each other's welfare. Joking and general horseplay are commonplace and the men help each other willingly and

requests for assistance are not denied. In fact the social bond among the
crew's members on many of the face crews is so strong that the removal of a
miner from one of these units even for temporary work with another crew is
often met with a strong protracted protest from the miner who has been
asked to change groups.

The transfer of a man from one work crew to another is usually
necessitated by the need for a man with a particular skill to fill in on
another crew. Generally, the cause for this move stems from absenteeism,
and the rate of absenteeism is high (about twenty percent, or each man on
average misses one day in five).[18] To alleviate the problem, men skilled
in operating the machinery of the absentees are simply shifted from their
own crews to where they are needed.

The miners usually feel uncomfortable in the new crew of workers and
their uneasiness is expressed many ways. For instance, at the break for
meals the newly arrived miners often eat by themselves, preferring to be
alone rather than to attempt to mix with a group of men who are practically
strangers to them.

Normally the men of these face crews take their meal break together,
and some of the men walk considerable distances so that the whole crew can
be together while eating. There is a good deal of joking and storytelling
at this time and the men enjoy this time together. Often men will share
food, sandwiches and desserts, with each other and a man who is low on
water will not hesitate to drink directly from another man's lunch bucket
or to transfer some water directly into his own. While most miners carry

their own snuff, it is common for a man to offer his mates a chew and for his friends to accept the offering.[19]

The conversations during breaks generally revolve around the personal activities of the men while away form work. Rarely is there talk of national political affairs or ideological disputes over the current topics of the day. Many conversations deal with farming, or animal husbandry since many of the miners own small farms or are generally familiar with the activities of rural people. Talk of sexual relations with women is frequent as well, with the miners relating tales of their exploits and the younger men inquiring from others about the virtues of a young lady that they may know. These accounts are very common and not infrequently will two younger "buddies" publicly discuss, half seriously and half in fun, their escapades directly before coming to work. Older miners too engage in this type of sexual talk, although less frequently, but they can on occasion develop as interested a group of listeners as the younger men.

Profanity is the rule rather than the exception in the miners' speech and most of the miners swear constantly in the course of their conversations. In the mines, men of all ages use this profane language although younger men appear to swear almost constantly. Profanity is not limited simply to people who consider themselves to be equals but is used between older and younger men as well as between "bosses" and "workers".

Speech patterns change dramatically as the miners leave the work place and it appears that as they ride up on the cage on their way home the swearing is already being reduced and that by the time they leave the area of the mine itself there is little evidence of it in their speech.

Swearing in the presence of women is generally considered unacceptable, although a man will occasionally use profanity for emphasis in front of his own wife.

The term "buddy" is used as a term of address when the men are talking to one another, and it is a particularly useful expression in a dark environment where it is sometimes difficult to recognize a man. It is also useful when the miner is working with strangers and does not know all the names of the men with whom he is working. When a man shines his light directly into the eyes of another man this usually elicits the response, "the fuckin' light's bright, buddy", and is a commonly heard expression which demands that miner stop shining his light into the speaker's eyes. The expression "buddy" softens the demand considerably and helps to keep harmony in the group while allowing the response to take place easily.[20]

As the work ends, there is usually a scurry of activity as the men hurry to finish and to get the work site in an acceptable condition for the next crew. This usually involves some quick rock dusting and the hanging of canvas to make the ventilation system work properly. The men are happy to be leaving, and within the crew there is a good deal of cooperation, and the men do more than just perform their own jobs. Not to assist the others would simply delay one's own departure, but more importantly it would be regarded as a socially unacceptable action. Once the face is cleaned up and readied for the incoming crew, the men quickly walk the several hundred yards to the portabus for the outgoing man-trip and soon they are in the cage ascending up to the bath house. Upon leaving the elevator, some of the men make quick comments to crew members going to the same location from which they have come. This interchange of information is important for the work to continue without serious interruption since the outgoing miners can instruct the men of the next crew about special conditions and can advise them to bring along special equipment if it is warranted.

Now the men of the work crew go their own way. As they remove their clothes, they may sit near a man who was on their crew and they may shower near a man on their crew, but by and large they simply move along at their own pace. After showering and dressing, they leave by themselves or perhaps with a man who is sharing a ride.

The nature of their work crew has been examined by other researchers who have offered two explanations of the social dynamics of these groups. One approach, which is partially at variance with my explanation, views the miner as individualists, isolated, and alienated from his work and from the men around him. This approach is a common one in studies of industrialization for it presumes in a correlative way that as mechanization increases the worker is simply more and more isolated, not only from his work, but from his fellow workers.[21] The technology of continuous mining with its own requirements for work organization is partially supportive of this view, and I have argued that the coal miner is a virtual stranger to the vast majority of men with whom he works. At the same time, however, the miner has close, interdependent relationships with the men of the work crew, and, in fact, the work crew must be described as having a high degree of social solidarity. As indicated, this view differs from the view generally held by those who have studied changes in mechanization leading to changes in the productive relationships among the

workers. Contrary to the most commonly held views, worker solidarity and
interdependence among the men of the production crews have increased with
more sophisticated and improved technology. Lewis and Knipe, although
exhibiting a certain ambivalence toward this opinion, do mention other
researchers who support this view.[22] They mention Rimlinger who, writing
on British coal miners, suggests that solidarity and interdependence are
produced within underground mines because of miners' separatism (the fact
of being isolated or separated from other men) and because of the intensely
felt need for cooperation and because of the psychological burden of danger
and hard work.[23] In addition, they cite Gouldner who claims that the
imminent dangers and need for cooperation lead to greater peer group
solidarity.[24] Their own findings, gathered through interviews and
questionnaires, while not conclusive in their own minds tend to support
this thesis too. In examining nine mines with different technologies in
the Virginia coal fields, they found that 56 percent of the 'hand loaders'
said they would prefer to work alone. At a higher technological level of
mining, the percentage of people preferring to work alone drops, suggesting
an increase in social solidarity and a preference to work cooperately.
They claim that only 14 percent of miners using conventional techniques
would choose to work alone and only 9 percent of continuous miners would
prefer to work alone.

If the coal miner is broadly and historically considered (from more
than just the perspective of him as a worker), the view which stresses the
coal miner's present alienation from work appears to be the more correct
view. After all, the coal miner today works basically with strangers, and

performs a somewhat repetitious job in the complex process of underground
coal production. By contrast, the coal miner of the past worked
cooperatively, and a sense of solidarity was present among the miners (see
Chapter V, section A and B) in spite of the fact that working with a buddy
on piecework meant that one's earnings were a function of his own efforts.
More importantly, the coal miner worked with his neighbors and the face to
face relationships that existed at work extended into the non-working
leisure time relationships in the isolated coal towns. The men's lives and
those of their families with their common employer, common housing, common
physical setting, nearly common wages, and in fact, common problems, were
intricately interwoven not only while they were at work but in most aspects
of their lives. While it has been suggested (Chapter III, section B, on
coal towns) that the coal towns were less than harmonious places,
cooperation, solidarity, and perhaps a sense of a common destiny did exist.
The effects of technological change, therefore, are better understood when
the coal miner is viewed broadly and historically in the setting of the
coal town, and he is considered in his total social and physical setting.

Lewis and Knipe refer to this type of perspective as representative of
the "human relations" school which concentrates on an effect of
technological change on the social and psychological relationships of men
at work. In contrast, their own view focuses much more intensely on the
details of the actual technological system (machines plus men actually
working), and they conclude that the changes in coal mining from
conventional to continuous mining have increased the interdependence of the
workers and have created, through increased worker interaction, more

solidarity on the work crews. However their explanation for this increase
in social solidarity differs from the human relations school. Here it is
necessary to return to the view of the coal miner at work in essentially a
large, complex organization, a coal factory if you will, amidst men whom he
only knows through the work situation and with whom he has very little
interaction when outside the work situation. Within this work setting,
there is only one place on a day to day basis where it is possible to
maintain a set of close relationships. This is in the work crew.

The modern coal mine while related in many ways to large factories and
mills in terms of its organization and complexity, differs significantly
from them because of the wide scale use of isolated work crews. It is in
these small, spatially isolated crews set among hundreds of other men who
are also working on crews, that the coal miner works. To the rest of the
men he remains for practical purposes a stranger. In a social sense then,
the work crew is of extreme importance to the modern coal miner.[25]

B.   SUPERVISORY PERSONNEL

The operational complexity of the large modern underground coal mine
is comparable to that of many large industrial complexes such as steel
mills or automobile assembly factories. The management organization of a
modern mine is complex, requiring people such as mining engineers,
economists, personnel officers, geologists and senior managers with
sophisticated business and technical skills.

It is evident that with the advent of mining on a large scale most
upper supervisory managers are well trained in the latest business

techniques. The small entrepreneur, who through hard work and practical

skill was able to develop a mine of modest size, let us say 50-100 miners,

is becoming extinct. Modern mining has evolved into a big business with

upper echelon managers meeting the demand of a sophisticated industry.

>"From 1940 to 1946, small mines proliferated. From 1947
>to the late 1950's, the industry lost its middle sized
>mines, with the small mines producing a relatively
>constant share of the production. Production became
>increasingly concentrated in the larger companies.
>The fifty biggest companies increased their market share
>from 45 percent in 1947 to 60 percent in 1960.
>Concentration has continued in the sixties, and the
>production and number of small mines have been
>decreasing."[26]

The Greenwich Collieries Company is representative of this industry-

wide changes. The number of top managers is small since a large staff for

advertising and selling the coal is not required. These two mines are

'captive' mines, which means all the coal is shipped to the power

generating plants of the parent company, and there is no competition on the

open market to sell the coal. The local management consists of a

president, vice-president, two personnel officers and two high level

bookkeeper-accountants who are responsible for much of the record keeping

and planning. They maintain their offices in Ebensburg, some twenty miles

south of the mines themselves, and their job is almost strictly concerned

with the business affairs of the company.

At the mine locations themselves are found the more technically oriented managers. These are the men who are directly responsible for coal production and safety. Each mine has a mine superintendent, to whom everyone at the mine location is responsible. Under his authority is a team of men who hold positions which are either technical or supervisory in nature. All of these men are referred to as "company men" and consequently their wages are not negotiated through union contracts.

Nearly all these men have had work experience as miners and have worked their way into supervisory and technical positions. Their backgrounds illustrate the situation which has long existed in the coal mining industry whereby a man could, through hard work and aptitude, move himself up from the position of worker to that of supervisor. This has been a pattern recognized within the industry for a long time and it is often mentioned by the supervisors as an incentive system for young miners. Since in the past there was little chance to recruit highly educated men to middle level supervisory positions, and because there were no training schools available, practical experience and "coming through the ranks" were the only way into management.[27]

The management personnel are almost all former miners themselves and there tends not to be any noticeable antagonism between those men who are management and those men who are labor. Rather, the workers appear to be relaxed in the company of bosses and, while there are subtle expressions of the inherent inequality between those men with authority and those without it and while the managers definitely do give orders to the other men, there is generally an easy relationship between the two groups.

When a man changes his position from that of actual miner to that of supervisor, he does not do so casually since he loses many of the benefits which the United Mine Workers' union gives to him. He places himself in a position of greater risk in terms of job security since his inability to perform satisfactorily as a supervisor could lead to his dismissal and he would lack the safeguards that the union could give to him in grievance procedures. A sizable number of men, therefore, are simply not interested in becoming a boss and in assuming the risks and responsibilities inherent in such a change in status, while some men have actually done "bossing" for a time and then have returned back to their former position as a union man, or ordinary miner.

Often one miner will urge a friend to take the exams to get one's "bossin' papers" for he believes his friend would be good for a job of that type. The point is that being a boss or being a worker is not a relationship in which one group of men has authority and power and the other group must react and join together in a union to avoid exploitation and harsh treatment. Rather the relationship is seen in practical terms. Both jobs--"bossin'" and "minin'"-- must be done and if a man feels that a supervisory job would be to his personal benefit, and if he has the qualifications, then he might as well take the job. The lower level supervisors and the miners appear to interact as equals and on some of the crews an experienced man who has demonstrated abilities will often dominate the decision making in dangerous situations or when special judgments are called for. Rarely would a young section foreman make a decision about what he regarded to be bad roof without consultation with the experienced miners on his crew.

The miners and the supervisors will often talk about particular positions or strategies which the union or the management have developed on various labor issues. Generally the discussions are good natured and both sides are interested in what the other will do in a particular instance. There is little secrecy and men talk openly about what they think is right and openly inquire about the position of the other side. At the Greenwich Mines, a fairly large percentage of the men are young and moderately militant about their rights as workers. Foremen can often be heard asking men what they think about certain things, and often they laugh at or mock, in a playful way, the young miners for demanding things which they as older men would not have asked for in years past. While many of the supervisors are convinced that miners have things fairly easy today, few begrudge the miners the money they make or the benefits which they have gained. The supervisors identify closely with the working miner and feel that as the life of the miner improves their own situation and the entire industry improves.

After work, it is not uncommon for management personnel and high level foremen to be seen socializing in bars in the Barnesboro area with working miners. The conversations are of those between equals and the buying of drinks, the joking, and the horseplaying associated with a social occasion in a barroom are noticeable.

In one other respect, the management personnel of the mine like the miners themselves conform to a pattern which is quite common in coal mining everywhere. Nearly all these men have fathers or uncles or brothers who are or have been miners. In addition, most of them have come from communities where coal miners constituted a sizeable percentage of the work force. Thus, the management personnel like the miners themselves have come from mining families and the environment of the mining towns and feelings of superiority based on one's position or on one's past for the most part do not exist.

1. The Role of the Supervisors

At the north mine there are three general foremen or, as they are sometimes called general assistant superintendents, who are responsible for the activities during one particular work shift. For example, one of these general foremen works the 8 AM to 4 PM workshift every day over the course of the five day work week and remains the "daylight" foreman. This means that in a three week cycle, the general daylight foremen will have all the men under his authority for one week since the men themselves rotate shifts while the general foreman does not.

One of the major functions of these men is to plan the activities which will go on during their shift. While the production crews perform essentially the same task each shift, variations due among other things to poor roof conditions or broken machinery do occur and do demand a change of plans. These foremen must act quickly to correct any problems which occur since it is considered poor management to leave groups of men idle for very long.

Since these men coordinate the running of the mine, their instructions must be given to the various groups of workers whose combined functions make up the overall operation. These men must display a good deal of judgment and possess a thorough knowledge of what is taking place in all areas of the mine because the work force must be carefully coordinated and priorities properly assigned.

The general foremen enter the mine itself after the working miners and remain within the mine for most of the shift. While their role is mainly to coordinate activities, they focus upon areas in which problems exist or upon tasks which are not done on a regular basis. Therefore, they actually address themselves to problems and display their practical knowledge to the men. While these general mine foremen never actually perform any work (this is forbidden in union contracts), they do interact closely with the men from time to time and it is not uncommon to hear the miners joking with the foremen or discussing issues of common interest.

One of the most important responsibilities of the general foreman is to organize the men when they report for work. This involves not only directing groups of workers to the various sections of the mine but also organizing the work crews themselves. Both these tasks are important and require a thorough knowledge of the mine and the men. The miners themselves are concerned about these job assignments because the miners are directly affected by the individuals with whom they work and to a lesser extent by the jobs they are assigned. Their assignments on a day to day basis remain relatively stable for the individual miner, but when a man is absent from work, it frequently is necessary to "borrow" a miner with the needed skills from another work crew in order to replace the absent miner. This requires the foreman to know a man's qualifications and capabilities as a worker and, whenever possible, to place him together with others who enjoy working with each other. This requires that the general foreman know the men from all three shifts, and so spending time in the mine actually problem solving or directing the work activity helps the foreman learn about the men.

2. The Section Foreman

Directly under the authority of the general mine foremen are the section foremen, or the face crew foremen. Unlike the general foremen, these men work directly with the miners on the production crews at the face. These section foremen, with six men under their authority, are assigned to one production area of the mine. Each foreman and his workers become recognized as a crew and receive a label based upon the area of the mine in which they work. For instance, they would be known as "main B, Right" or "B-4, Left", depending on their section of the mine. (Other bosses are responsible for overseeing other groups of men. For instance, one foreman organizes the mechanics and another organizes the trackmen.)

These section foremen are all former working miners and are now "company" men. Anyone can qualify for the position as section foremen after five years of mining experience and after the successful completion of an examination given by the federal and state governments. The foremen at the North mine tended to be older experienced miners in their forties and fifties although there was one foreman who was thirty-one years old.

Their responsibility is to oversee the activity of the men under them. They coordinate the work of the six men of the face crew and are responsible in a very direct way for the production of coal and the safety of the men and machinery. In a general way, they are responsible for all the important decisions at the face of the mine. They decide just what the men will do, which headings will be cut first, where the roof bolters will work, how the canvas will be set, etc. In short, they organize the work and make sure that the men carry it out.

While the production of coal is the basic activity of the face crews, the matter of safety is also a major concern for everyone. The foreman assumes a great deal of responsibility with regard to safety and must constantly be on the lookout for unsafe conditions. At the beginning of each work shift, he enters the area of the face while the men remain at some distance behind and checks for gas and dangerous roof conditions; at the same time he plans the work routine the men will follow when they themselves move up to the face area. Throughout the work day he makes periodic checks for gas and dust conditions and gives orders for the canvas to be reset in order to redirect the air which moves the gas and dust. In addition, it is his responsibility to insure that the men work in safe conditions and obey the rules with regard to safety.

Productivity is a result of the combined actions of all three work shifts as they work continually and sequentially, and a work crew and its foreman must continue the work from the point where the outgoing crew has stopped. At times, a particular aspect of a job may be completed and at these junctures in the work sequence a foreman must determine what will be done next. Generally, however, these decisions are not major ones since the work plan has been laid out well in advance and all the tasks must be done sooner or later.

The relationship of a particular work crew to the work crew on the following shift is interesting because its actions have a direct impact on the following crew. Two minor fears of the men coming to work are that the outgoing crew will have done a job improperly, so that it will need to be re-done, or that the outgoing crew will have "left them dirty". This second complaint can be heard from time to time and it simply means that the outgoing crew has left the work site in a condition which is not advantageous for the new crew to begin cutting coal easily. For instance, all the machines maybe poorly situated and may have to be moved considerable distances, taking considerable time, before any cutting can be done.

The foreman performs no labor but simply supervises the men.[28] This means that if the work is proceeding without problems the foreman can find periods of fifteen or twenty minutes at a time when he can sit and rest. Generally, however, the foreman must be moving throughout the area of the face and taking an active interest in the work. In addition to the planning of the overall activity of the day, he must be constantly re-evaluating the work as it is proceeding to make certain the men are being deployed efficiently. The foreman must have a general plan as to how the continuous mining machine is to be used during a shift, while he considers the position of other equipment and the fact that a new crew of men will be coming to replace his crew of departing men.

The work activities at the face are well understood by all the men, but the foreman assumes the responsibility for deploying the men and machines. For the experienced miner, this is really not too difficult but good judgment is required to do it efficiently. With the four large machines and with the electrical cables and water lines involved on some of these machines, it is necessary that the foreman direct the activity clearly and cleverly so as to minimize the amount of work and lost time.

In the event of a breakdown of machinery, the foreman will quickly summon the mechanic who has been assigned to work within this particular section of the mine.[29] The foreman must now use his judgement in re-evaluating the work activities. For instance, if the roof bolter is broken down, the production of coal can proceed since there is no interference with the continuous miner and shuttle cars. All that need be done is for the two miners doing the roof bolting to be assigned temporarily to new jobs, such as setting posts, or moving canvas or rock dusting. If a continuous miner is broken down, the problem or organizing the men into new jobs becomes much more difficult since this machine is the source of all production and its breakdown will eventually cause all the machines to stop. The foreman must make a series of judgments about this situation, and generally he puts the miners to work doing jobs such as rock dusting or moving supplies.

The foreman must be very cautious and exercise good judgment in the handling of the men in situations which involve a change in routine. The section foreman, like the foreman in many other industrial organizations, is management's representative who must deal directly with the workers.

From one perspective, he becomes a middleman, dealing with the demands of upper management to meet the production quota which they have determined, and on the other hand, he must deal directly with the men. Making a change in the work routine after a breakdown in machinery, the foreman must consider not only the efficient utilization of his men from the management point of view but also the miners' attitudes. Broken equipment means a change in routine for the miner and this can be unsettling. At first, there will be a period of rest as the foreman evaluates the situation and so the miners will remain near their machines. If it appears that the repair work will take a long time, orders will be given to do some other tasks, which, while not normally in the production activities, must be done from time to time.

The foreman's judgment and conduct in these situations becomes an important factor in his overall ability to handle the men. The idleness of men will not be tolerated by his supervisors and so he must direct his men into some useful action. The men, on the other hand, enjoy a rest and generally do not enjoy any of the peripheral or ancillary tasks which the foreman might suggest they do. The miners find most of these new jobs somewhat arduous since pulling canvas or carrying materials or just simply walking in a low coal mine is difficult. The coal miner expects to work hard but these extra tasks generally require a greater physical effort than the miner would normally expend. And for the older or overweight miners, these tasks can prove to be very difficult.

The section foremen fill out extensive reports at the end of each work day. After showering and dressing, they report to an office which they share with the other foremen. At their desks they work for about half-an-hour and write up in detail the events of the day. Not only do they report how many shuttle cars of coal have been collected and how many roof bolts installed, but, in the event of a breakdown, they must specifically account for the activities of each of the men on the crew because higher management demands activity reports for these periods.

A major issue for the foreman in executing his responsibility in the mine involves his ability to clearly issue orders to his crews. It is not an infrequent situation for the foreman to assign a job to several of the men only to have none of the men understand exactly what the order has been. This failure in communications is common and appears attributable to a number of factors. First, the noise level around the machines can be great if they are running. Second, since it is difficult to walk in a coal mine, the older foremen will often simply shout orders along a heading to their men and the soft coal absorbs the sound of their voice. Third, the verbal or communicative patterns of most of the men is characterized by such a brevity of words that misunderstandings are common and from the listener's standpoint, it is a common event for the men to ask for a fuller explanation about orders. This faulty communication causes little trouble when the routine tasks are being done because the working miner has a good knowledge of his job and easily adjusts to the general orders given him. However, when new jobs are assigned and the communication remains poor, confusion is often the result.

The result can be one of frustration for the working miner who after receiving a set of orders finds himself isolated in a section of the mine not knowing exactly what is expected of him. This can easily lead to antagonism between the foreman and the workers because a foreman expects the work which he has assigned to be completed, while the miner, having reported to a location within the mine, frequently has an incomplete description of what is required of him. The miner then must make a decision on his own as to what must be done and this can be a risky undertaking. The situation in which there is a break in the normal work routine is a particularly important time because the reaction of the foreman to the men is tested. The foreman must be reasonable with the men in his demands and reasonable in interpreting the results. While the men are willing to work hard the foreman must be careful in the way he directs orders, and he must take into account that the men often operate on their own.

The foreman occasionally undergo a two or three day training course on what amounts to simple psychology courses in how to manage men. The course teaches these supervisors to be friendly with the men, to win their confidence and respect and not to be stern and abrupt in their handling of the men. They are directed to take a personal interest in the lives of their men and to deal with them humanely. The situations where the normal routines are interrupted are the most obvious tests for the section foreman for it is here that they must direct the men to useful work while at the same time be reasonable in their demands.

The relationship of the foreman to the work crew varies noticeably among the crews. Generally, however, the relationship is characterized with friendliness, at least a surface friendliness, and the men rarely complain openly about any of their supervisors, whether section foremen or general foremen.[30]

The men frequently engage in friendly conversation with the foreman before work and even during the work activity, and it is not uncommon to see the foreman and the men enjoying a joke together. There is, however, a certain reserve which the foremen maintain with the men and this social distance is observable among all the foremen. In addition, all the foremen have separate locker rooms and showering facilities which they use before and after work. Since the foremen must fill out detailed reports on the events of the day, they leave work well after the men have gone home and do not see the men after leaving the cage. During the actual work activity, the foremen infrequently come in close contact with the men and except for an occasional order to outline the general scheme of the work the foremen would rarely stop to speak to a working miner. The foremen remain physically distant from the men and generally situate themselves in a central location where they can have a broad overview of the work activities. From time to time, they will move around to check on gas conditions or to see how members of the crew are doing, but generally they do not come in contact with the men unless it becomes necessary. Even the roof bolters, if they are in need of supplies, will simply have the shuttle car operators bring the supplies to them and not ask the foreman.

The foreman is listened to when he speaks and his orders are carried out quickly and without hesitation. It is a no nonsense relationship; the miner knows he is expected to work hard and expresses no resentment when he is assigned a task.

There is no particular respect afforded the foreman, nor any special
politeness shown. The men realize the foreman has some authority over
their actions but they show no signs of fear of the power of the foreman.
Rather, it seems that they want to cooperate with him. In many respects,
the foreman is an insider, having been a miner for a minimum of five years
and having worked his way up the career ladder into his current position.
He lives in communities like those of the miner and often he goes to the
same social clubs and bars as the men who work for him. His salary is not
much greater than the men of his crew and so even the financial differences
are minimized. He was formerly a member of a union and is likely to
believe in unionism as his men do. His formal education is nothing more
than high school, sometimes less, and this matches closely the formal
educational achievements of his workers. In short, the foreman is very
much like his workers; the men and the foreman feel comfortable in each
other's presence and work well together.

C.   ATTITUDES TO WORK

The work of the coal miner is considered neither boring nor
particularly difficult. It is considered to be a good job: one of the
better jobs within the area. With the current wage schedule and the steady
and even increasing demand for coal, the miner has a reasonably high degree
of assurance of job security and good wages.[30]*
While at work the miner generally works with a small crew of men which
forms a closely knit and generally very harmonious group and this provides
the miner with a sense of belonging and of identity. The work itself is

often performed in an isolated location and it requires a careful mixture
of some individual and some collective decision making and a considerable
amount of discussion to keep the work going smoothly. Taking these factors
into consideration, the miners generally agree that coal mining is good
work as well as reasonably enjoyable work.

Rarely does the modern miner have a brutally physical day at work.
The high degree of mechanization has made shoveling coal or carrying
equipment almost a thing of the past. The vast majority of miners operate
equipment of one type or another and generally the most difficult aspect of
coal mining is walking and working in the 'low' because the low height of
the mine transforms normally easy tasks such as walking or carrying bags of
rock dust into quite difficult ones. Occasionally, some of the non-
routine jobs such as cleaning belt (shoveling fine coal dust particles,
mixed with water, from under the conveyor belt onto the belt itself), or
unloading rock dust from the kersey, or unloading iron rails from the motor
can be very heavy and tiring work. With these few exceptions, however, the
physical aspects of the job have been so reduced that the miner, who is
generally physically strong, does not find the work particularly difficult.

The wet coal dust and the damp conditions insure that the miner will
be dirty after a day's work. This is simply an accepted part of the job.
It is claimed by some that the miner does not consider the coal dust itself
to be dirty but rather a sort of clean, albeit black, substance. This
attitude is evidenced by their occasional practice of actually chewing
pieces of coal while at work.[31]

With increased mechanization and stricter safety laws (and undoubtedly certain economies of scale) the industry trend has been for coal mining to become a large scale operation with hundreds of men working at one mine location. While mechanization requires fewer men to produce large amounts of coal, the extraordinary costs for equipment and the large investment in safety systems dictates that mining is done in large mines. The demographics of the coal towns have changed as a result so that today few men within the households of any given town are employed as miners. As a consequence the work crew serves as the most important unit with which the coal miners identify and clearly the convivial social relationships found among the crew members are very important to the individual miners.

The good wages and the steady work as well as the increased strength and militancy of the miners' union have combined, it would appear, to give the miner a greater sense of job security than ever before. Ironically, these same factors have also permitted increased rates of absenteeism and one of the major complaints of management today concerns this absenteeism. On some work shifts the problem is reported to be so great that the production rates are seriously and adversely affected. I overheard one miner being asked by a foreman why he persisted in working only three days a week. Boldly, he replied with one of the punch lines from a common joke heard among the men: "Because I can't make a living on two days a week." The result of this absenteeism from the miners' viewpoint is that the social relationships on the work crew which are so fundamental to his job enjoyment are constantly being disrupted by the absence of his friends who choose to stay home. Paradoxically, the good wages and steady work permits absenteeism which weakens the narrow social base of the work crew from which the miner derives enjoyment.

The modern miner differs from the miners of the past who strongly identified with the fact that they were coal miners. In fact, most older coal miners seem comfortable working in the mine and if asked about working outside the mine or working as a non-miner, they express a preference for the underground work. Undoubtedly, the reasons for this preference are complex and involve the factors of camaraderie and independence which have been mentioned. In addition there is a strong feeling that in order to be a coal miner one must actually work underground and there's a type of pride in one's occupation as well as a confidence derived from the high degree of knowledge and skill required to perform it. To be a coal miner in times past was to be a hard working man, a strong virile man, doing a job which few others dared to do or knew how to do. It was a source of identity and pride; it was the job of your father, and uncles, and neighbors; it was the job which provided a living for all the people of your isolated town; it was an important part of one's culture and a way of life. As one retired miner expressed it when asked if he liked coal mining: "Yah, I enjoyed it. I was young and coal mining in those days didn't have a whole lot of supervision. You had to be a good miner to get your place worked. I enjoyed it." While many of the older men still hold some of these views, the modern coal miner regards his job as a means of making a good income in a geographical area where there are not many alternative choices. The job is a means to the end of earning a living and the miner concerns himself primarily with the issues of money and fringe benefits. The job additionally affords the miner a means to live in a coal town, which as indicated in Chapter III, is a prized place of residence because the coal towns are regarded as comfortable and secure places to live and are greatly preferred to even small urban areas or suburban type areas. The miner no longer holds tightly to the old identity of the professional miner, knowledgeable in all phases of mining, having acquired his job through a long, often grueling apprenticeship begun in his mid or late teen-age years. The miner of today is seeking good employment in a geographical area he chooses to work in and coal mining provides him this opportunity.

The miner is well aware of the complexity of the modern operation, and while he himself performs only one task within a series of operations, he is aware of the overall size and sophistication of his industry. Among his fellow miners there is a shared knowledge and an appreciation for the complexity of the operation. The miner, however, realizes that the public outside the sphere of influence of mining is unaware of the current industry and the miner perceives the public at large as regarding him as the stereotypical, dumb, underground laborer possesses of a strong back and a weak mind. As a miner express it:

> "Outsiders look down on the coal miner. They don't think he is
> human. I can't say a coal miner is a low type person. I think
> these news reporters painted a picture of a coal miner as
> inferior. The coal miner was treated unfair in the past."

Today the modern miner is aware of the fallacy of this view, and he knows that his work requires a good deal of intellect not only to keep the complex machinery operating but to keep the work efficiently organized and effectively carried out.   The miner enjoys explaining his profession since it helps outsiders to gain a fuller appreciation of his job and to change the stereotypes about him.   In another sense, the public's lack of understanding and appreciation of the miners' work presents a situation in which the miner prefers to interact with men who are miners themselves or who have real knowledge of the modern coal industry.   Among themselves, at least, the miners have an appreciation for what they do.

As indicated, most coal miners live in small rural towns within the county.   Unlike the coal miners of Virginia described in reports of Lewis and Knipe these coal miners are not marginal members of their communities, either of their own individual coal towns or of the larger areas in which their coal towns exist.[32]   These towns were created for the miners to reside in and while most of the people of the region (excluding the city of Johnstown) were farmers at the time of the immigration of the early miners, the immigrant miners soon accounted for a substantial percentage of the population.   Even today approximately one-tenth of all the men of Cambria County are on the rolls of the United Mine Workers of America's Health and Retirement Fund.   From the point of view of involvement in his community, as a politician, school board member, church leader, or social club officer, the coal miner cannot be considered as being marginal, for not only has he assumed many of the values and attitudes of middle class America, but he has become indistinguishable from other men unless he is asked his occupation.   (Chapter VIII deals extensively with those features of personality and attitude which still distinguish the miner from other men.)

The older miners of today realize that the work is a good deal easier than it was in earlier times and they appreciate the improved conditions and increased wages which they receive. The younger men by contrast lack the historical perspective on the changes and do not seem to share this deep appreciation of the improvements.

The older men are mildly disdainful of the younger men. They know the younger men work simply for the money and that being a coal miner for the younger men is merely a means of getting money--not a way of life. They feel the younger men are "softies" and could never have withstood what they endured years ago. They resent in some ways the relative good fortune in terms of wages and working conditions which the young men now enjoy and they realize that the present situation is in part a result of their own prior labor struggles. When they were young men they appreciated their jobs because they were difficult to get and because it represented a way of life with which they identified. Today they realize the young miner does not feel the same way about coal mining as an occupation and as a way of life.

The older miners find the high rates of absenteeism among the new miners somewhat reprehensible and clearly outside their own set of values, and they consider this to be a form of weakness within the young miners. The fact that many wives of the young miners now work accounts, in their minds, for a good deal of the absenteeism since the men now have sufficient earnings to allow them a day off every now and then. But the feelings towards the younger men has other sides to it and the older men appreciate the spunk and militancy of the younger men. Their demands for improved working conditions and increased wages benefit the older miners too and, although the younger men possess a different set of attitudes towards their work, these changes which the younger men have helped bring about represent the fruition of the older miners' struggles to improve their own working conditions. In a sense, the young miners' attitudes, the management's reasonably evenhanded treatment of the miners, the good wages and the reduced difficulty of the work are all part of the substantial changes which have taken place and the young miners have had a hand in recent improvements.

Young men grow up and assume adult roles early in Cambria County (Chapter VIII on personality discusses this topic) and this results in the young men being viewed as adults with full responsibilities and capabilities by the older men almost as soon as they enter the mine. While the attitudes and life styles differ between the two groups the men generally feel comfortable in each other's presence and there's an easy interaction between them. In short, the men get along well together in spite of their age differences and in spite of the mildly critical attitudes of the older men towards the younger.

Interestingly, the younger men who often come from coal mining families have an acute awareness of the difficult times the older men went through and know very well that these men worked much harder than the men do today. In fact, they enjoy telling stories about the tough 'old days' as much as some of the older miners, and so older men who cannot work rapidly today are not maligned for their slower pace. There is an appreciation and a respect for what such older miners were capable of doing in times past and the younger men feel fortunate that they do not need to work in such difficult conditions.   In fact, they realize that the claims of the older men-that the young miners are softies-are correct.   The younger men appear not to be embarrassed about these views, while the fact that they generally perform the most technical jobs in the mine legitimizes their role in the context of modern mining.

As mentioned, the miners have no exaggerated fear of working in the mine although they are realistically aware that caution and a constant awareness of the dangers are necessary for continued safety.   They feel that outsiders such as the non-mining public over-emphasize the hazards of mining and to some extent, the coal miners enjoys the outsider's, including his wife's, exaggerated notions of the danger and difficulty of his work. This public perception of his difficult job is something, it appears, he finds pleasurable.   He maintains a masculine image--strong and brave--which he derived from the past and it seems he enjoys this image.   While the reality of hard work still exists in the mines, the job still offers a challenge to each miner, and the situation where a working miner has become alienated from his work, doing as little as he possibly can and assuming as little responsibility as he can, has not reached the coal industry in this region as it apparently has in so many the factory-type industries elsewhere in the United States.   Given that it is necessary to work, most coal miners enjoy their occupation and appreciate the good wages and benefits it provides them, and thus appear to work hard willingly.

VII. THE LEISURE TIME

Whether he is hunting, gardening or fixing an old truck in his back yard, today's coal miner is a man involved with his physical surroundings. He works with his hands, and in his recreation he turns to activities which again involve manual skills. It would be impossible to describe all the hobbies of coal miners but there are certain activities which are popular among large numbers of these men and thus worth mentioning.

Ranking high among the outdoor recreations is hunting, an activity enjoyed by many. Most of the men pursue small game hunting during the Fall hunting season; but the real popularity of hunting is shown by the noticeable increase in absenteeism among the men when deer season finally comes in late Fall. In the Spring, trout fishing attracts many men, and the enjoyment of such outdoor activities fills a major portion of their leisure time. Frequently, hunting or fishing involves a short overnight trip to some secret stream or place in the many nearby forests. Many of the men have their own campers which are well equipped with the full range of camping and cooking gear. Comparison of rifles and rods used in hunting and fishing is a constant topic of conversation among most miners. Another popular leisure time activity for the miner is tinkering with

171

motors and many of the men are expert auto mechanics and fine general
handymen.

A third favorite pastime for the coal miner is gardening. It is very
common to find a large vegetable garden in the yards at these men's homes
in addition to a well manicured lawn and a small flower garden. (Older
miners claim that very large vegetable gardens were a necessity in times
gone by to supplement the family's food supply.) The tools and equipment
associated with gardening are often discussed at work and the miner appears
as enthusiastic about the latest in gardening gadgetry as he is about
hunting and fishing gear.

New cars and trucks and motorcycles are favorite topics among the
younger miners and their fascination with machines and other motor vehicles
is displayed through these conversations. Although the miner is criticized
by some of his neighbors for spending his money unwisely on unnecessary
fads and gadgets, the young miner often has considerable disposable income
and he can purchase things easily. He rarely travels from the county or
vacations at resorts. He shows little interest in professional or
collegiate athletics or other cultural activities which might take him on
trips out of the county. In short, with the exception of brief hunting or
fishing trips, the coal miner's interests revolve around activities in his
immediate environment, and cars and guns are among the things he chooses to
spend his recreational money upon.

Hometown athletics are a major interest of many of the miners. There
is a great interest in high school football and wrestling, and to a lesser
extent, in basketball, baseball and track. Men often travel great

distances to watch these events, loyally following their hometown school teams for years even when their own sons are through participating. Conversations can easily be heard at the mine and at local restaurants and stores about the results of games and matches. (To a lesser extent emphasis is placed on girls' sports.) Some of the younger miners participate in summer softball leagues, with some teams being sponsored by mining companies.[1] However, the extent of this type of participation appears minimal when compared to the industrial and city teams in an urban area such as Johnstown.

For many of the miners, farming activities consume much of their non-working time and many raise cows, cattle, chickens or dogs and demonstrate considerable knowledge in these areas of husbandry. Others have small farms or help local farmers with their farm chores by haying or driving tractors.

Family affairs occupy a good deal of the miner's non-working time and many men spend much of their time at home working in the yard in warm weather or watching television in the cold weather. However, the miner today with a good income and a less demanding job than in times past finds himself with a substantial amount of leisure time. The coal miner is seen leaving his home to attend church, union, or social club meetings almost nightly and these occupy a good deal of his free time. Furthermore, it is a common practice for unannounced visiting to take place between miners and friends. A man, often accompanied by his wife, will simply drop in on friends and visit for an hour or two.

For some, church activities can be an enjoyable association, but for most of the miners involvement in church affairs is sporadic. Although at certain times of the year a good deal of church-related volunteer help is donated by the miners, especially in connection with large church picnics and summer carnivals, there appears that their church attendance rates are comparable to other communities in the United States. Roman Catholic Churches predominate numerically in the region although Orthodox Catholic Churches are also found. Protestant denominations are represented throughout the county as well and various types of Lutheran, Methodist, Presbyterian, Baptist, and Brethren denominational churches appear frequently. In addition, various fundamentalist protestant churches are found, some of which are small independent organizations. Seventh Day Adventist and Jehovah Witness Churches appear to be quite widespread too. Jewish Synagogues and Temples are found only in the city of Johnstown where there is one Orthodox and one Reform congregation.

By far the most popular form of organized activities is the social club. These clubs, found throughout the county, are composed of three types. First, there are the nationality based clubs, e.g. Hungarian-American club, Polish-American Club and Polish Falcons among the common ones. While not every area has a representation of each of these social clubs, they are widespread. Secondly, there are the clubs with national (political) affiliations, e.g. Veterans of Foreign Wars or American Legions. Thirdly, there are private clubs in which membership is simply a matter of a dues payment, with no restrictions based on nationality or

military service. These clubs appear to be located more frequently in
areas of Johnstown whereby walking to a neighborhood club is possible.

The widespread phenomenon of the volunteer fire companies should also
be mentioned in connection with the social clubs. These are found
throughout the county and their ostensible function is to provide a fire
fighting service in the townships and boroughs where there are not
publically supported companies. However, these volunteer fire companies
provide a source for neighborhood socializing since many men, coal miners
among them, spend much leisure time at fire halls.

These social clubs are a major outlet for socializing in the rural
areas of the county. While it is true that commercial bars are
commonplace, too, the social clubs offer the miner and his wife a place
where they can socialize together. The social clubs generally offer a full
range of social activities--dances, parties, inexpensive meals, and
cookouts and they are often busy places. While the clubs are open daily
including Sunday, unlike other commercial bars, and provide a quick stop-in
place for the man who wishes a beer or a shot of whiskey, it is the Friday
night fish dinners or the monthly polka dances which give the club a
special appeal as a family club for husbands, wives and children. Many
coal miners use these clubs almost exclusively for entertainment outside
their homes.

Most of the nationality clubs serve as institutions where traditional
cultural events and customs are promoted and these organizations serve an
important role in the transfer of so-called ethnic awareness to young
people. Generally the social clubs provide more than just social activity

for their members and consequently they receive a type of legitimacy from their activities which is not strictly social. For instance, the American Legions and V.F.W.'s participate politically to fulfill their organizations philosophies and goals.

It has been suggested in an earlier section that coal miners of the past drank far less than their reputation suggests. Today it appears that the situation is similar and the coal miner cannot be regarded as a particularly heavy drinker. The great distances that many men must drive to their homes from the mines discourage them from stopping after work for a few drinks. It is simply too dangerous an activity when so much driving is involved. Furthermore, the miners frequently have few close social relationships with other workers and so they hurry back to their home towns after work. This is not to suggest that coal miners display attitudes against alcohol or do not consumer reasonable amounts of it but merely to point out that their drinking behavior in public and in their homes seems to conform to a general pattern of moderation.

The biggest change in the coal miners' non-working habits corresponds to changes within the coal industry itself. Most significant is the fact that the coal miners now frequently socialize with men and women who are no longer directly connected with the coal mining industry. Socially this has led to an expansion of social contacts and awareness, and a trend toward what might be considered middle American values, attitudes and behaviors can now be detected within the coal mining society. Finally, the changes in mining, in terms of wages and the nature of the work, afford the miner

the financial means and the free time to pursue his rural, outdoor hobbies
and to socialize within the clubs of his rural town.

As perhaps expected, the miner pursues few artistic or literary
activities. Most men read nothing more than the daily newspaper, The
Tribune-Democrat, which comes from Johnstown, and occasionally monthly
magazines on hunting and fishing. Although the United Mine Workers Journal
is read by most men, at least in a cursory way, it seems to be the source
of little conversation. Television consumes a large part of the non-
working time of the miner particularly when the weather is cold, but rarely
are shows of a distinctly educational nature a viewing choice.[2]

It should be mentioned that this lack of interest in activities
outside their immediate environment is an indication of the provincialism
of many of the mining families, particularly of women. It is quite common
to find older adults who have not spent even one night outside their home
town areas, or who have never been to Pittsburgh, some ninety miles away.
Johnstown, a small city, looms as a large and confusing metropolis and so
many people avoid visiting it.

The coal miner, in summary, seems a well adjusted member of his
isolated community. He lives usually in his coal town with people much
like himself in terms of attitudes, outlook and behavior, and he finds
going outside his immediate environment both an unnecessary and unwanted
experience. He has financial and economic security now and undertakes a
full range of leisure time activities which reflect his rural life and his
bias toward mechanical interests. He does not desire city life, in fact,

he shuns it, feeling that in his own way he makes his life and his family's
life full and complete.

VIII.   THE MINERS' PERSONALITY AND WORLD VIEW

The description of the coal miners of Cambria County thus far has
given particular emphasis to the coal miners at work.   It is the task of
this chapter to look at the miner from a different perspective--to look at
his personality and world view as expressed through his actions and
attitudes.   It should be mentioned that the author assumes that the
personality of today's coal miner has been shaped by his life and his
parent's life in the coal towns and by his work as an underground coal
miner.   The evolution of this personality-type was obviously extremely
complex.   The original immigrant coal miners and Americans who entered the
mines obviously possessed attitudes and outlooks of their own prior to
entering the local coal industry.   However, the fact that these people
underwent common experiences was a very influential factor in the
development of their personality.

This chapter does not adhere to any rigid sequence of causality, nor
does it mean to imply in a mechanistic way that a coal mining culture leads
inevitably to a certain coal mining personality-type.   Rather, the intent
is simply to indicate that occupation and life in a coal town have
contributed dramatically to making the coal miners' personality and that it
is possible to describe this personality.

179

The underground bituminous coal mining industry, responding to advances in technology, has changed dramatically over the past seventy years. Life in the coal towns has changed too, and one of the greatest changes has been a reduction in the number of coal miners. The residence patterns within the coal towns today show the miners' homes mixed among those of men and women who work in different industries. This has substantially widened the miners' social contacts and social experiences and resulted in a shift in the coal miners' attitudes and outlooks toward that of the society at large. However, counteracting his phenomenon of broadened social contacts is the fundamental conservatism of his rural neighbors, coal families or not, and the demographic pattern, as discussed in chapter III, whereby people move out of and away from the coal towns, but rarely do people move into these towns. The personality of the coal miner today, while affected by the widened types of experiences and broadened range of social contact, bears the clear imprint of that of his parents. His rural, conservative environment even today has given him a legacy of attitude, outlook and personality from the coal mining days of the past.

As with all cultural phenomena, the following description of the coal miners' personality is an abstraction from the lives of many men--a pattern which represents no one man exactly and yet a pattern which facilitates an understanding of any member of the group. The description of personality logically begins with those traits which appear central to him in his everyday approach to life.

A. SUSPICION AND "TAKING IT PERSONALLY"

The coal miner displays two dominant personality themes, which in turn support other aspects of his personality. The coal miner is a man suspicious of other men. He is constantly questioning the motives and actions of others, and he is forever calculating the effects of a particular action taken by someone in all its ramifications, potential as well as real, and weighing the costs and benefits. Important in understanding this suspicion is the second dominant personality theme--the personal way in which the miner perceives his world. The coal miner deals with the world primarily through people-more explicitly through people and the power they have to affect the miner himself in a positive or negative fashion. These two themes are intertwined and supportive of each other and have important consequences for the coal miner's behavior.

The coal miner views the actions of others as motivated by personal gain and so believes that a man rarely takes action for idealistic reasons or as a matter of principle, except when the principle and personal gain are mutually supportive. If a man in authority makes a decision, whether it is the boss at the coal mine or a local politician, the miner is always calculating what might be "in it" for the leader and how might the miner himself benefit personally from the action. Conversely, if suggestions are made for improvement in a particular job at the mine or in local community service committees, the person in authority views the suggestions suspiciously and personally. He sees the suggestions as a personal criticism; he wonders why the suggestions could not have been made

privately instead of in an open forum like a meeting, and then he questions
what the real reasons behind the suggestions are.[1]

The personal approach to dealing with people means that the miners
must be extremely cautious and distrustful of all people except for very
close and proven friends. This personal view can result in people becoming
extremely loyal to each other. In fact, the bonds of friendship can become
so strong that criticism of a friend, even if he was clearly in the wrong,
is not made. Loyalty--blind personal loyalty--is given readily to true
friends and friends will stand by each other in spite of criticism or
adversity.

The evaluation of people is grounded once again in this personal
framework. A man's status and worth in the eyes of a coal miner is
determined only after the man is known through interactions over a long
time. The coal miner does not automatically feel a man is better or
smarter or deserving of any particular deference because he has more money
or has a better position than another man. The man must be seen and judged
basically for how he behaves not for the job he may hold or for the
reputation of his family. In fact, this approach to judging people is
sometimes so strong that people with money or position may not be able to
overcome these so-called advantages and be viewed fairly.

As indicated (in Chapter VI, Section B, The Role of the Supervisors),
the coal miners, young and old alike, can often be seen in bars or social
clubs drinking and having intimate conversations with men who are their
superiors at work, or have a high status or prestige in the community.

These events are not rare because men are taken for the kind of people they are judged to be, not because of their position.

Improving one's position in life is a struggle situated within this personal framework. While it is accomplished sometimes through hard work or luck, or even risk taking, it is most frequently a contest to align oneself with someone who can help you, or who can do a favor for you. The dealings for a better position, or for making more money or even for helping another friend, are not made on the basis of issues or on the basis of who objectively might be best qualified for a job, nor are things done idealistically for the good of the company or the institution. Politics are carried out for the gain of individuals, oneself or friends, and the process of political maneuvering is carried on secretively, behind closed doors. It is a framework which, while sometimes allowing issues to be aired and discussions to take place, proceeds on the basis of personal relationships and narrowly defined self-seeking goals.

People naturally learn how to work within and manipulate this type of framework. As stated, it is important to be at least minimally cautious and suspicious of others and to always search for the hidden meaning and motives behind their actions. In dealing with others, one frequently must avoid disclosing one's feelings about issues because if you were once known to support a particular cause or position it would be used against you at a latter time. The coal miner has learned to cautiously hide his opinions, to express little emotion in his tone of voice or on his face. He rarely appears enthusiastic or displays hearty approval or disapproval of an issue. Often he appears to be stoical and even stone-faced, refusing to tip his hand, to reveal his feelings, by smiling in agreement or laughing or passing the slightest clue, verbal or non-verbal. Under this facade, the coal miner is always calculating, measuring his own position in a situation, against and with others.

As evidence of the coal miners' skill in concealing his inner feelings, coal miners have been known to walk off the job in the middle of a work shift and to go on strike without any warning to management. These wildcat strikes are almost weekly occurrences in mines throughout Cambria County, at this time (The symbolic act is for a miner to kick over his lunch bucket, thus spilling his water supply, and then to walk out with all the men.) It is difficult to predict these events because the miners rarely give clues as to their true feelings of discontent, either verbally or through body language. A grievance simply grows more and more important among the men until a point is reached where decisive action is undertaken. But until this critical point is reached, there is little indication of what is actually happening. Reflecting this sentiment, one retired miner stated it this way:

> "I would say today's miners are hot headed, they are
> young and think they know it all. They would call a
> strike for the smallest thing. You never can tell
> about them."

Even violent and aggressive action by the miner can be carried out in this behavioral pattern because a man will often show no anger toward another man but then suddenly he may erupt violently into a fight to the surprise of all observers.

It should be noted that settling personal issues or scores through violent means, especially with one man directly fighting another, seems to

have been a commonplace happening in the coal towns in times gone by.
Several things seem to operate in this situation. The fist fight is
extremely personal, simply indicating one man's ability to physically beat
another man, and there is very little appeal to the right or wrong of an
issue. Furthermore, the isolated coal towns did not have police to
continually legislate disputes so that fighting and physically standing up
for one's interests were common. Today, this pattern is still found and
minor disputes are quite often worked out through fights or threats to
physical violence rather than through reasoned argument or through a law
suit. The common expression "I'm gonna stand him tall" is an allusion to
grabbing someone by the front of his shirt, under his chin, holding him
against a wall and beating him.

Since disputes between people are taken personally rather than
philosophically on the basis of the issues, the disputes quite often have
no end but linger in men's minds until the score has been settled. Grudges
are often held and a man will wait, literally years, to settle a score with
someone he has felt personal antagonism toward. There is frequent
reference to "setting people up" and to tricking them to even the score.

An interesting manifestation of this is the perception of the miner
within the work situation when a change in the nature of the work, for
instance, in its method or routine, is called for by a supervisor. Often
it is not seen as an attempt to improve the work through increased
efficiency but rather as a decision to punish or fix the men.

Life in the coal towns provided an atmosphere which was conducive to
the development of these personality themes, or minimally to the

reinforcement of them. (There is clear evidence that suspiciousness and a
"personal" world view were qualities of the early immigrants.) As
discussed in the chapter on life in the early coal towns, the mixing of the
various ethnic groups in small isolated towns, with languages often
unintelligible to each other, with customs so very different, and with
occupational goals often so diverse, resulted in an atmosphere
characterized by suspicion and prejudice. Increasing such prejudice was
the practice of frequently assigning better jobs to various ethnic groups,
at first to the Welsh and Scots, then to Protestants, then more broadly to
English speakers. Such practices exacerbated the social frictions which
already existed among the various groups and it was in the this climate
that the miner and his family learned, or perhaps relearned, caution and
suspicion of others. People learned too that one would pay a high price
for idealism and high principles. One must watch out for one's self first.
Even one's pay as a handloader was based on one's personal effort, and one
had to always realize that another man, like you, was looking out for
himself first. In this social climate, it is little wonder that suspicion
and an egocentric personal view of the world prevailed. In commenting on
the general situation of the social atmosphere in the towns, a miner said:

> "After the conditions improved it seemed as if the
> people were a little more friendly to each other. It
> figures, well naturally, well there wasn't probably one
> coal miner who didn't have a lot of problems. So at
> night they'd sit around and complain. So there weren't
> any pleasant faces in the crowd. So as working
> conditions improved, in disposition, they were
> happier."

B. INDIVIDUALISM AND CONFORMITY

A relationship emerges in this social climate which emphasizes two additional personality themes: individualism and conformity. The coal miner in the final analysis knows that he must watch out for his own welfare. In the distant past, work was irregular, with strikes or external economic conditions causing work stoppages which frequently put men out of work. The immigrants arriving with little money were greatly concerned with saving money but low wages and occasional unemployment made this a very difficult undertaking. The handloading techniques and the early techniques in conventional mining required a man to rely on his own efforts and abilities to earn money. The coal miner was in most ways a private entrepreneur functioning individually and one's wages corresponded to one's efforts.

The individualism of the coal miner persists today in a very subtle way. The coal miner is seen to have a few close or intimate friends--in fact, many men could be said to have only a range of acquaintances. He depends mainly on his family for emotional relationships. The coal miner will socialize with other men, and drink, hunt and play ball together, but there is a certain emotional reserve in his actions. He remains cautious in his emotional commitments to people as well as to issues. Often he appears to be willing to join others in undertaking an action only to change his mind and decide that he is no longer interested in the group effort. Finally, he is a man who will suddenly announce to his friends that he has made a major decision for himself, for instance, to quit his job for a new one or to move or to sell his house. While he may seek opinions on issues, he thinks for himself and decides questions for himself, and so, group discussions or collective decisions of a group are not necessarily influential.

He turns inward to his family for his only real intimate relations. This family is usually just his immediate family, his family of orientation, parents and siblings and/or his family of procreation, wife, children and later grandchildren. Relatives outside the range of these lineal relatives are sometimes enjoyed and socialized with, but as a rule these relationships are formal, like those of simple acquaintances. The coal miner spends a good deal of time with his family and children, particularly young children, who occupy a great deal of his attention.

More readily observable - and masking this sense of individualism - is the trait of conformity. In daily events conformity to the collective behavior of a group appears to be a major expression of the coal miner's personality. The molding process of common occupations, living arrangements and, in a broad sense, similar history, have left the miner remarkably like his neighbor in appearance, outlook and behavior. The homes of the miners, the furniture inside, the clothes worn, the automobiles owned, bare the clear stamp of similarity. But more importantly, it is in the more abstract aspects of his life, the ideas he holds and the attitudes he expresses, that conformity is observed. There is little tolerance for strange ideas, and men quickly learn what the sentiment of the group is and what ideas are acceptable.

In one way, conformity, at least the superficial appearance of conformity, operates to make the miner seem like all others, although he

may be harboring new ideas or attitudes. In the social environment of the
miner, conformity proves desirable, whether real or assumed.

C. ANTI-INTELLECTUALISM

Related to conformity is the anti-intellectualism of the coal miners.
In general, coal miners do not admire people with intellectual curiosity
(one would not want to be known as the "brain" in school) particularly if
the intellectual interests appear at all esoteric or are not grounded in
practical everyday events of one's life. Interest in literature or
abstract political ideas is rarely displayed but common sense and
cleverness in the everyday world are valued and admired.

This lack of intellectualism is exemplified by college students who
are the sons and daughters of coal miners. For them, college becomes a
way, as one of them expressed it, to get a "union card" which was a
guarantee of a job. Knowledge and learning per se are not respected nor
sought after for themselves and so vocational education and college majors
which appear most promising for employment are sought after. Students seek
academic majors in business administration, in the health related
professions or in education, while the humanities are much less popular.
Students who do seek degrees in the disciplines are frequently badgered by
their parents who perceive little value in these seemingly impractical
intellectual pursuits.

There is little conversation about abstract philosophical questions or
the sensitive political issues of the day among the miners. Their
interests usually revolve around local events, work or hunting. Ideas on

issues often are held on very shallow intellectual grounds, and have often little more than a personal prejudice. Most broad social and philosophical issues are not considered in any sophisticated framework and so the miners' views on issues are frequently inconsistent with other positions they have held. Generally, the coal miner simply asks how a particular event or action is going to affect him. If there appears to be no connection to himself, he has no interest and little opinion.

In everyday affairs the miner proves his common sense. He is very clever in his dealings with people and shrewd in his approach to life. It is difficult for strangers to put things over on the miner because new ideas are not received easily and strangers are always treated with caution until they are known or their intentions are well understood.

Outsiders to the life in the coal towns often had a false picture of the coal miners in general and of their intellectual capabilities in particular. One former mine superintendent said it this way:

> "Outsiders looked down on the coal miner. They didn't think he was human. I can't say a coal miner is a low type person. They just didn't understand the miner. The coal miner was treated unfair in the past. They just didn't understand."

D. ISOLATIONISM

Anti-intellectualism and conformity are supporting themes and produce a certain noticeable resistance to new ideas and life styles and a general resistance to change. Reinforcing this conservatism is the physical isolation of the coal towns which are located in the rural areas of the county and are little influenced by the cosmopolitan attitudes and life

styles of a major urban area such as Pittsburgh. This isolationism, as
argued previously, has abated as more men and women have obtained
employment in jobs outside of mining and have moved into the wider economy
of the county. However, the demographic patterns of the coal towns, with
people rarely moving into them and with the general population decline in
the county, have created a general lack of external influence upon the coal
miners' lives.

One man who grew up in a coal town recalled the story of seeing a well
known James Dean film, <u>Rebel</u> <u>Without</u> <u>A</u> <u>Cause</u>, in the summer of 1956. At
the time, the film appeared totally unrealistic, as if it were about
another country; such ridiculous treatment of cars seemed stupid and
wasteful; and wearing black leather jackets was a totally foreign and
strange thing to do. When this man went to college two months later at the
University of Pittsburgh's Johnstown Campus, some ten miles from his home
town, he noticed for the first time that, in fact, teenagers did race
around in cars and did in fact wear leather jackets. He claims that it was
a profound shock to learn how very different the world was outside his coal
town.

It has been mentioned that families from the small Cambria County
mining towns seldom go to Pittsburgh, or even Johnstown, but rather spend
their whole lives in their own communities, rarely spending one night away
from home. This often creates a very narrow and false picture of life in
the United States and the world in general. For instance, one man claimed
that as a boy in the 1940's he believed that his family was very well-to-
do, and today he claims his view was one where he considered himself in the

middle class or even upper middle class. In retrospect he sees with
amusement that his father was just a relatively successful miner with only
one child, a situation which gave the appearance that his family was secure
and financially fortunate. His father today, a man in his sixties,
indicates that in 1947 he earned about $3400 which was among the top
earnings for miners in the region. The isolation of the coal towns made
comparison to anything outside the towns unlikely.

One woman in commenting on life in the coal towns gave her impression
of isolation. She said:

> "Living in a coal town? For one thing, I'd say it was
> very depressing. You could never get ahead. And you
> had no transportation to go anywhere. You just stayed
> at home. It was just terrible. I just never knew
> anyone but my neighbors. And my parents didn't
> either."

E. AUTHORITARIANISM

This isolationism contributed in part to the authoritarianism found in
people's lives. Life in a coal town where everyone worked for the same
employer resulted in an authoritarian relationship between the common coal
miner and his boss whereby the miner simply knew his place. One was either
a boss and could order people around or one was a worker and expected to
take orders. There was very little questioning of the right of the boss to
use his authority. Simply, the position commanded authority and the miners
responded accordingly. It is interesting that when a man changed his
position from worker to company man and boss, he instantly commanded the
authority of his new position. As one young foreman expressed it:

> "When I did mining I did like I was told. But now the
> men gotta do as I tell them. There's no question.
> They know it. There's no problem. It should be that
> way."

In the daily lives of the miners, this authoritarianism is manifested in various ways. He generally responds unquestioningly and ungrudgingly to orders given to him within the work place even if orders do not appear to be reasonable. He is regarded as a good worker, since as a worker he normally responds easily to the authority over him. In other social relationships where he himself may have a position of authority, he demands in turn a response to his authority. At home, he tends to be a strict father, especially to young children, and displays a somewhat old world patriarchal relationship toward his wife and family. If elected to an office, or put in charge of some activity, he generally expects people to follow him unquestioningly.

The miners' seemingly automatic response to those with authority can on occasion mask their real feelings about a boss's instruction. And so, while the coal miner normally appears somewhat passive and even spiritless, the miner, always cautious and suspicious, is quite capable of refusing direct orders and sometimes erupts passionately to such an extent that he will walk off the job and out of the mine. In other words, the miner generally operates easily within an authoritarian set of relationship but he cannot be treated unreasonably.

F. RESIGNATION

On a day to day basis, the coal miner appears resigned to his
existence, to his job and his community, and therefore appears to be quite
at peace with himself. The miner knows that his position in life, and
certainly his short run situation, will be difficult to improve, and that
he is likely to be doing the same type of work and living roughly this same
type of life for the rest of his days. He realizes that there is little
probability that the world around him will improve substantially. He knows
too that no new industries are likely to come along and present new
opportunities to him. At the same time, he likes the rural life and
security of the coal town, while he views cities and other places as
confusing and inhospitable. He accepts being a coal miner without
complaint. In fact, he regards mining as a good job, and he sees chances
for substantial improvement in his life style as linked to major economic
changes which would encompass the entire region. He accepts his life
easily and is resigned to his work. He is not saddened or depressed about
his state in life: rather he enjoys many aspects of it and certainly his
resignation is not of the type where one withdraws from active living. Any
major improvements to his life, however, will come about through forces and
events outside his control and so he accepts his circumstances
realistically and without complaint and, like most people, he never
abandons hope that things will improve.

Since the coal miner tends to be cautious and suspicious, his impulse
is to fear new ideas and change. His conservatism is reinforced by his
resignation and a certain amount of pessimism because changes could always

be for the worse. However, the miner is capable of anticipating the positive side of change although not nearly as easily as would be found in the general population.

He appears to move through life without clearly articulated goals or plans. Since his ability to effectuate substantial changes in his life is small, he makes no grandiose plans for himself. He simply fills his life with a great deal of physical activity and his world view appears oriented to the present. He tends not to focus heavily on the future, and certainly not on the long range future, for his future is not likely to change much. He often buys material objects, e.g. television sets, cars, rifles, and new gadgets of every kind, almost on impulse. In times gone by, life was often very difficult and just making it through life from day to day was all that could be expected. In many ways, he behaves the same today: the only difference now is that he has money to spend and he does not hesitate to do so.

Manifestations of the coal miners' resignation are easily found. He is generally ambivalent in his attitudes toward his work, although always resigned to keep doing it, and often expresses opinions like the following:

> "No, I really never heard a coal miner say he really
> liked his job that much. I mean where was it gettin'
> him."

> "I wouldn't want my children to be coal miners neither,
> no way. It was just a dirty, back breaking job and no
> future to it. You have no satisfaction out of the job
> at all. It is just a means of supportin' the family.
> But you did it."

> "Life was really hard, but we had no choice. We didn't
> even see daylight. We went to work when it was dark,
> then worked in the dark, and came home in the dark. I
> hated it but I couldn't do nothin' about it."

In spite of the apparent resignation of the miner, it would be incorrect to label him as fatalistic. As indicated, he is aware of the possibilities of improving his lot, though at the same time he realizes that his chances are small. He assesses his own opportunities realistically and he knows that in his rural world, dominated by giant industries like coal and steel, a man is simply going to be a wage earner for the rest of his life. Opportunities for major change lie elsewhere and one must strike out to new parts of the country if one wants to improve one's situation. But most miners stay, and staying means a certain acceptance, if not resignation. It means doing about the same thing for a life-time and doing it in the same place; it means letting the events that will take place follow what appears to be their natural course with perhaps occasional human intervention, such as organized union efforts or technological advances changing the course of things ever so slightly.

It is clear that with the changes in the lives of the coal miners over the past thirty years, the degree of resignation has shifted somewhat. Two coal miners described the differences in world views:

> "When I was a boy in the 1940's, people who were in their twenty's seemed a lot older and middle age seemed to come sooner. Nowadays, people seem to be young a little longer and try to do a little something with themselves."

> "My father and mother just worked. Didn't seem like they wanted anything except to pay the bills. I don't know. Today, it seems like the fellows push a little to get things better. They think about bigger things."

And yet the views of most miners are not optimistic. Concerning his work, one miner described his resignation by saying, "To me, I just want to

get through my workin' life as fast as possible so I can sit and do
nothing." And college graduates from the rural areas of Cambria County,
when asked what they will do with their degrees, usually reply that they
are looking around home (an area clearly having few opportunities for
future white collar workers) for employment, and indicate little aspiration
to seek out opportunities which will lead to what might be considered big
jobs. This resignation, while subtle, can be so pervasive among the miners
and their children that this "sit and wait" approach to life, so often
devoid of aggressive action to force a change or to direct one's life,
becomes one of the main characteristics of their personality. There is a
tendency even in the young not to ask much from life; in fact, not to even
think in ambitious terms for oneself.

Curiously, retired miners who are now working in other jobs and who
suspect they qualify for black lung compensation (believing they suffer
from coal miners' pneumoconiosis) aggressively fight for the money that
they believe to be justly theirs. Often they will make appeal after
appeal, year after year, to win their compensation payments. If granted
these black lung payments, they are forced to stop all work, and their
total yearly incomes will generally be substantially lowered, but the dream
of sitting and being inactive for the remainder of their lives is very
appealing. There is little real drive to build fortunes or to extend their
influence--sitting and taking it easy, gardening, fishing and hunting, hold
many more attractions.

G. EARLY ADULTHOOD

     The children of coal miners, as they are socialized, learn very early
their roles as adults. The freedoms of childhood begin rather abruptly to
be replaced by the responsibility of adulthood when children reach about
fourteen years of age. By the time the teenager has completed high school,
he or she is generally prepared emotionally and attitudinally for the tasks
that lie ahead. The teenager is ready now to assume his place as an adult
worker and the notion of an extended adolescence with eight or ten carefree years before settling down is a virtually unknown pattern of
socialization. (One view is that when young men of fourteen or fifteen
went into the mines to work alongside their fathers, it was necessary that
they be emotionally stable and mature enough to withstand the rugged work
with its many drudgeries. One needed to assume the responsibility of a
mature man and to adjust to the seriousness of a working life. A child
could not make it.)

     The many manifestations of an early adulthood are still quite
observable in today's young coal miners. First, in the rural areas of the
county, young marriage is commonplace. It is a frequent occurrence to have
nearly all the students in a high school class married within a year or two
after graduation and many of the students marry in the summer immediately
following graduation.[3] Eighteen year olds are ready and willing to work
hard, and they come from a tradition where hard work is a part of life. If
job opportunities come along, they move into these jobs willingly. And
with employment and financial responsibility comes a great degree of
personal control of one's life and the abandonment of parental authority.

By the time a young man graduates from high school he is prepared in
many respects to be self-sufficient. Interestingly, parents, even when
they are financially able, will frequently cease to support or to give
financial assistance to their children. Children of eighteen or so are
supposed to be adult enough to take care of their own affairs, particularly
their financial affairs.[4]

This early 'adulthood' tends to make people less adventuresome than
youthful counterparts in comparable age groupings in society.
Responsibilities are accepted early and the model is to stand on one's own
and get into the business of life which is to work and marry and raise a
family. Being wild in one's behavior conflicts with the basic seriousness
of life and is to be avoided. Striking out on new and untried pathways
goes against the patterns of life which have been outlined. And so, the
assumption of adult roles early in life partially insures the replication
of the coal miners' personality and world view.

This chapter has outlined in a general way how the coal miner views
his world and approaches life's obligations. It is deficient in that it
does not deal thoroughly enough with the coal miner in the context of his
family (a point made in chapter II, on the limitations of the methodology),
but it does present a foundation for understanding the coal miner. As
stated, not all miners conform to the categories as described but no one
coal miner strays far from the composite picture.

The theme of suspicion within the framework of an egocentric world
view is the most salient personality characteristic of the coal miner and
his caution, conservatism, resignation, pessimism, anti-intellectualism and

acceptance of authority all serve to reinforce these dominant characteristics. And yet, for all his apparent conformity to the world around him, there lives an individual, aware of some opportunities for change and for making some gradual adjustments to the world as it changes around him.

What this view of the coal miner fails to convey is a sense of the pleasant derivatives of these characteristics which make association with coal miners an enjoyable experience. He is a man without airs. He does not pretend to be other than what he is. He presents himself to people straightforwardly and demands to be taken on his own merits. As a friend, he is loyal and reliable; he can be depended upon. He is a hard working man and will give a full measure of himself if he has entered into an agreement. He expects to take care of himself and requests little but fairness from others on his behalf. He is a good family man and protects and cares for his family intensely until his children are grown. And finally, his company is pleasant and non-threatening. He enjoys a good conversation and laugh, loves to talk about his work and hobbies, and can be generous and supportive of individuals or organizations which he likes.

IX. CONCLUSIONS

A. THE FINDINGS

The preceding chapters explain in considerable detail what the coal
miner does for a living, where he lives, how he enjoys himself, and what
kind of man he is. This is one of the major purposes of this study--to
simply describe the underground coal miner of Cambria County, Pennsylvania.
From this description emerge several conclusions which, along with a
framework for investigating illness and suggestions for further research,
are presented in this chapter.

The conclusions which emerge from the data include three general and
seven rather specific propositions. The first of the general conclusions
deals with the changing culture of the miners. Historical data indicates
that the coal miner of Cambria County is a member of a distinctive
subculture which sets him apart from other men. To be a coal miner means
sharing a history, life style, place of residence, personality and world
view with other miners. And so, the coal miner is distinct from other men
not simply because of his occupation but because of a series of cultural
components each additive to one another and each contributing to his
uniqueness.

201

Over the past seventy years the culture of the miner has changed dramatically as the technology of mining has changed. No longer are muscle power and individual initiative at the work place as necessary as they previously were for his survival. Today, the nature of his work in the large modern mines demands a high degree of technical skill. While he still lives in coal towns, most of his neighbors are not coal miners. Increasingly he comes in contact more with the main stream of life in the county and with people of different experience. While his leisure time reflects certain rural habits, his steady employment and good wages provide him with new means for recreation.

Because of these changes, a distinctive coal mining 'culture' is increasingly mixed with the greater society and is increasingly difficult to describe and define. His occupation continues to identify him, but his life style, place of residence and non-working activities have become the same as his neighbors. His personality and world view, although reflections of his uniqueness, are shared by most rural working class people who live alongside him, many having been former coal miners or the children of miners in new occupations. What is left of the coal miners' culture therefore is elusive and his occupation itself is only a practical indicator of his difference. While the occupation skill exists, the coal miner as a subculture is simply disappearing.

The second conclusion deals with the issue of coal miners as a community of workers in an industry which has undergone dramatic technological change over the past seventy years. It was within the towns themselves that occupation combined with residence to provide the miners with a sense of community. The boundaries of this community were defined essentially by territory, the physical boundaries of the coal towns, and were then reinforced by occupation and a common culture.

In today's situation, the miners live in towns with people no longer involved in the coal industry and so occupation no longer plays a major role in providing a sense of community. Rather, it is common residence along with personality, outlook and general life style which provides any existing sense of community. Coal mining as an occupation has lost its importance in this regard. The coal miners appear to be like workers in other large industrial occupations whose identity and feeling of belonging to a community of people are increasingly less derived from their occupation. But, interestingly, many historically created features of the subculture of the coal miner continue to exist and operate in spite of the lack of community among the miners.

The third finding of this study deals with the relationship between technological change and social change in the miners' lives. In sections of this study, it has been shown that the miners and their families have been brought into the main stream of life in the county and have increasingly assumed the values, attitudes and behaviors of their non-mining neighbors. There has been a shift in value orientation from the world view whereby a man was unable to control his destiny and was subjugated by his environment to a view whereby a person sees himself as directing his life and controlling the world about him. This change, as well as increased participation in community activity, greater ambitions for children, and increases in wages, has been due to the changes in mechanized mining and steady employment in recent years.

Lewis and Knipe in their research on the sociological impact of mechanization on coal miners ask in their conclusions: "How does our sample of the indigenous Appalachians compare with second and third generation Hungarians, Poles and Germans working in the coal fields of Pennsylvania, Ohio and West Virginia?"[1] (Their research had been conducted in the southwestern counties of Virginia on people who settled in the areas in the 1770's. These people were native born Americans from eastern Virginia, North Carolina and Tennessee and presumably are culturally different from their immigrant coal mining neighbors of Pennsylvania.) Their conclusions, while tentative, address themselves to the impact of coal mining on a traditional mountain community and they are comparable to the evidence in this study of northern Appalachians.[2] It is clear from their material on continuous mining that similar technological changes within the mining industry have been introduced to the miner of Cambria County as well as to the miners of southwest Virginia and these have resulted in very similar social changes, and these changes came about within two groups of people with diverse cultural backgrounds. Harris' ideas, as expressed in Chapter I, in which he claimed that similar technologies, applied in similar environments, produced similar arrangements of labor and similar kinds of social groupings which in turn rely upon similar systems of value and belief, are given substantial support by these findings.

It is evident that the coal miners of Cambria County have undergone a great deal of cultural change which has taken place as a result of technological changes within the underground coal mining industry. More importantly, however, is the observation that similar social arrangements seem to have been produced within groups of people with reasonably diverse cultural backgrounds. The idea of similar technology, impacting and resulting in similar types of social arrangements, as well as values and beliefs, is strengthened considerably.

There are additional conclusions of a more specific nature which can be drawn from this ethnography and are briefly discussed here.

First, the evidence demonstrates that the coal miners of Cambria County, Pennsylvania, and likely the miners throughout Pennsylvania and northern West Virginia, are more similar culturally to the miners of southern Illinois than to the miners of southern Appalachia. The work of Lantz on the miners from Illinois, who were relatively recent immigrants form western and eastern Europe, portrays people similar in personality, attitude and outlook (as described in chapter VIII) to the Cambria County's coal miners.[3] By contrast, southern Appalachians have value orientations which, while changing, appear to be different from those of northern Appalachians. These southern Appalachian orientations include traditionalism, individualism and fatalism.[4] Lewis and Knipe in their work on southern Appalachian coal miners concur with this description and, in fact, use these characteristics as a base from which to demonstrate change. The northern and southern Appalachian coal miners are culturally dissimilar people working within the same general industry. Consideration should always be given to allow for these differences when coal miners are discussed and considered; they are not a culturally homogeneous group of people.

Second, Cambria County coal miners are not marginal members of their communities but are active and fully involved in the activities of their townships and boroughs. This is in contrast to the conclusions of Lewis and Knipe who state on Virginia coal miners, "The miner is still a marginal member of the small towns of the area." Lewis and Knipe do not specify, however, whether the town's people are unwilling to accept the miner or whether the miner is culturally unprepared to participate in town activities.[5] The reasons for the participation of Cambria County's miners in the community life of the area are not fully clear but may be due to either the historical democratic traditions of many early coal miners who demanded a voice in matters concerning themselves or to the degree of contact between miners and other workers. On any account, the miners of Cambria County are not marginal members of the larger community but are active and full participants in the activities of the county.

Third, life in the coal towns is desirable from the miner's point of view. The coal miner and his neighbors live in their communities willingly and enjoy the security and comfort of knowing one's neighbors, of sharing a common history, and of being like one's neighbors.

Fourth, coal mining as an occupation is a highly sought after type of employment by men in the rural areas of the county. The good wages and the reduced difficulty of the work in a geographical region where there are few

other high paying jobs make mining an attractive job. Many men consider
themselves fortunate to have employment in the mines.

Fifth, underground bituminous coal mining as it is done today in large
modern mines is dramatically different from mining in the past, both in
terms of the type of work done and the social arrangements within the mine.
With portal-to-portal pay, and new technology, the work crew has become the
basic social unit with which the miner identifies himself. Otherwise,
working in the large mines has become impersonalized. The miners today no
longer work with neighbors and close friends but work in a sense with
strangers. The work in large coal mines with increased mechanization has
developed along lines similar to that found in large industries in the
United States. The work is easier, if more routine, and the pay is better,
but from the social point of view the work is less desirable. While good
wages are important it is the work crew which provides the miner with his
only real source of identification while at work and it is within the work
crew that he must find job satisfaction.

Sixth, the leisure time activities support the rural, isolated life
style of the coal miner. Hunting, fishing, farming, and high school
athletics occupy a great deal of the miner's non-working time. More
importantly, the miners rarely leave their rural environment to go to
cities or other parts of the country to pursue their hobbies or interests.
They appear happy within their environment, as reflected by their active
leisure time activities, and consequently new ideas and life styles are
slow to make their way into their lives. The miners remain conservative
with regard to change and provincial in their outlooks.

Seventh, the health situation for the coal miner is poor, in fact probably the poorest of any identifiable worker in the United States for which statistics are kept. The coal miner's access to good medical care, in spite of an extremely comprehensive health plan, is frequently limited because of a physician shortage and the poor distribution of physicians within the county. In terms of emergency care, availability of primary care physicians, and the high morbidity rates for a wide variety of diseases, the coal miner's health situation is far from satisfactory.

B. THE FRAMEWORK FOR INVESTIGATING ILLNESS

As stated, this study was intended in part to present a framework for investigating the morbidity and mortality of the coal miners. It is hoped that a deeper and more comprehensive understanding of the health situation can be derived from an analysis, within such a framework, of the data included in this study. This study has dealt with social and cultural factors which can be considered precursors of diseases, rather than the so-called objective factors such as dust levels, smoking habits and time spent in the mines, and it is these social factors which will be considered within the framework.

Although frameworks for investigating illness have been advanced by many medical sociologists and medical anthropologists, ranging from the so-called grand theorists to the empiricists, one such framework, presented by Steven Polgar, has been found suitable for analysis of the data contained within this study.[6]

Polgar's framework suggests two broad areas from which one should gather information: one, the popular health culture, including value orientations, notions and behavior of the laymen or people in question, and the other, the professional health culture, including value orientations, notions and behaviors of the health specialists. Although his framework has some additional features to it, the data of this study, particularly the chapter on the coal miners' personality and world view, provides information which can be employed in the first area of popular health culture.

The remainder of the information needed to fulfill the informational requirements of his framework could come from other health researchers (and anthropologists too) employing different research techniques. This information is more readily obtainable through questionnaires and through key informant interviewing of trained medical personnel. Medical anthropologists may or may not address themselves to these areas.[7]

Popular health culture is the health culture of the people investigated and refers broadly to their health practices as well as to their underlying health beliefs and their overall world view. According to Polgar's framework, there are three areas within the popular health culture which must be given consideration. These are: value orientations, notions, and behaviors. It is within the first of these three areas that the information of this study can be directly applied.

Value Orientations- All societies hold basic assumptions about the world around them. These can be referred to as the value orientations of a culture and they constitute a most basic disposition in all societies. A

full understanding of the popular health culture requires illumination of
these basic cultural assumptions. Polgar employs the work of Kluckholn and
Strodtbeck to provide him with the categories on values, while recognizing
the possibility of establishing other dimensions of value orientation.
Kluckholn's and Strodtbeck's categories lend themselves well to the data of
this study, so they will be employed here as well.[8]

(1)   The first orientation is: what is the character of innate human
nature? Is human nature basically evil, good or neutral? If human nature
is perceived as evil as in some variations of fundamentalist Christian
thought, then disease could be perceived as justly deserved, even if a man
did nothing evil himself. Health action would then be directed toward
seeking a release from this basic human condition. If human nature is seen
as neutral, or a mixture of good and evil, then health action could be
taken from a different approach, and perhaps directed toward bringing in
benevolent forces. (Kluckholn and Strodtbeck doubt that any societies
believe man is all good.)

This study has revealed that coal miners view others with suspicion and
caution. The hidden motive behind peoples' actions is usually sought out
and questioned. Their view is that people do things on behalf of others
because of some quality of human goodness but are forced by situations
outside their control to act as if they had evil intentions. The
introduction of better health facilities or new health education programs
or of additional health personnel is not likely to be accepted simply and
health planners should consider the miners' suspicion and possible
resistance in this regard.

(2)   The second orientation is: what is the relationship of man to nature? If man is subjugated to nature, he must avoid giving offense to nature and must petition the forces of nature to give him health or relief from illness. The many religious or magico-religious charms and amulets worn on one's body as in many western societies or pinned to the garments of saints in Mexican churches bear witness of this relationship. If man is in harmony with nature, he must struggle not to fall out of the delicate balances with his environment.[9] Illness can be attributed to the fact that man has fallen out of this balance. If man has mastery over nature, then he will not hesitate to take action to control it. This is the view of many middle-class Americans who have confidence that science and modern medicine can achieve good health for them.

The coal miners appear to be shifting toward this control-over-nature orientation as they become more involved in the main stream of life in the county. However, this shift is still incomplete and their basic orientation remains one in which they have imperfect control over their lives. They are resigned to their basic lot in life and accept that it is not likely to improve very much. It appears that they even expect to get pneumoconiosis if they work a full career in the mines. Although in their work environment the miners take an aggressive approach to maintaining safe conditions, they fully realize that in many situations no amount of human effort can assure their safety. They cannot fully control their lives or their environment and this awareness of nature's control permeates their attitudes toward health. Consequently, they do not possess a strong sense of confidence in the efficacy of scientific health care.

(3)   The third orientation is: what is the temporal focus of the
people? Is the past or the present or the future orientation the most
important? Some societies place great emphasis on the past by being
concerned with ancestors and their role in causing disease. Middle-class
American are future oriented with a willingness to endure hardships or to
work diligently in order to secure a better future. Cambria County's coal
miners do not fully share this middle class orientation, but rather are
more like lower class groups in industrial societies with an orientation to
the present. With regard to their health, this orientation has major
implications because the miner works in what he knows to be dangerous
health conditions (e.g. high dust levels) with full realization of the
likelihood of becoming ill. His future health concerns him little and his
present orientation allows him to work in these dangerous conditions. This
orientation is compatible with his acceptance of nature's control over him.
He does not agitate strongly to force stricter health regulations but
leaves this to public health officials. Furthermore, he is apt to continue
working even when his body indicates obvious signs of illness. His present
orientation is so strong that he does not view his condition, no matter how
unsatisfactory, as changing for the worse. It is as if his situation is
fixed.

(4)   The fourth orientation is: what is the modality of human
activity? In other words, does the modality of human activity stress being
or doing? For the coal miner, the dominant modality is one of being. His
health situation is viewed as a static condition. Through time his health
may slowly deteriorate or change abruptly as a result of an accident.

However, the maintenance of his health is not viewed as something that must be constantly worked upon. Health _per_ _se_ is not pursued by regular health programs; it just exists.

(5) The fifth orientation is: what is man's relationship to other men? There are three basic sets of relationships, lineal, collateral and individual within this orientation. Respectively, they are characterized as: 1) Unequal or stratified relationships among men; 2) equal or horizontal relationships in which solidarity is emphasized; 3) an every-man-for-himself orientation in which there is no emphasis given to man's relationships to others, either vertical or horizontal.

The coal miner's suspicion, caution and personalism does not allow him to build strong lateral relationships with many men and therefore the collateral orientation cannot be said to characterize him. Rather the individualistic and lineal relationship better characterize his value orientations. The coal miner asks what's "in it" for himself and weighs carefully the risks of any action he may take.

In terms of health, the individualistic orientation to other men allows the miner to separate himself from the condition of others. The fact that many men become ill or injured while mining disturbs the miner little since he does not necessarily link his fate to that of his fellow workers. Naturally, any health planning directed to the coal miner must consider this individualistic orientation.

Although the remaining two areas--notions and behaviors--go beyond the data presented within this study, a brief examination of their significance to health research will be given. Notions are the ideas, cognitions, explanations, rationalizations, sentiments and memories that people have about health.   Notions can be verbalized by people and can be more readily obtained, if the proper questions are asked, than value orientations. Notions in Polgar's framework are the conceptual bridge between value orientations on the one hand and observable behavior on the other.   Notions in popular health culture include such things as the way in which the body is regarded, anatomical knowledge, ideas about food and nutrition and diet, ideas about coping with particular sicknesses, etc.

The term behaviors simply means detailed descriptions used in curing. Many anthropologists have made detailed studies in so-called traditional societies and Polgar completes his descriptive framework on popular health culture by suggesting that this be done.

The final aspect of Polgar's framework is to repeat the descriptive process and examine the value orientations, notions and behaviors of the professional health actors.   Essentially, the same descriptions that were used for describing the popular health culture must now be applied to the health professionals. This section is now complete.   Polgar's work has provided a framework in which the data of this study can be presented.   The information presented for the miner's value orientations has been taken from this study, especially the chapter on personality and world view.   It illustrates an important role for the medical anthropologist in health research.

The following section deals with additional information and substantive findings derived from the health situation of the miners.

1. Suggestions for Health Planning

The following are three suggestions which should be considered by health planners who are involved in health research among Cambria County's coal miners. These suggestions for research are likely to be applicable when applied to other northern Appalachian coal miners as well.

First, health planning for underground coal miners should be done with the full realization of the cultural dissimilarities among different groups of miners. Northern and southern Appalachian coal miners, in spite of their similar occupations, are sufficiently different in personality and world view (and likely attitudes to health and illness) to warrant different research approaches both in the data gathering phase and in the planning health care delivery phase. (This generalization is most likely also true for coal miners in the mid-western and far-western coal fields of the United States.) Health planning or research into the causes of illness must account for these cultural differences among miners from the difference regions of the country.

Second, the personality and world view of the coal miner must be considered in any study of the miner's health situation. For the Cambria County coal miner (and likely other northern Appalachian coal miners) those factors of personality as outlined in chapter VIII can provide a basis for dealing with the miner in terms of his health situation. Important to any health delivery planning, or any research attempting to explain the causes of coal miners' illnesses, is an understanding of the coal miner's view of himself, of outsiders, and of his approaches to living.

Research should be conducted with an awareness of the suspicious nature of the miner as well as with a realization that he is apt to be extremely cautious about what is taking place and conservative with regard to trying new techniques or approaches to reducing illness. People well known to the miners may be influential in minimizing this suspicion, and when research is undertaken these types of people would be useful to researchers and research assistants. Furthermore, a mechanism introduced into the research design to mask the identity of an informant, such as questionnaires requiring no names from the respondents, would likely insure greater accuracy.

The research may utilize other personality themes in achieving the research purpose itself or in introducing new health and safety standards. For instance, in considering the miner's tendency toward authoritarianism, far better compliance to health and safety rules will be obtained through firm rules and regulations than through an appeal to some abstract notion about disease (or safety). The anti-intellectualism of the miner would make this latter approach less effective than the former.

Third, regarding the issue of illness itself, the miner must be understood in terms of his pessimism and resignation. Nearly every miner interviewed indicated that he expected to get black lung disease (coal workers' pneumoconiosis) sooner or later. For the miner, this was part of the job and he resigns himself to the likelihood of getting the disease. Attitudes and world views such as these must be taken into consideration when research is undertaken since they most likely differ from those of the trained health researcher and can lead to some erroneous conclusions.

To reiterate, it is suggested that a fuller understanding of the coal miner's personality and world view which differs in many respects from the outlooks of so-called middle America should form the basis, implicitly or not, of any health research.

And finally the serious illness situation for the coal miners is not likely to be changed significantly through improvements simply within the mines themselves. Control of dust levels and increased use of respirators may aid in reducing certain respiratory disorders but will not have a significant effect on the broader health situation as described in chapter VI. To improve the health picture, additional positive action is needed. The rural coal miner, inspite of a most comprehensive health plan, has poor medical facilities available to him. Recruitment of physicians to rural places, imaginative programs for visiting physicians, and the use of paramedical personnel and health educators are necessary for serving and for educating the coal miner about the broad range of illnesses to which he is susceptible and for instilling an attitude of prevention and positive health action. The rural coal miner is only slowly moving toward the value systems of so-called middle American and so health education must be brought to him. Improvement of conditions within the mines remain only one approach in approving the coal miners' health situation.

The three suggestions of this section provide a mere starting place from which researchers can begin to understand coal miners within a social and cultural context. With these points in mind, and with the value orientations somewhat clarified, the investigator can begin to reach for a more comprehensive understanding of the causes of morbidity and mortality

among the coal miners. In one sense, these suggestions are only a
beginning to understand the high morbidity rates among coal miners, but in
another sense they can prove to be useful in dealing with coal miners and
in planning health programs. The social and cultural factors, in short,
must be considered if the health situation for coal miners is to improve.

C. ADDITIONAL RESEARCH

The study of coal miners and coal towns offers an area fertile for many
types of academic research. In concluding this study, four research areas
which call for investigation are mentioned.

The labor history of western Pennsylvanian coal towns is very
inadequately understood. Oral histories should be collected immediately
from the coal miners themselves-- from their point of view. The rise of
unionism should be recorded and studied in detail.

One approach to understanding the labor history should deal with the
social and cultural dynamics of the coal towns. The question of how people
of various ethnic backgrounds came together in a common struggle invites
investigation. And finally, the question of how the various coal companies
(it appears) manipulated and managed these social and cultural differences
in order to diminish unity and to thwart unionizing efforts remains at this
time unanswered.

A second area in need of research is the question of the development of
the various social classes in the coal towns. These towns were not only
small and isolated but also based on a single industry. The abilities of
some men to earn greater amounts of money than others was, to some extent,

minimized by the nature of the work. Criteria other than income or "power"
appear to have been at work in class formation. The social strata, while
varying with the perspectives of the different ethnic groups, were
determined along ethnic lines. Finally, the relationships of the people
within a coal town to the people external to the town and not in the coal
industry should be investigated.

Ethnic studies is a third research area since coal mining towns provide
a good strategic base for study. The size of the towns, as well as their
isolation, provides a group of people with physical and social barriers.
In such a situation, various types of academic questions concerning ethnic
groups can be asked. Particularly advantageous in the study of coal miners
is that various ethnic social clubs are still active
in maintaining ethnic identity. These, coupled with a minimum degree of
social contact with people outside the coal towns, provide an excellent
subject for ethnic studies.

A fourth area for research lies in the expansion and manipulation of
the framework for investigating illness for the purpose of both applied and
academic health research. Coal miners offer a good study group since many
of the "objective" factors of illness are well understood and the
possibility of constructing a meta-theory of illness is quite possible.

NOTES

CHAPTER I

1.   Robert Munn, The Coal Industry in America: A Bibliography and Guide
to Studies (Morgantown: West Virginia University Library, 1965).

2.   Appalachian Bibliography, Volume I and Volume II (Morgantown: West
Virginia University Library, 1972).

3.   Archie Green, Only A Miner: Studies in Recorded Coal Mining Songs
(Urbana: University of Illinois Press, 1972), p. 26; Norman Dennis et al.,
Coal Is Our Life: An Analysis of a Yorkshire Mining Community (London:
Eyre and Spotiswoode, 1956). More recently, two works on English coal
miners have been published; Raphael Samuel (ed.) Miners, Quarrymen and
Saltworkers. (London: Routledge and Kegan Paul, 1977); Robert Moore, Pit-
Men, Preachers and Politics: The Effects of Methodism in a Durham Mining
Town, (London, Cambridge University Press, 1974). The supplementary
bibliography contained in this revised work lists most of the latest
material available.

4.   Herman R. Lantz, People of Coal Town (New York: Columbia University
Press, 1958).

5.   Edward E. Knipe, "Change in Mining Technology and Workers
Interaction," paper read at International Seminar on Social Change in the
Mining Community (Jackson's Mill, West Virginia, 1967); Helen M. Lewis,
"The Changing Communities in the Southern Appalachian Coal Fields," paper
read at International Seminar on Social Change in the Mining Community
(Jackson's Mill, West Virginia, 1967); Edward E. Knipe and Helen M. Lewis,
"Toward a Methodology of Studying Coal Miners' Attitudes," Open File Report
8-69 (Washington: United States Bureau of Mines, 1968); Edward E. Knipe and
Helen M. Lewis, "The Impact of Coal Mining on the Traditional Mountain
Subculture, in The Not So Solid South, ed. J. Kenneth Morland (Athens:
University of Georgia Press, 1971); Helen M. Lewis and Edward E. Knipe,
"The Sociological Impact of Mechanization on Coal Miners and Their
Families," Annual Council of Economics Proceedings Volume (American
Institute of Mining, Metallurgical, and Petroleum Engineers, Inc., 1969).

6.   George Korson, Coal Dust on the Fiddle, 2nd printing (Hatboro,
Pennsylvania: Folklore Associates, 1965); Minstrels of the Mine Patch, 3rd

220

printing (Hatboro, Pennsylvania: Folklore Associates, 1964). These are two of Korson's better known works.

6*. As indicated, this is a revised version of the original thesis. The coal industry in Cambria County is now in a desperate condition because steel making which used 'metalurical' coal is non existent in the area. Nevertheless, any revival of the coal industry must take into account the culture of the coal miners themselves.

6**. A new book has recently been published which addresses in considerable detail this issue. The author successfully writes of the life experiences and adaptations of ten eastern European ethnic groups in the Cambria County region and demonstrates that the pattern of adaptation is similar for all groups. See Ewa Morawska.

7. Marvin Harris, The Rise of Anthropological Theory (New York: Thomas Y. Crowell Company, 1968), p.4. For a critique of Harris and other technological determinists, see Alexander Alland, "Adaptation," in Bernard J. Siegel, Annual Review of Anthropology (Palo Alto: Annual Reviews Incorporated, 1975), pp.59-73.

8. Conrad M. Arensberg and Solon T. Kimball, Culture and Community (New York: Harcourt, Brace and World, 1965), p. 291.

9. Helen M. Lewis and Edward E. Knipe, "The Sociological Impact of Mechanization on Coal Miners and Their Families" op. cit., p.2.

10. E. Gable Jaco, Patients, Physicians and Illness (New York: The Free Press, 1958), p.2.

11. Edward A. Suchman, "The Addictive Diseases As Socio-Environmental Problems," ed. Howard E. Freeman, Sol Levine and Leo G. Reeder, Handbook of Medical Sociology (Englewood: Prentice Hall, 1963), p.124.

12. Irving J. Selikoff, Marcus M. Key and Douglas H.K. Lee, Coal Workers' Pneumoconiosis, Annals of the New York Academy of Sciences (New York: The New York Academy of Sciences, 1972). Some fifteen articles discuss the relationship of coal dust to morbidity.

13. Norman A. Scotch, "Medical Anthropology," Biennial Review of Anthropology (Stanford: Stanford University Press, 1960).

14. Talcott Parsons, Structure of Social Action (New York: The Free Press, 1949), pp. 28-29.

15. K. Bailey. "The Reconstruction of Controversial Theory: Human Ecology as a Case in Point," in E. Gartly Jaco, Patient, Physicians and Illness (New York: The Free Press, 1958), p. 28.

16.   Alvin W. Gouldner, "Theoretical Requirements of the Applied Social
Sciences," _American Sociological Review_, 22 (February, 1957), pp. 92-102;
George M. Foster, _Applied Anthropology_ (Boston: Little, Brown and Company,
1969), pp. 39-54.

17.   The reader should not be left with the impression that various
attempts have not been made at using social, cultural and psychological
factors to explain illness. S.H. King (1963) provides a good review
article, especially in the section entitled "Etiology and the Social
Environment", to illustrate various theories attempting to explain the
causes of illness.   In addition, Simons and Wolff (1954) relate social,
cultural and physical factors as a source of human illness and essentially
develop a stress theory of disease; Leighton (1959) theorizes a
relationship between human striving and psychiatric illness. More
recently, Alland (1970) has developed an ecological explanation of disease
which views man as a biological organism adapting by means of culture to an
environment.   Changes in either the environment or the culture, e.g.,
through culture contact, necessarily affect the strategies of adjustment
and consequently change the cultural patterns. The epidemiological
approach has been illustrated by many. Cassel (1964) illustrates a number
of situations where the disease organisms alone failed to provide more than
a _necessary cause_ of illness and that illness only occurred when _sufficient
causes_, certain social and cultural factors, were present as well.   Other
studies which demonstrate obvious relationships between illness and
cultural factors include: Suchman (1963) on addictive diseases, Hughes and
Hunter (1970) on "development diseases," Newman (1962) on "overnutrition,"
Rao (1967) on diseases of old age.

       Alexander Alland, _Adaptation in Cultural Evolutions: An Approach to
Medical Anthropology_ (New York: Columbia University Press, 1970); John A.
Cassel, "Social Theory as a Source of Hypothesis in Epidemiological
Research," _American Journal of Public Health_, 54 (1964), p. 1482-1488;
Charles Hughes and John M. Hunter, "Disease and 'Development' in Africa,"
Social Sciences and Medicine, 3 (1970), p. 443-493; Stanley H. King,
"Social Psychological Factors in Illness," in H.E. Freeman, Sol Levine and
Leo G. Reeder, _Handbook of Medical Sociology_ (Englewood: Prentice-Hall,
1963), pp. 99-121; Marshall T. Newman, "Ecology and Nutritional Stress in
Man," _American Anthropologist_, 64 (1962), pp. 22-34; Sharadombe Rao,
"Culture and Mental Disorder: A Study in an Indian Mental Hospital,"
International Journal of Social Psychiatry, 12 (1966), pp. 139-148; Leo W.
Simmons and Harold G. Wolff, _Social Science in Medicine_ (New York: Russel
Sage Foundation, 1954); Edward A. Suchman, "The Addictive Diseases as a
Socio-Environmental Health Problem," in H.S. Freeman, Sol Levine and Leo G.
Reeder, _Handbook of Medical Sociology_ (Englewood: Prentice-Hall, 1963), p.
124.

18.   It should be noted that there is some evidence that due to the new
machinery involved in modern mining that the dust levels have increased
making the physical environment even more dangerous from the standpoint of
health than in the recent past.

19.   Everett C. Hughes, Men and Their Work (New York: The Free Press,
1958); Studs Turkel, Working (New York: Pantheon Books of Random House,
1972).

20.   Oscar Lewis, "The Culture of Poverty," Scientific American, 216, No.
4 (1966). Lewis says the primary identity in industrial society tends to
be based on occupation.

21.   A.B. Shostak and William Gomberg, Blue Collar World: Studies of the
American Worker (Englewood: Prentice-Hall, 1964).

22.   One exception is a recently published monograph, William W. Pilchner,
The Portland Longshoremen: A Dispersed Urban Community (New York: Holt,
Rinehart and Winston, 1972).

CHAPTER II.

1.   Claude Levi-Strauss, Structural Anthropology (New York: Basic Books,
1963), p. 17.

2.   Wives of retired miners have proved particularly useful in describing
life in coal towns.

3.   Annual Report of the Office of Mines and Land Protection 1973
(Harrisburg: Pennsylvania Department of Environmental Resources, 1974), p.
155.

4.   This figure is determined by adding together the totals of membership
roles from all the union locals in Cambria County. Unpublished report,
Election Information for U.M.W.A. District 2, December 12, 1972.

5.   Nationally, the number of working coal miners shows an increase from
124,532 in 1909 to 145,664 in 1971, with 99,269 and 109,311 being the
respective figures for underground miners. In District One of the National
Coal Association, of which Cambria County is a part, the working miners
increased from 10,974 to 13,501 in 1971. Bituminous Coal Data (Washington:
National Coal Association, 1972), pp. 29-30.

6.   Annual Report of the Office of Mines and Land Protection, 1973
(Harrisburg: Pennsylvania Department of Environmental Resources, 1974), pp.
261-265, p. 296.

7.   John J. Honigmann, "Sampling in Ethnographic Field Work," A Handbook
of Method in Cultural Anthropology, eds., Raoul Naroll and Ronald Cohen
(New York: Columbia University Press, 1973), p. 266.

8.   Margaret Mead, "National Character," <u>Anthropology</u> <u>Today</u>, ed., A.L. Kroeber (Chicago: University of Chicago Press, 1953), pp. 642-667.
9.   In Cambria County, starting at the beginning of 1974, a handful of women have become underground coal miners and as of June 1974, five women are employed by the Bethlehem Mining Corporation. <u>Pittsburgh</u> <u>Press</u>, June 23, 1974.

10.   It is usual for the mines to close down completely, except for skeleton crews, during the last week in June and the first week in July and for all miners to be on vacation at one time.

10*. This labor history research project was completed and later published. See, Bruce T. Williams and Michael D. Yates. <u>Upward</u> <u>Struggle</u>.

11.   Many of these tapes are cataloged and are available at the University of Pittsburgh at Johnstown Library.

11*. One major user of these tapes was Professor Ewa Morowska in her monumental work on ethnic groups in Johnstown, Pennsylvania. See, Ewa Morawska, <u>For</u> <u>Bread</u> <u>With</u> <u>Butter</u>.

12.   Herman R. Lantz, <u>People</u> <u>of</u> <u>Coal</u> <u>Town</u> (New York: Columbia University Press, 1958).

CHAPTER III.

1.   <u>Economic</u> <u>and</u> <u>Social</u> <u>Study</u> (Ebensburg: Cambria County Planning Commission, 1973), p. 2.

2.   <u>ibid</u>., P. 3.

3.   <u>ibid</u>., p. 3.

4.   <u>ibid</u>., p. 4.

5.   <u>ibid</u>., p. 4.

6.   <u>ibid</u>., p. 12.

7.   <u>ibid</u>., p. 2.

8.   <u>ibid</u>., p. 16.

9.   The information in this entire section comes principally from two sources: Henry Wilson Story, <u>History</u> <u>of</u> <u>Cambria</u> <u>County</u>, Volume I and Volume II (New York: Lewis Publishing Company, 1907); John E. Gable,

History of Cambria County Pennsylvania (Topeka: Historical Publishing Co., 1926).

10. The information on this section on the coal industry comes entirely from John E. Gable, History of Cambria County, Pennsylvania (Topeka: Historical Publishing Co., 1926), pp. 215-259.

11. Economic and Social Study (Ebensburg: Cambria County Planning Commission, 1973), p. 129.

12. ibid., p. 130.

13. Pennsylvania County Industry Report, Cambria County (Harrisburg: Pennsylvania Department of Commerce, 1972), p. 5-7.

14. loc. cit.

15. Pennsylvania County Industry Report, op. cit., p. 17-19.

16. ibid., p. 18.

17. Economics and Social Study, op. cit., p. 35.

18. John E. Gable, op. cit., p. 69.

19. ibid., p. 70.

20. ibid., p. 70.

21. ibid., p. 71.

22. ibid., p. 71. Clearly World War I curbed the flow of immigrants into Pennsylvania dramatically.

23. Heber Blankenhorn, The Strike for Union (1924; rpt. New York: Arno and The New York Times, 1969), Appendix B.

24. ibid.

25. ibid., Appendix B.

26. Pennsylvania County Industry Report, op. cit., p. 9.

27. 1970 Census of Population, Pennsylvania (Washington: United States Bureau of Census, 1972), p. 40-739.

28. Pennsylvania County Industry Report, op. cit., p. 9.

29. Suzanne Jaworski, "Health Care for Cambria County Coal Mining

Families," unpublished report, Johnstown: United Mine Workers Health and Retirement fund, March, 1975.

30.   Eli Cvijanovich, "An Addendum Report, A Comparative Study of the Medical Communities of Cambria and Blair Counties, unpublished (Johnstown, 1975).

31.   Draft Ambulatory Care Plan (Cambria-Somerset Counties: Ambulatory Care Plan Development Committee), 1975, p. 12.

32.   ibid., p. 40.

33.   A physician equivalent is defined as the amount of time, or percentage of time, a physician devotes to rendering primary care. In other words, a man practicing full time in general practice is 1 physician-equivalent, and a man practicing half time as a general practitioner is .5 physician-equivalents in each category. Or, a nearly retired physician may be .25 physician-equivalents within a particular category. So clearly there is at this time a shortage of physician manpower within the county.

34.   Suzanne Jaworski, op. cit.

35.   ibid.

36.   Suzanne Jaworski, op. cit.

37.   Suzanne Jaworski, op. cit.

38.   Suzanne Jaworski, op. cit.

38*.   In the past ten years, since the time of the original study, great changes have taken place in the health industry of Cambria County. Increased competition of the area's three major hospitals has lead to the recruitment of many new physicians and many of these are specialists. In addition, the Health and Retirement Funds which served the miners so well in the past have deteriorated greatly.

39.   Henry N. Doyle, "Pneumoconiosis in Bituminous Coal Miners," Pneumoconiosis in Appalachian Bituminous Coal Miners, ed. W.S. Lainhart et al. (Cincinnati: United States Department of H.E.W., 1969).

40.   M.M. Key, L.E. Kerr and M. Bundy, Pulmonary Reactions to Coal Dust (New York: Academic Press, 1971).

41.   Jan Lieben, E. Pendergrass and W.W. McBridie, "Pneumoconiosis Study in Central Pennsylvania Coal Miners," Journal of Occupational Medicine, 3 (1961), pp. 493-506; E.J. Baier and R. Kaikun, "Pneumoconiosis Study in Central Pennsylvania," Journal of Occupational Medicine, 3 (1961), pp. 507-521.

42.   Henry N. Doyle, op. cit., p. 18.

43.   Philip E. Enterline, "Mortality Rates Among Coal Miners," American Journal of Public Health, (1964), pp. 758-768.

44.   Further supporting evidence, although coming some twenty years earlier, supports these figures. Although coal miners were not treated separately, the data indicated a death rate 1.8 times as great as the employed population of the U.S. as a whole. L. Guralnick, "Mortality by Occupation and Causes of Death," Vital Statistics Special Reports, 53, No. 4 (1963), p. 20.

45.   Women generally were efficient household managers and continual debt to the company store, in fact, appears to have been somewhat rare. Laws were passed at various times during the 1920's and 1930's guaranteeing that a man receive two dollars, and later up to five dollars, on each payday regardless of his indebtedness to the company store.

46.   Some mining houses were made of stone, others of brick and others of large cement blocks.

47.   There is some confusion as to whether "Johnny Bulls" referred to just Englishmen, or to all English speakers. Among eastern and southern Europeans it appears generally to have referred to English speakers, but among the English speakers themselves there was discrimination between English, Irish, Scottish and Welsh.

48.   In the City of Johnstown, for example, there is one small section with six Roman Catholic Churches, five of which are nationality churches.

49.   The evidence for this comes from two sources: first, the taped interviews of older miners and their wives; second, Peter Roberts, Anthracite Coal Communities (1904; rpt. New York: Arno Press and The New York Times, 1970). Roberts documents the large amounts of money the eastern and southern Europeans saved in the eastern anthracite coal fields of Pennsylvania.

49*.   Ewa Morawska in For Bread With Butter: Life Worlds of East Central Europeans in Johnstown, Pennsylvania 1890-1940, exhaustively explores this issue and concludes that approximately 35% of Eastern Europeans in the greater Johnstown area did return to Europe.

50.   The exact nature of the relationships between the various groups has not been worked out and may never be, but it is clear that suspicion and discrimination based on nationality and religion were widespread and deeply rooted.

51.   The result of this social climate is observable even today in the personalities of the miners and neighbors. In chapter VIII, the miners' personalities and world view will be discussed and related to these early social conditions.

52.   It is interesting to note the United Mine Workers never had a contract with miners in southern Cambria County or Somerset County, to the south, until the early 1930's. Coal miner individualism remained quite prevalent.

CHAPTER IV.

1.   Coal Mines Safety Amendments of 1966 and Coal Mine Health and Safety Act of 1969. The period 1953-1965, it is claimed by some, was a time of increasing federal regulatory authority compared to previous times. The argument is that from 1952 to the present was a time of increasing regulation with this process accelerating in the late 1960's. W.H. Andrews and C.L. Christenson, "Some Economic Factors Affecting Safety in Underground Bituminous Coal Mines," Southern Economic Journal, Volume 40, No. 3 (January, 1974), pp. 364-376.

2.   The problem is simply that the amount of capital needed to meet federal standards for ventilation, roof support, mine subsidence and mine acid water drainage proved prohibitive for the small entrepreneur.

3.   Annual Report, Anthracite, Bituminous Coal and Oil and Gas Divisions, 1971-72 (Harrisburg: Pennsylvania Department of Environmental Resources, 1973), pp. 492-499, p. 52.

4.   Annual Report, Office of Mines and Land Protection, 1973 (Harrisburg: Pennsylvania Department of Environmental Resources, 1974).

5.   ibid., p. 155.

6.   Intra-company employment sheet, August, 1974.

7.   Cambria County is also part of District 2 of the United Mine Workers of America. Also, Cambria County is in production District 1 as defined by the Bituminous Coal Act of 1937. The National Coal Association includes Cambria County within District 1 when compiling data for the coal industry.

8.   Robert D. Sponsellar, Analysis and Measured Sections of Pennsylvania Bituminous Coals, Mineral Resource Report 66, Fourth series (Harrisburg: Pennsylvania Geological Survey, 1973).

9.   In the early days of coal mining, the widespread occurrence of coal beds or seams was not recognized, and so these seams were assigned local names. Through time, geological surveys have been made so that these local names have been correlated to some extent. However, correlations are not known for all the coal beds, and in some areas local names are still in use.

10.   Later in this chapter it will be made clear why this was not done.

11.   Since mining activity is constantly going on within the mine, both the "length" and "width" are constantly changing.

12.   Occasionally there will be small places in the mine which have been cut to greater heights. For example, an overcast is in an area where a conveyor belt carrying coal passes over one of the headings. The conveyor belt is enclosed by cement blocks, and it is raised up high so that the miners can walk under it. This means that more rock must be cut from this section of the mine.

13.   Because of the potentially high dust levels and the fear of explosions, no fires and no machines with internal combustion engines are allowed within the mine. Consequently, electricity is the only source of power used other than human effort. As a condition of employment, the company officials maintain the right to search miners for matches or other devices which might produce a flame. To the best of my knowledge, such a search was never conducted where I was employed, but the possibility existed.

14.   It is argued that after miners' holiday, which is the last week of June and the first week in July, the machinery is apt to cause a great deal more mechanical and electrical trouble, since it has not run for two weeks and it has been damp for a long time. This is not the situation when the machines are running nearly twenty-four hours per day, five to seven days a week.

15.   Because the mine is ventilated, there is a constant wind or draft in the mine. In those sections of the mine or the main haulageway where the mine is high, the draft from the moving air is stronger. Therefore, the chill factor of the air is higher. The miners in these areas of the mine are subject to more rapid chilling than men in less windy parts of the mine after they have stopped working.

16.   The methane gas seeps out of the coal seam itself. It is poisonous and explosive. In times past, the miners claim they brought canaries into the mines to test for this gas. If the canary died, there was gas and danger.

17.   A great deal of research (and technology) has been put into 1) inhibiting dust formation, by designing better bits on the coal cutting machine and 2) inhabiting dust dispersion, by the use of water sprays. Kenneth M. Morse, "Recent Progress in Dust Control in Bituminous Coal Mining," in Coal Workers' Pneumoconiosis, Annals of The New York Academy of Sciences, ed. Irving J. Selikoff, Marcus M. Kay, and Douglas H.K. Lee (New York: The New York Academy of Sciences, 1972), pp. 676-690.

18.   There are measurements taken of the percentage of the surface covered by limestone dust because these measurements are specified in the state and federal safety conditions.

19.   Historically, this was one reason why so much of the land was cleared in this mountainous area and why today there are so many saw mills in the area.

CHAPTER V.

1.   McAlister Coleman, Men and Coal, (New York: J.J. Little and Ives Company, 1943,), p. 30.

2.   ibid., p. 33.

3.   Howard N. Eavenson, The First Century and a Quarter of the American Coal Industry (privately printed: Pittsburgh, 1942), p. 450, in Historical Summary of Coal Mine Explosions in the United States, 1810-1958, H.B. Humphrey, Bulletin 586 (Washington: United States Bureau of Mines, 1960), p. 10.

4.   Albert H. Fay, Coal Mine Fatalities in the United States, 1870-1914, Bulletin 115 (Washington: United States Bureau of Mines, 1916), pp. 84, 104, 105.

5.   H.B. Humphrey, op. cit., p. 21.

6.   Bituminous Coal Facts, 1972 (Washington: National Coal Association, 1973), p. 58.

7.   Bituminous Coal Data 1973 (Washington: National Coal Association, 1974), p. 33._

8.   Bituminous Coal Data, 1973 Edition, op. cit., p. 49.

9.   ibid., p. 49.

10.   McAlister Coleman, op. cit., p. 13.

11.   Bituminous Coal Data, 1973. op. cit., p. 49.

12.   John Brophy in his autobiography on coal mining in Cambria County in the early part of this century uses the term "butties" but this appears simply to be a variant of buddies. John Brophy, A Miner's Life: John Brophy, ed. John O.P. Hall (Madison: University of Wisconsin Press, 1964), p. 36.

13.   ibid., Chapter 4.

14.   Daniel Devan, taped interview, May, 1975, by Daniel Devan, Jr.

15.   John Brophy, op. cit., p. 47.

16.   W.P. Tams, Jr., The Smokeless Coal Fields of West Virginia
(Morgantown: West Virginia University Library, 1963), p. 37.

17.   ibid., pp. 36-50.

18.   John Brophy, op. cit., p. 46.

19.   W.D. Tams, Jr. op. cit., p. 39.

20.   John Brophy, op. cit., p. 46.

21.   With stricter mining laws, the practice changed and this rock was
removed from the mines.

22.   H.B. Humphrey, Historical Summary of Coal Mine Explosions in the
United States, 1810-1958, op. cit., p. 14.

23.   ibid., p. 21.

24.   ibid., p. 21.

25.   ibid., p. 39.

26.   ibid., op. cit., p. 37.

27.   ibid., p. 21.

28.   ibid., p. 42.

29.   L.C. Ilsley and A.B. hooker, "Permissible Electric Cap Lamps, 1895-
1932", Information Circular, 6760. Washington: United States Bureau of
Mines, 1934.

30.   ibid., p. 161.

31.   ibid., p. 42.

32.   Carter Goodrich, The Miner's Freedom (Boston: Marshall Jones
Company, 1925) in McAlister Coleman, op. cit., p. 9.

33.   McAlister Coleman, op. cit., p. 9.

34.   ibid., p. 9.

35.   ibid., p. 9.

36.   Bituminous Coal Facts, 1972, National Coal Association, Washington, 1972, p. 46.

37.   McAlister Coleman, op. cit., p. 11.

38.   Appalachian Joint Wage Agreement, April 1, 1941 to March 3, 1943, Executed in Washington, D.C. on June 19, 1941. Agreement between the United Mine Workers of America and the Appalachian Joint Conference.

39.   ibid., Schedule A.

40.   ibid., Schedule B.

41.   A sizable percentage of miners, mostly young ones, were opposed to portal to portal when it was first introduced since they felt they could make out better financially with tonnage work.

42.   H.B. humphrey, op. cit., pp. 37-38.

43.   ibid., p. 159-165.

44.   U.S. Congress, Coal Mine Inspection Act, Public Law 49, 77th Congress, May 7, 1941.

45.   U.S. Congress, Federal Coal-Mine Safety Act, Public Law 552, 82nd Congress, July 16, 1952.

46.   H.B. Humphrey, op. cit., pp. 236-240, 277-278.

47.   Helen M. Lewis and Edward E. Knipe, "The Sociological Impact of Mechanization on Coal Miners and Their Families", op. cit., pp. 19-20.

48.   Bituminous Coal Data, 1973, op. cit., p. 24.

CHAPTER VI.

1.   Some non-union mines in the area do give outright money incentives to the men and consequently some men who had worked at non-union mines claimed that with incentives they made more money than at union mines.

2.   It is necessary for a miner to obtain miner's papers which allow him to work alone in a mine. A miner is to be accompanied by an experienced miner at all times if he has no miner's papers. The miner is supposed to work for one year at the face and to have a work record to support this fact before applying for these papers.

3.   The hammers which the miners carry also aid them while walking in low areas.   The hammer is grasped on the head end and the top of the handle is placed on the bottom, or ground, to serve as an extension of the miner's arm, thus serving as a sort of long third leg so that he need not bend so far forward.   Consequently, about one-half of the miners carry hammers. Many men simply grab cap pieces, or small triangular wooden wedges which are used to help "prop" the top up.

4.   Casual visitors to the mine and even newspaper reporters who have visited mines are frequently horrified at the possibility of cave-ins and often seem to project their own fears to the miners when writing of coal mining.   By way of contrast, autobiographies by former experienced coal miners display none of this emotionalism.

5.   Helen M. Lewis and Edward M. Knipe, "The Sociological Impact of Mechanization on Coal Miners and Their Families", op. cit., p. 31.

6.   ibid., p. 32.

7.   ibid., p. 31.

8.   Annual Report, Anthracite, Bituminous Coal and Oil Gas Divisions, 1971-1972, op. cit., p. 448.

9.   ibid., p. 77.

10.   ibid., p. 456

11.   Annual Report of the Office of Mines and Land Protection, 1973, op. cit., p. 154.

12.   Annual Report, Anthracite, Bituminous Coal and Oil and Gas Divisions, 1971-1972, op. cit., pp. 343-386.

13.   Annual Report, Anthracite, Bituminous Coal and Oil and Gas Divisions, 1971-1972, op. cit., p. 456.

14.   ibid., p. 77.

14*.   In 1984, there was a major explosion from gas at the North Mine of the Greenwich Colleries and three men were killed.

15.   Bituminous Coal Data, 1972, op. cit., pp. 42-44.

16.   Portal-to-portal pay was introduced by the UMWA in the middle and late 1940's.

17.   Annual Report of the Office of Mines and Land Protection, 1973, op. cit., pp. 198-205, 295-296.

18.   Exact figures could not be obtained. This information was obtained
verbally from personnel officers from two large mining corporations in the
district.

19.   Many of the men smoke while above ground, but since smoking is now
forbidden within the mines, snuff becomes the tobacco substitute.   In
addition, one's hands can be kept busy while still chewing. The snuff is
placed between the lower lip and in front of the lower teeth. A great deal
of saliva is produced while chewing snuff so the miner is constantly
spitting. Interestingly, a bit of folklore is connected with chewing. The
contention is that chewing snuff is good for you since it cuts down on the
dust that gets into your lungs. The idea is that the saliva somehow
captures the dust as one inhales.

20.   The expression is used commonly throughout the county and may have
originally come from the expression of the miner's buddy. At the turn of
the century the expression was probably "butty". John Brophy, op. cit. p.
36, mentions this. Furthermore, this appears consistent with evidence from
English, Welsh and Scottish slang.

21.   E.L. Trist and K. Bamforth, 'Some Psychological Consequences of the
Long Wall Method of Coal Getting", Human Relations, 4 (January, 1951), pp.
3-38.

22.   Helen M. Lewis and Edward E. Knipe, "The Sociological Impact of
Mechanization on Coal Miners and Their Families," op. cit., pp. 19-20.

23.   G.U. Rimlinger, 'International Differences in the Strike Propensity
of Coal Miners: Experiences in Four Countries," Industrial and Labor
Relations Review (April, 1959), pp. 389-405.

24.   Alvin W. Gouldner, Patterns of Industrial Bureaucracy (Glencoe: The
Free Press, 1954).

25.   The arguments put forth here are further enhanced when seen in terms
of Chapter IV, which demonstrates the changes in coal mining, and in terms
of Chapter VII, which describes the activities of the miners outside the
work activity.

26.   Darold T. Barnum, The Negro in the Bituminous Coal Mining Industry,
Industrial Research Unit, Department of Industry, Wharton School of Finance
and Commerce (Philadelphia: University of Pennsylvania Press, 1970), p.
10.

27.   This is beginning to change. Pennsylvania State University has a
School of Mining Engineering to train college graduates for the technical,
supervisory and business positions needed in a mine.

28.   It is a condition of the union contract that the foreman is not allowed to work. The union position is that if a foreman were allowed to work he would be taking a job away from a man who needed work. This applies to the general foremen as well.

29.   Generally he will send one of the men to walk to the area where he believes the mechanic to be. For a major repair, he would telephone the mechanics' shanty which is located near the bottom of the elevator shaft, and request extra mechanics or special equipment. The shanty itself is simply a cut in the seam of coal and in this "room" the mechanics store tools and equipment.

30.   On one crew on which I worked there was a noticeable exception. The foreman yelled frequently and was constantly impatient with the men. The men always talked about him and were scheming to walk off the job at some time.

30*. As indicated, by 1987 the coal mining activity in the area is less than half of what is was at the time of the original study. The salaries of those miners who are still working are still regarded as being very good for the area.

31.   My theory is that chewing coal may act as an antacid. Many of the miners suffer from heartburn because they must bend over while working and the top of their stomach and their esophagus is subjected to the stomach acid which eventually becomes very irritating. Many of the miners consequently chew antacids like Tums and Rolaids while at work, and many refuse to eat fruit while working.

32.   Helen M. Lewis and Edward E. Knipe, "The Sociological Impact of Mechanization on Coal Miners and Their Families," op. cit., p. 19.

CHAPTER VII.

1.   In the 1930's and 1940's, company sponsored softball teams were widespread. The decline in the number of miners seems to have contributed to the reduction of this activity.

2.   During the televised Watergate trials, I found it nearly impossible, whether in a private home or in bars, to get miners to watch these presentations, rather than the standard fare of serialized comedies, etc.

CHAPTER VIII.

1.   In dealing with men of authority, it was often helpful to meet privately to discuss issues before meetings in order to avoid the charge that you are criticizing them. On the other hand, "bombshell" suggestions were a good way to attack secret enemies.

2.   Rebel Without A Cause, Warner Brothers, directed by Nicholas Ray, 1955.

3.   After observing a group of eighteen year old miners and hearing them talk of their mortgages, car payments and pregnant wives, it was obvious to me that they were reasonably well adjusted to their grown up roles and "man sized" jobs.

4.   At the University of Pittsburgh at Johnstown, a large percentage of students work as they go through college. Many reveal, through my conversations with them, that getting money for college from their parents never occurred to them. It is simply understood that they would pay their own way through college.

CHAPTER IX.

1.   Helen M. Lewis and Edward E. Knipe, "The Sociological Impact of Mechanization on Coal Miners and Their Families," op. cit., p. 38.

2.   Edward E. Knipe and Helen M. Lewis, "The Impact of Coal Mining on the Traditional Mountain Subculture," op. cit., pp. 25-37.

3.   Herman R. Lantz, People of Coal Town, op. cit.

4.   John C. Campbell, The Southern Highlander and His Homeland (New York: Russell Sage Foundation, 1921); Marion Pearsall, Little Smoky Ridge (University, Alabama: University of Alabama press, 1959); John B. Stephenson, Shiloh: A Mountain Community (Lexington: University of Kentucky, 1968); Jack E. Weller, Yesterday's People: Life in Contemporary Appalachia (Lexington: University of Kentucky Press, 1965).

5.   Edward E. Knipe and Helen M. Lewis, "The Impact of Coal Mining on the Traditional Mountain Subculture," op. cit., p. 19.

6.   Steven Polgar, "Health Action in Cross-Cultural Perspective," in Handbook of Medical Sociology, eds. Howard E. Freeman, Sol Levine and Leo G. Reeder (Englewood Cliffs: Prentice-Hall, 1963), pp. 397-4197.

7.   Polgar's framework emphasizes the social roles of individuals involved in health action systems. He employs the term health action to bring into a single analytical framework "the procedures used by laymen and specialists to promote health, prevent sickness and remedy sickness." The

judgments that are employed to identify the conditions which might call for health action are sociocultural (hence the anthropologist's contribution to understanding what these conditions are) and can be seen as an interpersonal network involving the health actors, ranging from physicians to personal friends, and the clients.

There are four phases within the health action system, each requiring empirical observation. The first is the <u>self-addressed phase</u> in which an adult perceives some changes in the way he feels and then takes action to improve his condition. In this phase, the same person is performing both the client role and the health actor role. The second phase is the <u>lay health actor phase</u> and the person solicits help from another. The type of advice given and the symptoms expressed which elicit advice conform to a cultural pattern.

If the client's health, however culturally defined, is not restored, the client enters into the <u>professional actor phase</u> and seeks the help of a trained professional (or traditional health practitioner in a non-western society). The advice given can be empirically observed, and in the case of the coal miners would presumably be the advice of a trained physician or nurse. The fourth phase is the <u>indirect health action phase</u> and concerns itself with areas like the training of the health specialists themselves. For instance, the teacher in a medical school does not deal directly with clients (in this case the coal miners) but he does influence the physicians who do deal directly with the clients.

Polgar's concepts of popular health culture and professional health culture cut across these four health action phases. Data must be collected within these two conceptual areas in order to have a comprehensive understanding of the four phases.

8.   F.L. Kluckholn and F.L. Strodtbeck, <u>Variations in Value Orientations</u> (New York: Harper and Row, 1961).

9.   The Navajo conception of health and the classical Chinese medical beliefs of balance between the "Yang" and "Yin" are examples of the harmony-with-nature orientation.

APPENDIX D

1.   <u>Annual Report</u>, 1971-1972, <u>Op</u>. <u>Cit</u>., pp. 492-499, p. 521.

2.   In 1971, Greenwich Collieries was included in District 15.

3.   <u>Annual Report of the Office of Mines and Land Protection</u>, 1973, Commonwealth of Pennsylvania, Department of Environmental Resources, Harrisburg, June 30, 1974, pp. 198-205 and pp. 295-296

4.   In 1971, Greenwich Collieries was included in District 15.

APPENDICES

APPENDIX A

Interview Guidelines

I. To standardize the interviews, ask the following questions at the
    beginning of the tape session:

    A.) Name
    B.) Birthdate
    C.) Birthplace and nationality
    D.) Spouse's birthplace and nationality
    E.) Number of children
    F.) Where did you live? Briefly, how long in various places, both
        before and after marriage.
    G.) Your age and your spouse's age at marriage
    H.) Education
    I.) Ask any questions you feel comfortable with of a general, but
        personal, nature. For instance, your religion, divorces, deaths
        in family, where you met your spouse (hometown, church, etc.)

II. To help you with the interview process, I have set up a series of
    guideline questions which I urge you to follow when tapping. If
    all members in the project follow the guideline questions, we will
    build a reasonable amount of reliability, or "repeatability" into
    our data. NOTE: these guideline questions are simply reminders to
    you of subject areas where information should be gathered. It is
    not suggested that you use the phrasing in the questions. The
    specific way you ask a question, or elicit information is left to
    your skill and the specific direction of your actual conversation.
        Also, don't forget that you should not feel constrained by
    these guideline questions. If a interviewee appears to have a lot
    of knowledge in one particular area, please explore this fully with
    a large number of questions.

    A.) To learn about the "nature" of coal communities:

        1.) What ethnic groups were found in your home community (or
            one of the communities you know best). At what point in
            time are you describing this town. Give a break down by
            age and sex. Estimate.
                Many "older" people. What was the largest group
                in the town, 2nd largest, 3rd etc.

        2.) Were all the men of the town coal miners? Did a woman
            and children remain, if she was a widow?

        3.) Did the various families move around a lot? From one town
            to the next? Why did they move? Explore? Loss of jobs,
            social problems, worker-management problems.

B.)   To learn about how the people got along, and how they regarded each other:

4.)   How did the people get along? Did the various ethnic groups "trust" each other or not? Did they socialize together? In what ways? What cooperative activities took place in these towns? E.g. clearing ballfields, building clubs, etc.

5.)   Were the people suspicious of each other for one reason or other? Was one group of people less trusted than another? A specific ethnic group or a class of workers (e.g., foremen, etc.)? Why, over what issues, did suspicions develop?

6.)   What was your (and other coal miners') attitudes toward:
      a.)   foremen, bosses, owners
      b.)   storekeepers, etc.
      c.)   company men
      d.)   people outside the town
      e.)   police, firemen, etc.
      f.)   teachers

7.)   Talk about the social clubs, ethnic clubs, sport teams, social activities. Were the clubs active? What ones existed in your town? What social activities were important? How often were they held? What team sports existed? What was the participation of women in these activities? Were any activities specifically for women?

8.)   Did the men drink a lot? Everyday or just (more or less) on payday? What was the pattern.

9.)   How has the coal town changed since 1940 to present?
      a.)   % of men in mining, etc., ages of men
      b.)   ethnic groups, etc.
      c.)   social clubs
      d.)   jobs men work in
      e.)   women's jobs
      f.)   men's, women's, and children's social activities
      g.)   how have children and teenagers changed

10.) Were the people of coal towns suspicious of outsiders? What was the demographic pattern of the towns? Check, to see if most people moved out (born in the town and moved away) and very few moved in. Do you live in a coal town today? Why? Do people enjoy these towns? Why?

C.)   To learn a little more about work:

11.) What was mining like (was it hard, easy, so-so)? Try and get a descriptive statement on the nature of the work it-self. What was good about coal mining? What was bad?

Did you enjoy the relationship to the other men? The challenge of the work? The individualism?

12.) For women, ask the same question about her perception of mining.

13.) For women, describe her activities, and ask the questions of number 11.

14.) Did you prefer working with a buddy or with a crew of men? Did you like hardloading or day wages? Was mining better after the new machinery (about 1940-47) or before? Did the new machinery make the work easier? Do you think the men were "closer" before the new machinery or after?

15.) Do you think the miners today ask for too much? What things?

16.) Do you think coal miners (and their wives and families) are different from non-miners? How? Did the non-miners think the miners were somehow different? In what ways? Does (did) a coal miner need a special set of attributes from other people? E.g., physical-strength or certain personality traits. Describe a "real coal miner". The idealized description. Describe a "real coal miner's wife". Was there pride in being a miner? Did most miners simply do this type of work because they had no other options and would stop at the first opportunity?

17.) When your children were small, what did you hope they would grow up to be? Be realistic and truthful. What possibilities did you see for their success?

18.) When you were a child, or first married, did you manage to save money, no matter how little? Did you ever hear of your parents talking about returning to the old country if they got the money together?

19.) Have you remained close to your brothers and sisters, and nephews or nieces? How often do you visit?

20.) What value or set of values are most important to install in your children?

21.) If some men succeed in getting rich, or getting ahead, how did they do it? Luck, "apple-polishers", hard work, sold out?

22.) Did the owners (and bosses) appear cruel and mean - or were they fairly reasonable, and in a way, cared for the men? Describe.

23.) Was there pride in being able to get a lot more coal (and therefore, more money) than other miners? Was there a sense of competition?

24.) During the Depression, was there a sense of community? For example, did people share food (women baked bread for those who needed it), of clothes or homes, etc.? Did people loan money? In other words was there less competition outside the mine, than inside?

25.) Describe what you felt like when you joined a union. You took an oath, was it like a "religious" or "very specifial" kind of thing? Why did you take an oath?

26.) What type of things did you read? (UMW Journal, books, newspapers, very little, only listened to the radio)

27.) Were the homes crowded? Lots of families in a house? During what periods?

28.) Make some general comments.

APPENDIX B

Map of Cambria County

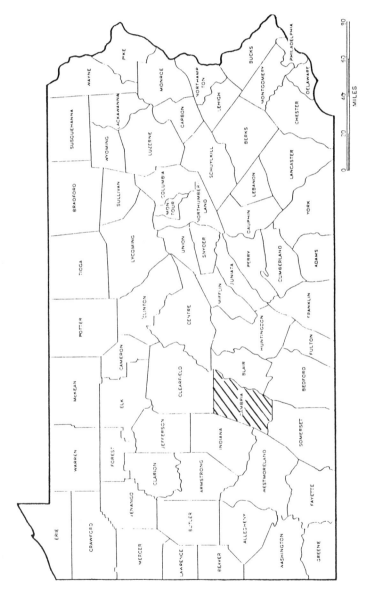

APPENDIX C

Geological Map of Cambria County

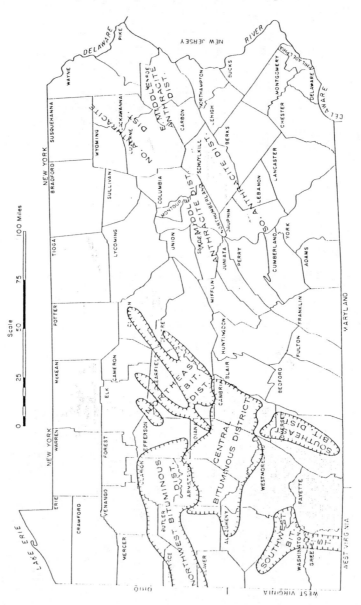

APPENDIX D[1]

Mines in Cambria County - 1972

Operators and Mines	Total Production of Coal	Ave. Days Worked	No. of Employees	Nonfatal Accidents
District 17				
Northern Cambria Fuel Company				
Hastings No. 7	147,467	228	30	3
Hastings No. 7 Cleaning PL	-	228	5	-
TOTAL	147,467		35	3
District 18				
Barnes & Tucker Company				
Lancashire No. 24B	573,116	263	254	29
Lancashire No. 24D	589,639	265	315	74
Lancashire No. 25	614,325	262	297	71
Lancashire No. 25 Cleaning PL	-	262	25	-
TOTAL	1,777,080		891	174
Garay, Wm.				
Sterling No. 9	2,062	158	2	-
Hillsdale Mining Company				
Hillsdale No. 1	36,601	253	11	-
Sponsky, Wm. F.				
Sponsky No. 1	1,342	180	3	1
District 19				
Bethlehem Mines Corporation				
Mine No. 32	518,835	247	392	6
Eastern Assoc'd Coal Company				
Colver "B"	399,032	257	214	19
Colver Cleaning PL	-	257	26	-
TOTAL	399,032		240	19
District 20				
Bethlehem Mines Corporation				
Mine No. 31	463,949	255	371	2
Brookdale No. 77	258,208	252	177	-
No. 77 Cleaning PL	-	252	10	-
TOTAL	722,157		558	2

Operators and Mines	Total Production of Coal	Ave. Days Worked	No. of Employees	Nonfatal Accidents
Vinton Coal Company				
Vinton No. 3	1,834	159	4	–

District 21

Bethlehem Mines Corporation				
Ehrenfeld No. 38	265,256	259	169	5
Solomon Run No. 73	178,681	248	71	1
TOTAL	443,937		240	6
Cimbam, Hinks, W.				
Harmony No. 1	–	229	5	1
Cooney Brothers Company				
Sonman Processing PL	–	200	12	–
Dalton Run Coal Company				
Mine No. 3	2,275	41	5	–
Island Creek Coal Company				
Bird No. 2	293,236	257	189	13
Bird No. 3	358,659	256	185	9
Bird No. 3 PL	–	256	21	–
TOTAL	651,895		395	22
Jandy Coal Company Inc.				
Eureka No. 40	138,720	214	73	5
Cleaning Plant	–	214	11	–
TOTAL	138,720		84	5
Longwall Mining, Inc.				
No. 1	155,968	244	45	5

District 24

Barnes & Tucker Co.				
Lancashire No. 20	782,666	270	314	77
Cleaning Plant	–	270	33	–
TOTAL	782,666		347	77
Bethlehem Mines Corp.				
Cambria Slope No. 33	912,269	252	613	11
Preparation Plant	–	252	84	1
TOTAL	912,269		697	12
Stella Maris Coal Co.				
Stella Maris	870	280	1	–

Operators and Mines	Total Production of Coal	Ave. Days Worked	No. of Employees	Nonfatal Accidents
District 19 [2]				
Greenwich Collieries Company				
Greenwich No. 1	410,874	236	358	51
Greenwich No. 2	483,196	236	381	62
Greenwich Cleaning PL	–	–	16	–
TOTAL	894,070		755	113

Mines in Cambria County – 1973 [3]

District 17

Operators and Mines	Total Production of Coal	Ave. Days Worked	No. of Employees	Nonfatal Accidents
Kristianson & Johnson Coal Co.				
Westover Tipple	–	300	4	1
North Cambria Fuel Co.				
Hastings No. 7	115,130	244	25	2
Hastings Cleaning PL	–	244	10	–
TOTAL	115,130		35	2

District 18

Operators and Mines	Total Production of Coal	Ave. Days Worked	No. of Employees	Nonfatal Accidents
Barnes and Tucker Company				
Lancashire No. 24B	611,590	232	234	51
Lancashire No. 24D	503,397	321	313	79
Lancashire No. 25	403,433	223	277	77
Lancashire No. 24 PL	–	232	32	–
Lancashire No. 25 PL	–	223	47	–
TOTAL	1,518,420		903	207
Garay Coal Co.				
Sterling No. 9	899	90	3	–
Hillsdale Mining Company				
Hillsdale No. 1	50,115	246	11	–
Sponsky, Wm. F.				
Sponsky No. 1	821	128	2	–

District 19

Operators and Mines	Total Production of Coal	Ave. Days Worked	No. of Employees	Nonfatal Accidents
Bethlehem Mines Corporation				
Mine No. 32	468,311	236	369	6

Operators and Mines	Total Production of Coal	Ave. Days Worked	No. of Employees	Nonfatal Accidents
Eastern Assoc'd. Coal Company				
Colver "B"	332,958	245	221	34
Colver Cleaning PL	–	245	24	–
TOTAL	332,958		245	34
Starford Coal Corporation				
Oak Hill	7,925	169	11	–
District 20				
Bethlehem Mines Corporation				
Mine No. 31	378,159	256	371	10
Brookdale No. 77	313,232	263	176	2
Brookdale No. 77 PL	–	263	10	–
TOTAL	691,391		557	12
Vinton Coal Company				
Vinton No. 3	1,885	199	4	–
District 21				
Bethlehem Mines Corporation				
Ehrenfeld No. 38	233,009	254	157	2
Solomon Run No. 73	120,611	255	70	3
Ehrenfeld Proc. PL	–	240	10	–
TOTAL	353,620		273	5
Cooney Bros. Coal Co.				
Sonman Processing Plant	–	260	12	–
GMK Co.				
Redbird Refuse	29,643	239	9	–
Redbird Proc. PL	–	203	–	–
No. 37 Refuse	346,494	256	14	–
No. 37 Prep. Plant	–	236	–	–
TOTAL	376,137		23	
Harmony Mining Co.				
Harmony No. 1 (a)	–	235	6	–
Island Creek Coal Co.				
Bird No. 2	319,013	251	175	2
Bird No. 3	255,812	251	148	2
Bird Proc. Plant	–	258	27	–
TOTAL	574,825		350	4
Jandy Coal Co., Inc.				
Eureka No. 40	204,393	231	73	6
No. 40 Upper Proc. PL	–	256	12	–
TOTAL	204,393		85	6

Operators and Mines	Total Production of Coal	Ave. Days Worked	No. of Employees	Nonfatal Accidents
Longwall Mining Inc.				
No. 1	156,684	250	52	5
M. & K. Coal Co.				
No. 40 Refuse	132,839	253	13	–
No. 40 Proc. PL	–	248	16	–
St. Michael Proc. PL	–	186	8	–
TOTAL	132,839		37	

District 24

Operators and Mines	Total Production of Coal	Ave. Days Worked	No. of Employees	Nonfatal Accidents
Ace Drilling Coal Co., Inc.				
Loading Dock	–	105	7	–
Barnes & Tucker Co.				
Lancashire No. 20	859,687	271	338	85
Lancashire No. 20 CL/PL	–	271	33	2
TOTAL	859,687		371	87
Bethlehem Mines Corporation				
Cambria Slope No. 33	1,044,332	235	700	12
Cambria Slope Prep. PL	–	249	86	1
TOTAL	1,044,332		786	13
Stella Maris Coal Co.				
Stella Maris	850	265	1	–

District 19 [4]

Operators and Mines	Total Production of Coal	Ave. Days Worked	No. of Employees	Nonfatal Accidents
Greenwich Collieries Co.				
Mine No. 1	957,358	222	464	80
Mine No. 2	639,112	224	461	67
Greenwich CL/PL	–	224	22	–
TOTAL	1,590,470		947	147

APPENDIX E

Data for Wage Classifications

Grade	Concentration of Classifications 1/	Standard Daily Wage Rate 2/ Nov. 12,'71	Nov. 12,'72	Nov. 12,'73	Standard Hourly Wage Rate 3/4/ Nov. 12,'71	Nov. 12,'72	Nov. 12,'73	Weekly Earnings Five Day Week 4/ Nov. 12,'71	Nov. 12,'72	Nov. 12,'73
	Underground at Deep Mines 3/									
6	Continuous mining machine operator;electrician;mechanic;firebcss;longwall machine operator;welder, first class.	$41.50	$45.75	$50.00	$5.188	$5.719	$6.250	$207.50	$228.75	$250.00
5	Cutting machine operator;dispatcher;loading machine operator;designated machine operator helper;general inside repairman and welder;roof bolter.	40.25	43.75	47.25	5.031	5.469	5.906	201.25	218.75	236.25
4	Driller-coal;shooter;precision mason-construction;faceman;dumper.	38.75	41.75	44.75	4.844	5.219	5.594	193.75	208.75	223.75
3	Motorman;shuttle car operator.	37.45	40.45	43.25	4.681	5.056	5.406	187.25	202.25	216.25
2	Beltman;bonder;brakeman;bratticeman;general inside labor;electrician helper;mason;mechanic helper;pumper;timberman;trackman;wireman.	37.25	40.00	42.75	4.656	5.000	5.344	186.25	200.00	213.75
1	Laborer - unskilled.	37.00	39.75	42.25	4.625	4.969	5.281	185.00	198.75	211.25
	Strip and Auger Mines 3/									
6	Coal loading shovel operator;overburden stripping machine operator;master electrician.	42.00	46.00	50.00	5.793	6.345	6.897	210.00	230.00	250.00
5	Electrician;machinist;mechanic;welder, first class;shovel and dragline oiler.	39.00	42.50	46.00	5.379	5.862	6.345	195.00	212.50	230.00
4	Mobile equipment operator;Repairman;stationary equipment operator;welder,driller and shooter;groundman.	37.90	40.90	43.75	5.228	5.641	6.034	189.50	204.50	218.75
3	Tipple attendant;electrician helper;mechanic helper;machinist helper;repairman helper.	37.00	39.50	42.00	5.103	5.448	5.793	185.00	197.50	210.00
2	Car dropper;car dumper;car trimmer;sampler;truck driver service;utility man.	36.50	39.00	41.50	5.034	5.379	5.724	182.50	195.00	207.50
1	Laborer - unskilled.	36.35	38.85	41.25	5.014	5.359	5.690	181.75	194.25	206.25

APPENDIX E

Preparation Plants and Other Surface Facilities for Deep and Surface Mines [3]

Grade	Concentration of Classifications [1/4/]	Standard Daily Wage Rate [2/4/]			Standard Hourly Wage Rate [3/4/]			Weekly Earnings Five Day Week [4/]		
		Nov. 12,'71	Nov. 12,'72	Nov. 12,'73	Nov. 12,'71	Nov. 12,'72	Nov. 12,'73	Nov. 12,'71	Nov. 12,'72	Nov. 12,'73
5	Electrician;machinist; mechanic;welder, first class; preparation plant central control operator.	$38.00	$41.50	$45.00	$5.241	$5.724	$6.207	$190.00	$207.50	$225.00
4	Mobile equipment operator; repairman;stationary equipment operator;welder;railroad car loader operator.	37.30	40.40	43.50	5.145	5.572	6.000	186.50	202.00	217.50
3	Tipple attendant;dock man; electrician helper;machinist helper;mechanic helper;repairman helper.	36.55	39.15	41.75	5.041	5.400	5.759	182.75	195.75	208.75
2	Car dropper;car dumper;car trimmer;sampler;bit sharpener; truck driver, service;equipment operator, service;preparation plant, utility man;surface utility man.	36.05	38.65	41.25	4.972	5.331	5.690	180.25	193.25	206.25
1	Laborer - unskilled.	35.80	38.40	41.00	4.938	5.297	5.655	179.00	192.00	205.00

APPENDIX F

Fatality Figures for the Coal Industry

Year	Production (Net Tons)*	Stripping Production	Employes	Fatalities	Production Per Fatality	Fatalities Per 1000 Employes	Fatalities Per 1,000,000 Tons Produced	No. of Mine Inspectors
1938	76,881,944	—	115,347	119	646,067	1.03	1.55	25
1939	89,397,222	2,792,966	117,959	120	744,977	1.02	1.34	25
1940	111,416,916	2,808,607	117,832	188	592,643	1.60	1.69	25
1941	127,469,207	6,479,207	124,941	166	767,887	1.33	1.30	23
1942	142,759,573	10,303,160	115,451	187	763,420	1.62	1.31	27
1943	139,801,363	17,177,054	105,903	178	785,401	1.68	1.27	26
1944	144,408,418	22,211,661	99,942	164	880,539	1.64	1.14	25
1945	130,696,854	26,675,095	98,764	141	926,928	1.43	1.08	27
1946	123,587,065	31,027,425	103,894	128	965,524	1.23	1.04	27
1947	144,761,964	35,946,734	109,202	134	1,080,313	1.23	0.93	27
1948	130,627,789	33,483,099	110,326	114	1,145,857	1.03	0.87	27
1949	87,351,892	21,320,389	100,119	65	1,343,875	0.65	0.74	29
1950	103,439,887	25,460,343	94,514	83	1,246,264	0.88	0.80	29
1951	106,680,097	22,688,543	86,369	70	1,524,011	0.81	0.66	28
1952	87,308,999	19,462,498	76,676	63	1,385,857	0.82	0.72	30
1953	91,938,156	19,538,037	69,126	67	1,372,211	0.97	0.73	30
1954	70,623,985	19,954,885	55,405	44	1,609,636	0.79	0.62	29
1955	85,042,677	19,212,849	52,103	50	1,700,854	0.96	0.59	27
1956	88,595,658	21,694,916	50,529	51	1,737,170	1.01	0.53	26
1957	84,064,493	20,558,733	46,989	53	1,586,123	1.13	0.63	30
1958	67,398,564	19,548,293	41,309	32	2,206,205	0.77	0.47	31
1959	65,627,585	20,506,999	37,337	35	1,875,074	0.94	0.53	31
1960	65,595,999	21,028,887	33,396	26	2,522,923	0.78	0.40	29
1961	63,171,313	20,892,753	29,633	22	2,871,423	0.74	0.35	26
1962	65,648,015	22,235,984	27,264	59	1,112,678	2.16	0.90	28
1963	71,258,957	24,233,668	26,226	21	3,393,284	0.80	0.29	30
1964	77,321,793	24,019,760	26,008	18	4,295,655	0.69	0.23	30
1965	80,119,548	23,661,102	25,206	33	2,427,865	1.31	0.41	30
1966	61,449,647	24,701,150	24,729	28	2,908,916	1.13	0.34	32
1967	79,101,385	21,729,033	23,811	27	2,929,681	1.13	0.34	33
1968	75,714,611	20,512,477	23,117	29	2,610,849	1.25	0.38	33
1969	78,185,036	21,652,731	22,969	25	3,127,401	1.09	0.32	33
1970	80,091,922	24,161,015	24,667	30	2,669,731	1.21	0.37	33
1971	71,776,681	26,861,508	26,549	32	2,243,021	1.21	0.45	42
1972	75,863,137	25,717,040	25,627	19	3,992,797	0.74	0.25	42
1973	76,796,661	29,326,629	26,722	17	4,517,450	0.64	0.22	45

APPENDIX G

Fatality Figures for Pennsylvania

County	Deep Production	Strip Production	Auger Production	Refuse Production	Total Production	Deep Employes	Strip Employes	Auger Employes	Refuse Employes	Tipple & Preparation Plant Employes	Total Employes	Fatals
Allegheny	3,213,253	420,273	—	26,704	3,660,230	1,325	86	—	14	109	1,534	2
Armstrong	3,420,778	3,214,476	92,062	—	6,727,316	1,180*	511	46	—	119	1,856	2
Beaver	182,368	23,905	—	—	206,273	94	4	—	—	23	121	1
Bedford	—	53,113	—	—	53,113	—	19	—	—	—	19	—
Blair	—	1,977	—	—	1,977	—	5	—	—	—	5	—
Bradford	42	—	—	—	42	1	—	—	—	—	1	—
Butler	102,643	1,351,596	105,189	—	1,559,428	149	272	7	—	59	487	3
Cambria	5,579,854	1,295,118	—	811,212	7,676,184	3,658	269	—	87	387	4,401	2
Centre	475,598	526,308	—	—	1,001,906	161	120	—	—	48	329	1
Clarion	—	5,062,848	840	—	5,063,688	—	746	2	—	124	872	1
Clearfield	784,811	7,014,372	14,317	—	7,813,500	222	1,156	3	—	236	1,617	1
Clinton	—	459,561	—	—	459,561	—	88	—	—	19	107	—
Elk	—	751,208	22,053	—	773,261	—	122	9	—	5	136	1
Fayette	708,505	1,836,242	5,212	128,805	2,678,764	338**	373	4	6	247	968	—
Greene	7,462,785	824,535	—	—	8,287,320	3,540	107	—	—	203	3,850	—
Huntingdon	7,019,347	1,951,098	56,441	—	9,026,886	3,577	375	15	—	185	4,152	—
Indiana	73,380	1,574,178	15,854	—	1,663,412	33	324	11	—	52	420	1
Jefferson	—	500,321	19,421	—	519,742	—	133	6	—	7	146	—
Lawrence	—	457,239	—	—	457,239	—	58	—	—	9	67	—
Lycoming	—	312,871	—	—	312,871	—	24	—	—	7	31	—
Mercer	1,305,100	3,890,399	30,353	271,242	5,487,094	690	689	17	3	255	1,654	—
Somerset	—	426,534	—	—	426,534	—	90	—	—	8	98	—
Tioga	—	466,969	—	—	494,903	—	64	—	—	—	64	—
Venango	—	—	7,934	—	494,903	—	70	3	—	—	73	—
Washington	10,967,934	2,115,066	—	—	13,083,000	4,501	333	—	—	370	5,204	5
Westmoreland	1,028,825	1,523,965	—	52,907	2,605,697	416	439	—	41	61	896	—
REGION TOTAL	42,325,223	36,056,422	369,676	1,290,870	80,042,191	19,885	6,416	123	151	2,533	29,108	20

* Includes 40 coke employes.
** Includes 9 coke employes.
£ Includes one coke plant.

Year	Production (Net Tons)*	Stripping Production	Employes	Fatalities	Production Per Fatality	Fatalities Per 1000 Employes	Fatalities Per 1,000,000 Tons Produced	No. of Mine Inspectors
1938	76,881,944	-	115,347	119	646,067	1.03	1.55	25
1939	89,397,222	2,792,966	117,959	120	744,977	1.02	1.34	25
1940	111,416,916	2,808,607	117,832	188	592,643	1.60	1.69	25
1941	127,469,207	6,479,207	124,941	166	767,887	1.33	1.30	23
1942	142,759,573	10,303,160	115,451	187	763,420	1.62	1.31	27
1943	139,801,363	17,177,054	105,903	179	785,401	1.68	1.27	26
1944	144,408,418	22,211,661	99,942	164	880,539	1.64	1.14	25
1945	130,696,854	26,675,095	98,754	141	926,928	1.43	1.08	27
1946	123,587,065	31,027,425	103,894	128	965,524	1.23	1.04	27
1947	144,761,964	35,946,734	109,202	134	1,080,313	1.23	0.93	27
1948	130,627,789	33,483,099	110,326	114	1,145,857	1.03	0.87	27
1949	87,351,892	21,326,389	100,119	65	1,343,875	0.65	0.74	29
1950	103,439,887	25,460,343	94,514	83	1,246,264	0.88	0.80	29
1951	106,680,097	22,688,543	86,369	70	1,524,011	0.81	0.66	28
1952	87,308,999	19,462,498	76,676	63	1,385,857	0.82	0.72	30
1953	91,938,156	19,538,037	69,126	67	1,372,211	0.97	0.73	30
1954	70,823,985	16,954,885	55,405	44	1,609,636	0.79	0.62	29
1955**	85,042,677	19,212,869	52,103	50	1,700,854	0.96	0.59	27
1956	88,595,658	21,694,916	50,529	51	1,737,170	1.01	0.58	26
1957	84,064,493	20,558,733	46,989	53	1,586,123	1.13	0.63	30
1958	67,398,564	19,548,293	41,309	32	2,105,205	0.77	0.47	31
1959	65,627,585	20,506,999	37,337	35	1,875,074	0.94	0.53	31
1960	65,595,999	21,028,887	33,396	26	2,522,923	0.78	0.40	29
1961	63,171,313	20,892,758	29,633	22	2,871,423	0.74	0.35	26
1962	65,648,015	22,235,984	27,264	59	1,112,578	2.16	0.90	28
1963	71,258,957	24,233,668	26,216	21	3,393,284	0.80	0.29	30
1964	77,321,793	24,019,760	26,008	18	4,295,655	0.69	0.23	30
1965	80,119,548	23,661,102	25,206	33	2,427,865	1.31	0.41	32
1966	81,449,647	24,701,150	24,729	28	2,908,916	1.13	0.34	33
1967	79,101,385	21,729,033	23,811	27	2,929,681	1.13	0.34	33
1968	75,714,611	20,512,477	23,117	29	2,610,849	1.25	0.38	33
1969	78,185,036	21,652,731	22,969	25	3,127,401	1.09	0.32	33
1970	80,091,922	24,161,015	24,667	30	2,669,731	1.21	0.37	42
1971	71,776,681	26,861,508	26,549	32	2,243,021	1.21	0.45	42
1972	75,863,137	25,717,040	25,627	19	3,992,797	0.74	0.25	45
1973	76,796,661	29,326,629	26,722	17	4,517,450	0.64	0.22	45

County	Deep Production	Strip Production	Auger Production	Refuse Production	Total Production	Deep Employes	Strip Employes	Auger Employes	Refuse Employes	Tipple and Preparation Plant Employes	Total Employes	Ya-tails
Allegheny	3,645,054	592,802	-	36,408	4,275,264	1,311	96	-	18	85	1,510	1
Armstrong	4,136,755	2,609,570	75,667	-	6,821,992	1,289*	372	29	-	109	1,799	1
Beaver	126,082	11,918	-	-	138,000	53	7	-	-	11	71	1
Bedford	322	553	-	-	875	3	2	-	-	-	5	-
Blair	-	57,373	-	-	57,373	-	8	-	-	-	8	-
Bradford	40	-	-	-	40	1	-	-	-	-	1	-
Butler	52,082	988,996	98,845	583,809	1,139,923	101	287	14	29	39	441	2
Cambria	6,063,233	1,071,955	-	-	7,718,997	3,562	204	-	-	354	4,149	2
Centre	468,512	477,591	-	-	946,103	144	76	-	-	68	288	-
Clarion	-	5,151,871	16,905	-	5,168,776	-	697	3	-	141	841	1
Clearfield	709,333	5,746,170	13,547	-	6,469,050	213	1,075	6	-	160	1,454	1
Clinton	-	465,957	-	-	465,957	-	76	-	-	14	90	-
Elk	-	594,892	26,004	-	620,896	-	94	10	-	4	108	-
Fayette	770,925	1,314,403	4,293	10,989	2,100,610	321**	244	6	9	229	809	2
Greene	8,232,313	435,531	-	-	8,667,844	3,313	89	-	-	200	3,602	2
Indiana	7,329,685	1,665,333	37,385	-	9,032,403	3,343	288	12	-	144	3,787	1
Jefferson	70,784	1,394,605	19,224	-	1,484,613	28	248	12	-	49	337	-
Lawrence	-	519,204	10,492	-	529,696	-	110	3	-	6	119	-
Lycoming	-	132,315	-	-	132,315	-	22	-	-	10	32	-
Mercer	-	241,304	-	-	241,304	-	24	-	-	17	41	-
Somerset	1,343,482	2,890,527	5,752	198,156	4,437,917	609	590	6	6	207	1,418	6
Tioga	-	575,992	-	-	575,992	-	91	-	-	14	105	-
Venango	-	440,928	-	-	440,928	-	65	-	-	4	69	-
Washington	12,127,909	1,307,795	-	-	13,435,704	4,237	224	-	-	349	4,810	5
Westmoreland	1,249,658	639,044	3,305	2,072	1,894,089	556	203	2	14	53	828	-
REGION TOTAL	46,327,179	29,325,629	311,419	831,434	76,796,661	19,084	5,192	103	75	2,267	26,722	17

* Includes 38 coke employes
** Includes 10 coke employes

BIBLIOGRAPHY

Alland, Alexander. "Adaptation." Annual Review of Anthropology. ed.
    Bernard J. Siegel. Palo Alto: Annual Reviews Incorporated, 1975.

_____. Adaptation in Cultural Evolution: An Approach to Medical
    Anthropology. New York: Columbia University Press, 1970.

Andrews, W.H. and C.L. Christensen. "Some Economic Factors Affecting
    Safety in Underground Bituminous Coal Mines." Southern Economic
    Journal. Volume 40, No. 3 (January, 1974). pp. 364-376.

Appalachian Bibliography, Volume I and Volume II. Morgantown: West
    Virginia Library, 1972.

Appalachian Joint Wage Agreement. (Washington: United Mine Workers of
    America and Coal Producers from Pennsylvania, Michigan, Ohio,
    Maryland, West Virginia, Virginia, Northern Tennessee and Eastern
    Kentucky, 1941).

Arnesberg, Conrad M. and Solon T. Kimball. Culture and Community. New
    York: Harcourt, Brace and World, 1965.

Baier, E.J. and R. Daikun. "Pneumoconiosis Study in Central Pennsylvania."
    Journal of Occupational Medicine. 3 (1961), pp. 507-521.

Bailey, K. "The Reconstruction of Controversial Theory: Human Ecology as
    a Case in Point." Unpublished paper presented at Pacific Sociological
    Association meeting, Seattle, 1969, in Physicians, Patients and
    Illness. E. Gartly Jaco. New York: The Free Press, 1958.

Barnum, Darold T. The Negro in the Bituminous Coal Mining Industry.
    Industrial Research Unit, Department of Industry, Wharton School of
    Finance and Commerce. Philadelphia: University of Pennsylvania
    Press, 1970.

Bituminous Coal Data, 1972 Edition. Washington: National Coal
    Association, 1973.

_____. 1973 Edition. Washington: National Coal Association, 1974.

256

Bituminous Coal Facts, 1972 Edition. Washington: National Coal
    Association, 1973.

Blankenhorn, Heber. The Strike for Union. 1924; rpt. New York: Arno and
    The New York Times, 1969.

Brophy, John. A Miner's Life: John Brophy. ed. John O.P. Hall.
    Madison: University of Wisconsin Press, 1964.

Cambria County Planning Program. Economic and Social Study. Ebensburg:
    Cambria County Planning Commission. 1973.

Campbell, John C. The Southern Highlander and His Homeland. New York:
    Russell Sage Foundation, 1921.

Cassel, John A. "Social Theory as a Source of Hypothesis in
    Epidemiological Research." American Journal of Public Health, 54,
    1964, p. 1482-1488.

Coleman, McAlister. Men and Coal. 1943; rpt. New York: Arno and The New
    York Times, 1969.

Commonwealth of Pennsylvania. Annual Report, Anthracite, Bituminous Coal
    and Oil and Gas Divisions, 1971-1972. Harrisburg: Pennsylvania
    Department of Environmental Resources, 1973.

_____. Annual Report of the Office of Mines and Land Protection,
    1973. Harrisburg: Pennsylvania Department of Environmental
    Resources, 1974.

_____. Pennsylvania County Industry Report. Harrisburg.
    Pennsylvania Department of Commerce, 1972.

Cvijanovich, Eli, "An Addendum Report, A Comparative Study of the Medical
    Community of Cambria and Blair Counties." Unpublished. Johnstown,
    1975.

Dennis, Norman, Fernando Henriques and Clifford Slaughter. Coal Is Our
    Life: An Analysis of A Yorkshire Mining Community. London: Eyre and
    Spotiswoode, 1956.

Doyle, Henry N. "Pneumoconiosis in Bituminous Coal Miners."
    Pneumoconiosis in Appalachian Bituminous Coal Miners. ed. Wm. S.
    Lainhart et al., comps. Cincinnati: United States Department of
    Health Education and Welfare, 1969.

Draft Ambulatory Care Plan. Cambria-Somerset Counties: Ambulatory Care
    Plan Development Committee. 1975.

Eavenson, Howard N. *The First Century and a Quarter of the American Coal Industry*. Privately printed: Pittsburgh, 1942. *An Historical Summary of Coal Mine Explosions in the United States*, 1810-1958. H.B. Humphrey. Bulletin 586. Washington: United States Bureau of Mines, 1960.

Enterline, Philip E. "Mortality Rates Among Coal Miners." *American Journal of Public Health*, 54 (1964), pp. 758-768.

Foster, George M. *Applied Anthropology*. Boston: Little, Brown and Company, 1969.

Gable, John E., *History of Cambria County, Pennsylvania*. Topeka. Historical Publishing Co. 1926.

Goodrich, Carter. *The Miner's Freedom*. Boston: Marshall Jones Company, 1925; in McAlister Coleman. *Men and Coal*. 1943; rpt. New York: Arno and The New York Times, 1969.

Gouldner, Alvin W. *Patterns of Industrial Bureaucracy*. New York: The Free Press, 1954.

_____. "Theoretical Requirements of the Applied Social Sciences." *American Sociological Review*, 22 (February, 1957), pp. 92-102.

Green, Archie. *Only A Miner: Studies in Recorded Coal Mining Songs*. Urbana: University of Illinois Press, 1972.

Guralnick, L. "Mortality by Occupation and Causes of Death." *Vital Statistics Special Reports*. Washington: United States Public Health Service, 53, No. 4 (1963), p. 20.

Harris, Marvin. *The Rise of Anthropological Theory*. New York: Thomas Y. Crowell Company, 1968.

Honigmann, John J. "Sampling in Ethnographic Field Work." *A Handbook of Method in Cultural Anthropology*. Eds. R. Naroll and R. Cohen. New York: Columbia University Press, 1973, p. 266.

Hughes, Charles and John M. Hunter. "Disease and 'Development' in Africa." *Social Sciences and Medicine*, 3, 1970, p. 443-493.

Hughes, Everett C. *Men and Their Work*. New York: The Free Press, 1958.

Humphrey, H.B. *Historical Summary of Coal Mine Explosions in the United States, 1810-1958*. Bulletin 586. Washington: United States Bureau of Mines, 1960.

Ilsley, L.C. and A.B. Hooker. "Permissible Electric Cap Lamps, 1895 to

1932," Information Circular, 6760 (Washington: United States Bureau of Mines, 1934), pp. 2-5.

Jaco, E. Gartly. _Patients, Physicians and Illness_. New York: The Free Press, 1958.

Jaworski, Suzanne. "Health Care for Cambria County Coal Mining Families." unpublished report. Johnstown: United Mine Worker Health and Retirement Fund. March, 1975.

Key, Marcus M., Lorin E. Kerr, Merle Bundy. _Pulmonary Reactions to Coal Dust_. New York: Academic Press, 1971.

Kluckholn, F.L. and F.L. Strodtbeck. _Variations in Value Orientations_. New York: Harper and Row, 1961.

Knipe, Edward E. "Change in Mining Technology and Workers Interaction." paper read at International Seminar on Social Change in the Mining Community. Jackson's Mill, West Virginia, 1967.

Knipe, Edward E. and Helen M. Lewis. "The Impact of Coal Mining on the Traditional Mountain Subculture." _The Not So Solid South_. ed. J. Kenneth Morland. Athens: University of Georgia Press, 1971.

_____. "Toward a Methodology of Studying Coal Miners' Attitudes." Open File Report 8-69. Washington: United States Bureau of Mines. 1968.

Korson, George. _Coal Dust on the Fiddle_. 2nd printing. Hatboro, Pennsylvania: Folklore Associates, 1965; _Minstrels of the Mine Patch_. 3rd printing. Hatboro, Pennsylvania: Hatboro Associates, 1964.

Lantz, Herman R., _People of Coal Town_. New York: Columbia University Press, 1958.

Levi-Strauss, Claude. _Structural Anthropology_. New York: Basic Books, 1963.

Lewis, Helen M. "The Changing Communities in the Southern Appalachian Coal Fields." Paper read at International Seminar on Social Change in the Mining Community. Jackson's Mill, West Virginia, 1967.

Lewis, Helen M. and Edward E. Knipe. "The Sociological Impact of Mechanization on Coal Miners and Their Families." _Annual Council of Economics Proceedings Volume_. American Institute of Mining, Metallurgical and Petroleum Engineers, Inc., 1969.

Lewis, Oscar. "The Culture of Poverty." _Scientific American_, 216, No. 4. (1966).

Lieben, Jan, E. Pendergrass, W.W. McBride. "Pneumoconiosis Study in Central Pennsylvania Coal Mines." Journal of Occupational Medicine, 3 (1961), pp. 493-506.

Mead, Margaret. "National Character." Anthropology Today. ed. A.L. Kroeber. Chicago: University of Chicago press, 1953.

Morse, Kenneth M. "Recent Progress in Dust Control in Bituminous Coal Mining." Coal Workers' Pneumoconiosis, Annuals of the New York Academy of Sciences. ed. Irving J. Selikoff, Marcus M. Key, and Douglas H.K. Lee. New York: The New York Academy of Sciences, 1972.

Mann, Robert. The Coal Industry in America: A Bibliography and Guide to Studies. Morgantown: West Virginia University Library. 1965.

Newman, Marshall T. "Ecology and Nutritional Stress in Man." American Anthropologist. 64, 1962, pp. 22-34.

Parsons, Talcott. Structure of Social Action. New York: The Free Press, 1949.

Pearsall, Marion. Little Smoky Ridge. University, Alabama: University of Alabama Press, 1959.

Pilchner, William W. The Portland Longshoreman: A Dispersed Urban Community. New York: Holt, Rinehart and Winston, 1972.

Polgar, Steven. "Health Action in Cross-Cultural Perspective." Handbook of Medical Sociology. eds. Howard E. Freeman, Sol Levine and Leo G. Reeder. Englewood Cliffs: Prentice-Hall, 1963. pp. 397-419.

Rao, Sharadomba. "Culture and Mental Disorder: A Study in Indian Mental Hospital." International Journal of Social Psychiatry, 12, 1966, pp. 139-148.

Rimlinger, G.U. "International Differences in the Strike Propensity of Coal Miners: Experiences in Four Countries." Industrial and Labor Relations Review (April, 1959), pp. 389-405.

Roberts, Peter. Anthracite Coal Communities. 1904; rpt. New York: Arno Press and The New York Times, 1970.

Scotch, Norman A. "Medical Anthropology." Biennial Review of Anthropology. Stanford: Stanford University Press, 1963.

Selikoff, Irving J., Marcus M. Key, Douglas H.K. Lee. Coal Workers' Pneumoconiosis, Annals of the New York Academy of Sciences. New York: The New York Academy of Sciences, 1972.

Simons, Leo W. and Harold G. Wolff. <u>Social Science in Medicine</u>. New York:
    Russel Sage Foundation, 1954.

Sponsellar, Robert D. <u>Analysis and Measured Sections of Pennsylvania
    Bituminous Coals</u>. Mineral Resource Report 66, Fourth series.
    Harrisburg: Pennsylvania Geological Survey, 1973.

Stanley H. King. "Social Psychological Factors in Illness." <u>Handbook of
    Medical Sociology</u>. ed. H.E. Freeman, Sol Levine and Leo G. Reeder.
    Englewood: Prentice-Hall, 1963.

Stephenson, John B. <u>Shiloh: A Mountain Community</u>. Lexington: University
    of Kentucky, 1968.

Storey, Henry Wilson. <u>History of Cambria County</u>. Volume I and Volume II.
    New York. Lewis Publishing Co. 1907.

Suchman, Edward A. "The Addictive Diseases as Socio-Environmental
    Problems." <u>Handbook of Medical Sociology</u>. ed. Howard E. Freeman,
    Sol Levine and Leo G. Reeder. Englewood: Prentice-Hall, 1963.

Tams, W.D. Jr. <u>The Smokeless Fields of West Virginia</u>. Morgantown: West
    Virginia University Libraries, 1963.

Trist, E.L. and K. Bamforth. "Some Psychological Consequences of the Long
    Wall Method of Coal Getting." <u>Human Relations</u>, 4 (January, 1951), pp.
    3-38.

Turkel, Studs. <u>Working</u>. New York: Pantheon Books of Random House, 1972.

United States Congress. <u>Coal Mine Inspection Act</u>, Public Law 49, 77th
    Congress, May 7, 1941.

_____. <u>Federal Coal-Mine Safety Act</u>, Public Law 552, 82nd Congress,
    July 16, 1952.

Weller, Jack E. <u>Yesterday's People: Life in Contemporary Appalachia</u>.
    Lexington: University of Kentucky Press, 1965.

SUPPLEMENTAL BIBLIOGRAPHY

Bauman, John F. "Ethnic Adaptation in a Southwestern Pennsylvania Coal
    Patch, 1910-40." The Journal of Ethnic Studies, 3:3 (1979), pp. 1-23.

Becker, Edmund R. "Black Bituminous Coal Miners in Southern Appalachia
    1890-1970." Sociological Spectrum, 4:4 (1984), pp. 461-476.

DeYoung, Alan J. "Economic Development and Educational Status in
    Appalachian Kentucky." Comparative Educational Review, 29:1 (1985),
    pp. 47-67.

Ewen, Lynda Ann. "Politics of Health and Safety in the Coal Mines."
    Association Paper of the Society for the Study of Social Problems,
    West Virginia Institute of Technology, Montgomery, West Virginia,
    1981.

Friedl, John. "Explanatory Models of Black Lang: Understanding the Health-
    Related Behavior of Appalachian Coal Miners." Culture, Medicine and
    Psychiatry, 6:1 (1982), pp. 3-10.

Haines, Michael R. "Fertility, Marriage, and Occupation in the
    Pennsylvania Anthracite Region 1850-1880." Journal of Family History,
    2:1 (1977), pp. 28-55.

Krebs, Girard. "Technological and Social Impact Assessment of Resource
    Extraction: A Case of Coal." Environment and Behavior, 7:3 (1975),
    pp. 307-329.

Moore, Robert. Pit-Men, Preachers and Politics: The Effects of Methodism
    in a Durham Mining Town. London: Cambridge University Press, 1974.

Morawska, Ewa. "The Internal Status Hierarchy in the East Central European
    Immigrant Communities of Johnstown, PA 1890-1930's." Journal of
    Social History, 16:1 (1982), pp. 75-107.

_____. For Bread with Butter: Life Worlds of East Central Europeans
    in Johnstown, Pennsylvania, 1890-1940. New York: Cambridge University
    Press, 1985.

Neff, James Alan. "Community Dissatisfaction and Perceived Residential Alternatives: An Interactive Model of the Formulation of Migration Plans." Journal of Population, 2:1 (1979), pp. 18-32.

Nyden, Paul J. "Rank and File Organizations in the United Mine Workers of American." The Insurgent Sociologist, 8:2-3 (1978), pp. 25-39.

Perry, Charles S. and Max Marx. "The National Bituminous Coal Wage Agreement of 1950 and Trends in Bituminous Coal Mining 1923-1967." Association Paper of the Rural Sociology Society, University of Kentucky, Lexington, Kentucky, 1983.

Samuel, Raphael (ed.). Miners, Quarrymen and Saltworkers. London: Routledge and Kegan Paul, 1977.

Williams, Bruce T. and Michael D. Yates. Upward Struggle, Johnstown Regional Central Labor Council, Johnstown, Pennsylvania, 1976.

_____. "Labor in Johnstown," Johnstown: The Story of a Unique Valley, Karl Berger (ed.), private printing, Johnstown Flood Museum, 1984.

Yarrow, Michael N. "A Reexamination of Braverman's Thesis on the Basis of an Analysis of a Deviant Case: Coal Mining." Association paper of the Society for the Study of Social Problems, Livingston College of Rutgers University, New Brunswick, New Jersey, 1979.

INDEX

264